Re-Visioning Education

Series Editor
Shirley R. Steinberg

Vol. 555

Douglas Kellner

Re-Visioning Education

Cultural Studies, Critical Media and Digital Literacies, and Democracy

New York · Berlin · Bruxelles · Chennai · Lausanne · Oxford

Library of Congress Cataloging-in-Publication Control Number: 2024022666

Bibliographic information published by the Deutsche Nationalbibliothek.
The German National Library lists this publication in the German
National Bibliography; detailed bibliographic data is available
on the Internet at <http://dnb.d-nb.de>.

Cover design by Peter Lang Group AG

ISSN 1058-1634 (print)
ISBN 9783034349987 (paperback)
ISBN 9783034349963 (ebook)
ISBN 9783034349970 (epub)
DOI 10.3726/b21953

© 2024 Peter Lang Group AG, Lausanne
Published by Peter Lang Publishing Inc., New York, USA

<info@peterlang.com> – <www.peterlang.com>

All rights reserved.
All parts of this publication are protected by copyright.
Any utilization outside the strict limits of the copyright law, without the permission of the publisher, is forbidden and liable to prosecution.
This applies in particular to reproductions, translations, microfilming, and storage and processing in electronic retrieval systems.

This publication has been peer reviewed.

TABLE OF CONTENTS

1 Neoliberalism, Technology, and Radical Pedagogy for the
Re-Construction of Education in the 21st Century 1
Steve Gennaro and Douglas Kellner

2 Multiple Critical Literacies and Radical Pedagogy in a Multicultural
Society 15

3 Key Components of Critical Cultural Studies 41

4 School Shootings, Crises of Masculinities, and Challenges
to Education 85

5 Douglas Kellner, "Dangerous New Dimension to Mass Shootings in
America," Interview with Joanie Harman 103

6 The Conflicts of Globalization, Cosmopolitanism, and Democracy 111

7 Critical Reflections on Marcuse, Freire, and Radical Pedagogy 127

8 Concluding Thoughts on Multiple Critical Literacies and the
   Reconstruction of Education   149

Afterword   169

· 1 ·

NEOLIBERALISM, TECHNOLOGY, AND RADICAL PEDAGOGY FOR THE RE-CONSTRUCTION OF EDUCATION IN THE 21ST CENTURY

Steve Gennaro and Douglas Kellner

The matrix of technological revolution, globalization, and neoliberal capital has produced intense change, conflict, and upheaval in society, culture, politics, and education throughout the 21st century. The recent events of the global COVID-19 pandemic have only further increased the polarity between economic haves and have-nots while at the same time doubling down on education, and even more so public education, as a battleground for where neoliberalism and the extreme right must be confronted. In this article, we argue that radical pedagogy today must arm students and citizens with new skills to negotiate and participate in the present age's global and techno-society and culture and that critical media and techno-literacies are becoming more crucial for the development of educated and critical individuals and citizens of a democratic society.

In particular, the centrality of globalization, technology, and neoliberalism in contemporary experience, and the need for adequate conceptualizations and responses, require critical theory and radical pedagogy to engage the conjuncture of technology and globalization in the context of neoliberalism to maintain their relevance in the present age. Critical educators need to comprehend the effects of globalization and technology on education over the last half-century, work to democratize education in the present moment, and develop pedagogies adequate to the challenges of an age of neoliberal capital and corporate models of education that we need to contest and offer alternatives.

In addition, the COVID-19 pandemic has presented a challenge to the future of education at the same time as it has opened opportunities for contestation and transformation to make schooling serve the needs of students and teachers, as opposed to neoliberalism that wants to commodify education and make it subservient to global capital and the ruling elites. Specifically, the rapid move toward online education during the ongoing Covid pandemic of the 2020s has raised new questions about the sites, pedagogies, and education goals in the 21st century. In this context, Educators need to do a radical critique of online education and subject current online pedagogical practices to critical examination, which depicts its possible benefits while criticizing the problems it raises. Further, educators should develop radical pedagogies that will reconstruct education in the Deweyean and Freirean traditions of promoting democracy and enabling students and citizens to be active creators of their lives and societies rather than passive subjects of media spectacles, virtual worlds, and digital learning.

This requires revalorization of in-class teaching supplemented by digital education and the need for new critical media and digital literacies while at the same time producing in-class face-to-face educational practices that promote discussion, engagement, and participation in the educational project inspired by Dewey, Freire, Marcuse, and others who were aware of the impact of capitalism, technology, and schooling as preparation for labor and conformity to techno-capitalist societies and who called for the reconstruction of education to make students and citizens able to participate democratically in their social and political worlds – which today involves both our lived bodily experience in natural and social worlds, as well as our participation in virtual worlds.[1]

Globalization, Neoliberalism, and the Reconstruction of Education

In the face of expanding globalization and digital technologies of information and communication in the context of neoliberalism, critical educators continue to develop transformative educational strategies to understand and counter the oppressive forces and effects of neoliberal globalization in conjunction with possibilities for democratization to empower individuals to understand and act effectively in a globalized neoliberal world, and to struggle for social justice. At the same time, the 2020s have seen a fierce attack on education in the United

States, with conservative groups and politicians attempting to ban the teaching of race, sexuality, and even history that takes a critical look at U.S. society. Conservatives are banning books, throwing out essential parts of school curricula, and firing teachers and administrators who teach books or ideas that offend students or their conservative parents and right-wing opposition groups who want to enforce a conservative agenda on schools. Florida Governor Ron DeSantis – with his eyes on a 2024 U.S. Presidential run – has been leading the charge, banning books and the teaching of any critical race studies, gender or sexuality studies ("don't say Gay"), forcing rightwing curriculum on schools, firing teachers that do not conform to his strictures and claiming that Florida in the place where "Woke dies here."[2].

Rightwing culture wars against education means that teaching books critical of U.S. society and history and addressing controversial issues of race, gender, class, sexuality, and critical thinking must be defended against the conservative culture war on education; at the same time, we should focus on teaching the essential literacies of reading, writing, and thinking, supplemented by new critical media and digital literacies to address the current developments and issues of U.S. society.

The project of transforming education will take different forms in different contexts. For example, in post-industrial or "overdeveloped" countries, individuals need to be empowered to work and act in a high-tech information economy and thus should learn skills of critical media and digital literacies to survive in the novel social environment. Traditional crafts of knowledge and critique should also be fostered so that students can name the system, describe the changes occurring in the evolving neoliberal global order, and engage in critical and oppositional practice in the interests of democratization and progressive social and cultural transformation. This requires a vision of alternatives to the present order and the necessity of struggle and organization to realize progressive goals. The discourse of critique, hope, and praxis must thus supplement languages of competition, grading, and achievement in education to promote critical students and citizens working toward social justice, participatory democracy, a sustainable environment, and a better world for all.

Transforming education in Neo-liberal globalization requires addressing educational issues in response to an unprecedented climate crisis ravishing the earth, creating intense catastrophic weather events, and threatening all life on the planet, human and natural (Klein 2014). In a recent interview, Naomi Klein called for climate justice and global activism to address the climate crisis, arguing: "We live in a time of multiple overlapping crises: we have a health emergency; we have a housing emergency; we have an inequality emergency; we have a racial injustice emergency; and we have a climate emergency, so we're not going to get anywhere if we try to address them one at a time. We need responses that are truly intersectional. So how about as we decarbonise and create a less polluted world, we also build a much fairer society on multiple fronts?" (Klein 2023).

Neoliberal capitalism puts profit over people and expands production over preserving natural resources and the environment. This is a global problem that requires a global solution. In an earlier stage of multinational capital, the United States and overdeveloped countries played a significant role in the climate crisis and continue to suffer growing climate disasters. The National Centers for Environmental Information (NCEI) dramatizes the dangers and costs of the climate crisis, stating: "Since 1980, the United States has experienced 323 in climate and weather related disasters, which have cost more than $2.195 trillion in total. According to NOAA's National Centers for Environmental Information (NCEI), 2021 witnessed 20 climate-related disasters, each exceeding losses of $1 billion (NOAA 2023). In a significant statement, the United Nations warns:

> Climate change is the defining crisis of our time and is happening even more quickly than we feared. But we are far from powerless in the face of this global threat. As Secretary-General António Guterres pointed out in September, 'the climate emergency is a race we are losing, but it is a race we can win.'

No corner of the globe is immune from the devastating consequences of climate change. Rising temperatures are fueling environmental degradation, natural disasters, weather extremes, food and water insecurity, economic disruption, conflict, and terrorism. Sea levels are rising, the Arctic is melting, coral reefs are dying, oceans are acidifying, and forests are burning. It is clear that business as usual is not good enough. As the infinite cost of climate change reaches irreversible highs, now is the time for bold collective action (UN75 2020 and Beyond).

Considering the significant role of science and technology in the modern world (stressed by Dewey and Marcuse), threats to the environment, and the need to preserve and enhance the natural as well as social and cultural worlds, it is scandalous how illiterate some overdeveloped societies, like the US, are concerning science, nature, and even people's bodies. An **eco-literacy** should thus appropriately teach competency in interpreting and interacting with our natural environment, ranging from our bodies to natural habitats like forests, oceans, lakes, and deserts.

Already eco-pedagogy is addressing important environmental issues and teaching students about the danger of climate crisis, the need for a sustainable economy, and ways to enjoy and preserve our natural world (Kahn 2010). Eco-pedagogy requires knowledge of the threats to the environment and natural and human worlds from the global climate crisis, the urgency of addressing the crisis, and the necessary changes to increase our possibilities of human survival. This also requires knowledge of globalization and neoliberalism and how unregulated neo-liberal capitalism contributes to the climate crisis, as Naomi Klein (2014 and 2023) and others have argued for decades.

For decades now, there has been a battle between climate crisis scientists who have warned about the urgency of the problem and climate deniers who downplay the crisis and twist the facts. This urgent issue of public concern requires both the media and citizens to be climate aware, educated, and active in discerning climate information from disinformation, as critical news literacy requires distinguishing information from lies, propaganda, and disinformation.

Under the regime of neo-liberalism, corporate media have traditionally played down climate crisis and focused on the debate over those who warn climate change is producing a dangerous climate crisis and those who deny the crisis. Since neo-liberal corporations are significant producers of the climate crisis, it is no secret that corporate media often ignore the severity of the climate crisis, and entire networks like Fox News and other right-wing media downplay the extent of the crisis. The Trump administration (2016–2020) promoted climate denial and even exited the Paris climate accords while stalling action on the climate crisis for four crucial years (Daley 2020). With the Biden Administration reaffirming the Paris climate accords, the media have increased coverage of climate crises in the face of worsening environmental crises, with extreme weather events expanding and intensifying in severity and frequency.

In this situation of conflicting accounts of the climate crisis, education must produce the critical and digital literacies that enable individuals to distinguish between information and misinformation, and scientific evidence contrasted to propaganda and lies, as well as developing eco-literacies that produce solid knowledge of the extent, nature, and remedies for the climate crisis. This requires the development of critical media and digital literacies to appraise media sources and distinguish between information and misinformation, scientific knowledge, and corporate propaganda and ignorance.

Toward Critical Media and Digital Literacies

Critical media and digital literacies and pedagogies presuppose digital technology and media access. However, even as access to mobile technology continues to rise globally, the rates of growth and access are unequal. For example, while a 2019 PEW research report noted that more than five billion people have access to mobile devices, and more than half of these are smartphones (Silver 2019), recent work from UNICEF in April 2020 on pandemic education documents how despite 188 countries adopting a digitally-based continuation of education during the pandemic using technologies such as internet, TV, and radio, one-third of schoolchildren worldwide (over 463 million) could not be reached by the broadcast – and Internet-based remote learning policies (UNICEF April 2020).

This poses different challenges for transforming education in underserviced regions, such as the global south. In *How Many Children and Youth Have Internet Access* at Home, UNICEF reported that two-thirds of children and young people aged 25 years or less (over 2.2 billion) are without a home connection to the Internet (UNICEF December 2020). The data is startling. In West and Central African Nations, only 5% have internet access at home compared to the 33% global average. Differences continue to grow between rich and developing countries, with only 6% of children and young people in low-income countries having internet access compared to 87% in high-income countries. A progressive reconstruction of education that is done in the interests of democratization would demand access to emergent technologies for all, helping to overcome the so-called digital divide and divisions of the "haves" and "have-nots" both in the overdeveloped countries and countries that do not yet have adequate access to digital technology (see Kellner 2002 and 2021).

Interestingly, one of the earliest proponents of critical pedagogy, Paulo Freire, was also an early advocate for critical media literacy. Freire noted, "It is not the media themselves which I criticize, but the way they are used" (1972: 136). He argued for the importance of teaching media literacy to empower individuals against manipulation and oppression and using the most appropriate media to help teach the subject matter (1972: 114–116). For Freire, media technologies offered potential tools for empowering citizens simultaneously as they also offered the potential to act as instruments of domination when exclusively controlled by ruling elites.

A critical theory of technology maintains that there is utopian potential in information and communication technologies and the possibility for increased domination and the hegemony of capital. While the first generation of computers were large mainframe systems controlled by big government and big business, later generations of "personal computers" and networks created a more decentralized situation in which ever more individuals own their computers and digital devices, using them for their projects and goals. A current generation now exists both physically and digitally in the world via handheld smartphones and emergent social media platforms that finds 95% of American teenagers claim access to a smartphone, and almost half of all American teens claim to be online "almost constantly" (Andersen & Jiang, 2018). The utopian potential for the current technology can be seen in the global networks of young people who are using smartphones as a tool to organize, mobilize, and contest the most significant challenges of their contemporary moment, such as climate change, de-gendering S.T.E.M and racial inequity with movements such as Black Lives Matter (Gennaro & Miller, 2020).

In this ever-expanding technoworld, developing critical media and digital literacies requires evaluating media and digital sources to distinguish between information and disinformation, propaganda and sourced knowledge, and at heart between truth and lies. Regarding critical media literacy, it requires discerning the biases and ideological slants of different media and news organizations in both the domains of news and entertainment (Kellner 1995 [2020]) and Kellner & Share, 2019). Within the last half-century, a dramatic shift has occurred in how media organizations deliver news content to the American public. For example, in the 1980s and early 1990s, throughout the Reagan and George H.W. Bush administrations, the three major television networks in the U.S. were marked by centrist corporate neo-liberalism with no significant ideological differences between ABC, NBC, and CBS broadcasting networks (see Kellner 1988).

However, the emergence of cable news networks, like CNN, Fox, and MSNBC, in the mid-1990s altered the news media landscape. News networks focused on segmented media audiences. Fox News coverage has tended to support the Republican Party (and more recently, even the extremism of the Trump administration), MSNBC features liberal and Democratic Party voices and positions, and CNN attempts to hold some form of middle ground. YouTube and Internet news now offer a witch's brew of voices and polemics within an intensified social media cauldron. "The sensationalized one-liner headline written to lure the reader to the news corporation home site or independent YouTube channel becomes naturalized as news itself and takes on the perception of truth – even when the perception is an empty and hollow symbol" (Gennaro 2020). Now, every individual can bloviate any opinion, from the extreme right to the extreme left, and it is presented as legitimate and consumed, often without critique, as people consume information in tribal bubbles.

Critical media and techno literacy pedagogies exploring social media require understanding the ownership, politics, audiences, and voices across Facebook, Twitter, YouTube, Tic-Toc, and the other proliferating media of the digital technoscape. This space is constantly mutating as ownership and polities of social media shift, as in the case of Elon Musk taking over Twitter, reinstating Donald Trump on the medium, and even encouraging Twitter's users to vote Republican in the 2022 midterms after having previously primarily supported Democrats, a development we documented in an earlier study (see Gennaro and Kellner, in print). The proliferation of media and digital sources requires every student and citizen to become media and digitally literate to function as an individual in a democratic society properly and to keep from being a victim of propaganda, misinformation, and lies.

Critical and participatory citizenship thus involves cultivating abilities to read and critique the text of one's own and other cultures, including political and media discourses, social media, television programming, popular music, advertising, and other cultural forms. Thus, a public pedagogy articulates critical cultural studies that require critical educators to rethink the concepts of literacy and the very nature of education in any high-tech and rapidly evolving society. Literacy must be expanded to develop novel cultural and technological literacy forms. In contrast, technological revolution, significant demographic and socio-political changes, and culture wars and political battles occur in the United States and elsewhere.

Toward Multiple Critical Literacies

We have delineated some critical literacies necessary to utilize and deploy information and communication technologies, including an expanded role for essential media and digital literacies and multimedia literacies that provide literacy in reading, researching, and producing in the evolving multimedia world. However, radically reconstructing education requires techno-literacies often neglected in schooling. The challenge for education today is to develop multiple critical literacies to empower students and citizens to use emergent technologies to enhance their lives and to create a better culture and society based on respect for multicultural differences and to aim at fuller democratic participation of individuals and groups excluded from wealth and power in the previous modern society, and to deal with climate crisis effectively.

Since a multicultural society is the context of education for many in the contemporary moment, innovative forms of social interaction and cultural awareness are needed that appreciate differences, multiplicity, and diversity. Therefore, an expanded multicultural literacy is required to respect diverse groups' cultural heritage, histories, and contributions and educate all citizens on the histories of dominant ethnic groups in the country. Whereas one can agree with E.D. Hirsch (1987) that we need to be literate in our shared cultural heritage, we also need to become culturally literate in hitherto invisible cultures, as Anthony Appiah, Henry Louis Gates, and their colleagues have been arguing in their proposals for multicultural education (1999).

Engaging the politics of representation includes decoding images, discourses, and narratives encompassing race, class, gender, sexuality, and the other cultural dimensions of media ranging from sports to film, popular music, and television. Media consumers need to distinguish between racist, sexist, homophobic, classist, and other bigoted discourses, images, and narratives and more progressive entertainment. Of course, many artifacts of media entertainment contain contradictory mixtures of messages. Still, it is essential to recognize flat-out racism, sexism, homophobia, and other biases when in a volatile political environment, hate speech and biased news and entertainment has led to increasing hate crimes against people of color, Jewish and Muslim people, women, the LGBT2Q+ community, and other targets of hate speech and discriminatory representations.

Indeed, as we write in 2023, intense culture wars have been fought over education, taking the form, first, of a battle over critical race theory (CRT), which conservatives claim was "grooming" students to focus on racial differences and was dividing society into "woke" subcultures that were attacking mainstream conservative values and institutions. One of the first national politicians to manipulate critical race theory to mobilize his conservative base against CRT in public schools was Republican gubernatorial candidate Ralph Youngkin of Virginia, who deployed a war on CRT to win his bid for Governor in the 2020 election successfully (Schneider & Vozella, 2022). At the time, there was little or no understanding of critical race theory among the conservative politicians attacking it, nor did the conservatives crusading against CRT know where and how it was taught and what actual impact it was having on K-12 or higher education. There were, but a few University schools of Education that were teaching CRT, and there were few documented programs of

CRT in K-12 at the time. So this attack was a political red herring that conservative demagogic politicians used.

The attack on critical race studies intensified when Republican Governor Ron DeSantis of Florida vowed to prevent schools from teaching a College Board-approved advanced placement (AP) course in African American studies, claiming "it violated state law and 'significantly lacks educational value.'" DeSantis's "Florida education department then cited examples in the pilot of what it termed 'woke indoctrination' that would run afoul of recently passed Florida laws that clamp down on class discussions about racism" (Chan 2023).

DeSantis' vicious attack on education continued outlawing "subversive" books like *Huckleberry Finn*, banning any discussion of gay and lesbian issues in schools ("Don't Say Gay!"), and attacking the Walt Disney Corporation for having gay characters in their entertainment, bragging that "Woke Will Die in Florida." (Gross 2023). Of course, DeSantis was eyeing a presidential bid for the Republican Party nomination in the 2024 election and was playing to the Trump hard right to present himself to conservative Republicans and extreme right Trumpsters as the anti-Woke candidate for sleepy Republican who wanted to dream themselves back to the antebellum period where women, people of color, and alternative sexualities knew their place and would not dare shake up the toxic Patriarchy that rightwing cultural warriors and their armies of reactionaries are dreaming of returning to.

Not surprisingly, the rightwing culture wars over education are mobilizing an alliance of students, teachers, and concerned citizens who value the importance of education and the need to deal with issues of contemporary importance, not be subjected to school censorship by rightwing know-nothings, and to have a multicultural and critical education from K-12 to college and beyond opened to the most relevant and vital books, ideas, course subject matter, and pedagogies putting pressure on critical pedagogy to address these highly sensitive and intense debates and culture wars of the present over higher education.

A public pedagogy involves teaching citizens what is happening in our and other democratic and nondemocratic societies, threats to democracy, and citizenship demands. Training individuals for citizenship involves training in rhetoric, public speaking, and the fundamentals of reading and writing. It also requires cultivating critical tolerance in a multicultural society that affirms respect and tolerance for all while being critical of social institutions and groups that themselves promote fundamentalism and assault tolerance or that use terrorism, militarism, and violence to promote their ends.

Tolerance should be linked with cultural cosmopolitanism that affirms the value of world culture and multiculturalism, and that is not chauvinistic and noncritical toward one's own culture and society. While democratic patriotism can help cultivate respect for the positive features of a culture or society and help create solidarities in times of trouble, blind nationalistic patriotism can lead to submission to aggressive and nondemocratic policies and practices of political manipulation.

In addition to Multicultural Literacy, Social Literacy should be taught throughout the educational systems, focusing on how to relate and get along with various individuals, negotiate differences, resolve conflicts, and communicate and socially interact in multiple ways and situations. Social literacy involves ethical training in values and norms, delineating proper and improper individual and social values (which may differ in different regions and countries). It also requires knowledge of contemporary societies and thus overlaps with social and natural science training. Harkening back to John Dewey (1997 [1916]) and his notion of education and democracy, students should be taught democratic values and the need for citizens to participate in local, national, and global social life in the interests of social justice, a democratic polity, and a sustainable environment.

Ideals of a future society would thus involve the creation of a more egalitarian and democratic society in which more individuals and groups were empowered to participate in a sustainable economy and protected environment. Francisco Fereirra noted recently for the International Monetary Fund, "The severe impact of the COVID-19 pandemic is seen in the numbers: more than 3.1 million deaths and rising, 120 million people pushed into extreme poverty and a massive global recession. As suffering and poverty have risen, some data show an increase in another extreme: billionaires' wealth." *Forbes* noted in April 2021 that "U.S. billionaires have gotten about $1.2 trillion richer during the pandemic."

A related problem is that media companies are owned by mega-corporate conglomerates that control news and information, thus controlling the public sphere and adjudicating the limits of public debate. This means that it is rare that giant media conglomerates will discuss taxation and regulation that will distribute wealth, significantly increase the budget and quality of education, or advance proposals that will significantly protect the environment from pollution, destruction, and the predatory practices of overdevelopment, appropriating valuable and limited natural resources, and dangerous transport and store dangerous industrial waste and poisonous chemicals.[3]

In light of the neoliberal projects to dismantle the Welfare State, colonize the public sphere, and control globalization, it is up to citizens, activists, and educators to create alternative public spheres, politics, and pedagogies. In these spaces, which could include progressive classrooms, students and citizens could learn to use information and multimedia technologies to discuss what kinds of society people today want and to oppose the society against which people resist and struggle. This minimally demands more education, health care, welfare, and benefits from the state and work to create a more democratic and egalitarian society. Yet one cannot expect charitable corporations and a beneficent state to make the bounties and benefits of the globalized information society available to citizens. Instead, it is up to individuals and groups to promote democratization and progressive social change.

Conclusion

The concept of multiple critical literacies and radical public pedagogy that we envisage maintains that it is not a question of *either/or* classifications that position media, technology, and education only through binary lenses, i.e., pedagogy must *either* adhere to classical traditions *or* jump full-on into emerging technologies, whereby curriculum can *either* focus on print-based learning *or* multi-media literacy. We are not claiming that traditional educational skills and new critical media and digital literacies happens more successfully *either* in the traditional classroom *or* online in virtual spaces since we advocate a public pedagogy geared to creating democratic citizens and social justice in the spirit of Dewey, Freire, and Marcuse.

We want to overcome the dichotomy which posits that since we are *either* passive consumers of media messages *or* active producers of media meaning by increasing critical media and digital literacies whereby a public pedagogy helps create active participants who can access relevant information and active and critically engage media and information sources *and* be active democratic citizens fighting for a more just, sustainable, and equable society.

In opposition to the neoliberal globalization of corporate and state capitalism, we would advocate an oppositional democratic, pedagogical, and cosmopolitan globalization. This requires the *both/and* approach advocated by intersectionality, which moves past binaries of knowledge and the hierarchical, patriarchal, and colonizing power dynamics they preserve and perpetuate. This approach supports *both* individuals *and* groups using emerging media technologies to create a more multicultural, egalitarian, democratic, and ecological education system. Where emergent technologies might exacerbate existing inequalities in the current class, gender, race, and regional power configurations and give dominant corporate forces ever more powerful tools to advance their interests, it is up to education to train students and citizens with new skills to use technologies to promote democratization, social, and environmental justice. Changes in the economy, politics, and social life demand a constant and radical rethinking of democratic education as a response to ever-changing historical conditions.

Notes

1 Themes concerning Dewey, Freire, and Marcuse will run through the studies to follow, while Chapter 8 will highlight their relevance for radical pedagogy and the reconstruction of education today.
2 See Matt Dixon and Gary Fineout, "'Where woke goes to die': DeSantis, with eye toward 2024, launches second term. Inaugural speech had national focus, signaled continued focus on culture war fights." *Politico*, January 3, 2023 at <https://www.politico.com/news/2023/01/03/desantis-2024-second-term-00076160> (accessed March 25, 2023) DeSantis' "Woke goes to die" speech can be found at YouTube at <https://www.youtube.com/watch?v=nuE0WLNZzEY> (accessed on March 25, 2023).
3 As we write in Spring 2023, there have been numerous spills of toxic chemicals and environmental waste through train crashes, storage site fires, and industrial accidents. See Carey Gillam, "Revealed: the US averages one chemical accident every two days. *Guardian* analysis of data in light of Ohio train derailment shows accidental releases are happening consistently." *The Guardian*, February 25, 2023 at <https://www.theguardian.com/us-news/2023/feb/25/revealed-us-chemical-accidents-one-every-two-days-average> (accessed March 1, 2023). In the summer of 2023, there were unprecedented heat waves, highly destructive fires from Canada to Greece, and other extreme weather events like floods, earthquakes, and other catastrophes of Biblical proportion that have given the lie to climate deniers and created a situation that anyone who does not see the dangers of climate catastrophe and support a progressive and rational agenda to confront it is a clear and present danger to the survival of the human race.

References

Anderson, M. and Jiang, J. (2018). "Teens, Social Media, and Technology". PEW Research Center. <https://www.pewresearch.org/internet/2018/05/31/teens-social-media-technology-2018/#vast-majority-of-teens-have-access-to-a-home-computer-or-smartphone> (accessed October 1, 2021).
Appiah, A. A. and Gates, H. L. (1999). *Africana: The Encyclopedia of the African and African American Experience*. New York: BasicCivitas.

Aronowitz, S. and Giroux, H. (1993). *Education Still Under Siege*. Westport, Conn.: Bergin & Garvey.
Daley, J. (2020). "U.S. Exits Paris Climate Accord after Trump Stalls Global Warming Action for Four Years," *Scientific American*, November 4, 2020 at <https://www.scientificamerican.com/article/u-s-exits-paris-climate-accord-after-trump-stalls-global-warming-action-for-four-years/> (accessed March 6, 2023).
Dewey, John (1997 [1916]). *Democracy and Education*. New York: Free Press.
Ferreira, F. (2021). "Inequality in the Time of Covid-19". International Monetary Fund. <https://www.imf.org/external/pubs/ft/fandd/2021/06/inequality-and-covid-19-ferreira.htm> (accessed October 4, 2021).
Gennaro, Steve, and Blair Miller. *Young People and Social Media*. 1st ed. Wilmington, DE: Vernon Art and Science Inc, 2021. Print.
Gennaro, S. (2020) "Is Information Knowledge in the Digital World?" Source: Evaluation in Science and Correlated Areas, European Academy of Sciences of Ukraine. https://source.euasu.org
Richard Kahn (2010). *Critical Pedagogy, Ecoliteracy, and Planetary Crisis: The Ecopedagogy Movement*. New York: Peter Lang.
Kahn, R. and Kellner, D. (2003). "Internet Subcultures and Oppositional Politics", in D. Muggleton (ed.), *The Post-subcultures Reader*. London: Berg.
Kellner, D. (1995a; second edition 2020). *Media Culture*. London and New York: Routledge.
Kellner, D. (2002). "Technological Revolution, Multiple Literacies, and the Restructuring of Education," in Ilana Snyder (ed.), *Silicon Literacies*. London and New York: Routledge: 154–169.
Kellner, D. (with Jeff Share 2019). *The Critical Media Literacy Guide: Engaging Media and Transforming Education*. Rotterdam, The Netherlands: Brill-Sense Publishers.
Kellner, D. (2021). *Technology and Democracy: Toward a Critical Theory of Digital Technologies, Technopolitics, and Technocapitalism*. Wiesbaden: Springer Publications.
Klein, N. (2014). *This Changes Everything: Capitalism vs. The Climate*. New York, NY: Simon & Schuster.
Klein, N. (2023). "It's Inequality that Kill': Naomi Klein on the Future of Climate Justice. Canadian Author and Professor of Climate Justice Cautiously Hails Loss and Damage Agreements at Cop27," *Guardian*, February 13, 2023 at <https://www.theguardian.com/books/2023/feb/13/its-inequality-that-kills-naomi-klein-on-the-future-of-climate-justice> (accessed on March 6, 2023).
UN75, 2020 and Beyond. "The Climate Crisis: A Race We Can Win," at <https://www.un.org/sites/un2.un.org/files/2020/01/un75_climate_crisis.pdf> (accessed March 6, 2023).
UNICEF. (August 2020). "COVID-19: Are Children Able to Continue Learning During School Closures? A Global Analysis of the Potential Reach of Remote Learning Policies". <https://data.unicef.org/resources/remote-learning-reachability-factsheet/> (accessed on October 4, 2021).
UNICEF. (December 2020). "How Many Children and Young People Have Internet Access at Home? Estimating Digital Connectivity during the COVID-19 Pandemic". <https://data.unicef.org/resources/children-and-young-people-internet-access-at-home-during-covid19/> (accessed on October 4, 2021).

· 2 ·

MULTIPLE CRITICAL LITERACIES AND RADICAL PEDAGOGY IN A MULTICULTURAL SOCIETY

We are amid one of the most dramatic technological revolutions in history that is changing how we work, how we communicate with each other, and how we spend our leisure time. This technological revolution centers on information technology as a key factor in a knowledge society and therefore ascribes education a central role in every aspect of life. This Great Transformation poses tremendous challenges to education to rethink its basic tenets, to deploy new technologies in creative and productive ways, and to restructure schooling in the light of the socio-cultural metamorphosis we are now undergoing.

While we are undergoing a technological revolution, significant demographic and socio-political changes are occurring in the United States and worldwide. Emigration patterns have witnessed an influx of new people into the U.S. in recent decades, and the country is now more racially and ethnically diverse and multicultural than ever before. This creates the challenge of providing people from diverse races, classes, and backgrounds with the tools to enable them to succeed and participate in an ever more complex world. Critical pedagogy considers how education can strengthen democracy, create a more egalitarian and just society, and deploy education in the process of progressive social change.

In this chapter, I argue that we need multiple critical literacies for our multicultural society, that we need to develop literacies to meet the challenge of the emergent technologies, social media, and digital culture, and that literacies of diverse sorts – including even more fundamental importance for print literacy – are of crucial importance in restructuring education for a high-tech and multicultural society. I argue that education today needs to foster multiple critical literacies to empower students and make education relevant to the present and future demands. Emergent technologies and social media are altering every aspect of our society, and we need to use them to understand and transform our world.

In the next section, I discuss how radical pedagogy can promote multicultural education and sensitivity to cultural differences. Then, I focus on developing critical media and technoliteracies to critically engage the wealth of media and cultural materials that currently immerse us. Pedagogy today must become radical because of the radical change produced by growing technological and multicultural societies. The explosion of new technologies and media combined with the growth of contemporary multicultural societies demand an increased focus on the dynamics of race, class, gender, and sexuality, exploring how, in a multicultural technoculture and society, phenomena like racism, classism, sexism, homophobia, and other biases deeply affect education and culture, while providing new challenges for teachers and schools.

These developments require radical pedagogy to engage the assaults on teaching and education organized by rightwing and reactionary forces and the role of class, race, gender, and sexuality in these struggles. To be radical is to go to the roots, so radical pedagogues must go to the roots of racism, sexism, classism, and homophobia and teach students and citizens to combat these pernicious forces and to struggle for a more multicultural, egalitarian, and democratic society, aimed as social justice for all.

Radical pedagogy include critical media and digital literacies that involve teaching the skills that will empower citizens and students to become sensitive to the politics of representations of race, ethnicity, gender, sexuality, class, and other cultural differences to promote critical thinking and enhance democratization (Kellner and Share 2019). Accordingly, I will delineate a wide range of multiple critical literacies to deal with the exigencies of the cultural and technological revolution that we are currently involved in, ranging from digital literacy to multimedia literacy to new forms of cultural literacy. Such concerns are part of a radical pedagogy that summons educators, students, and citizens to rethink established curricula and teaching strategies to empower individuals to participate democratically in our increasingly multicultural and technological society.

The Question of Multiculturalism

It is ever more apparent that we live in a multicultural society, and the term multiculturalism has for decades become a buzzword for our time, used in multiple contexts in many ways. It is a highly contested term with diverse social groupings and political forces either appropriating it for their agendas or virulently challenging it to preserve established modes of culture, schooling, and society. The term means quite different things in different contexts and is thus overloaded with diverse and sometimes conflicting meanings articulating different political agendas and discourses. In Canada, for instance, multiculturalism is the official government policy of a state with liberal emigration policies and diverse races. It is thus a legitimating ideology, serving much as melting pot ideologies functioned in the United States in an earlier era. In South Africa, the term was initially used to support segregation between Africans and Europeans, but is now also an official government policy that functions more progressively to get different racial groups to put aside the virulent hatred and racism of an earlier period.

In the United States, the term is contested between conservatives who would vilify it as a threat to traditional canons of education and as a cover for liberal reform of education and society. Overall, in post-1960s U.S. society, "multiculturalism" signifies a mode of affirming otherness and difference and the importance of attending to marginalized, minority, and oppositional groups and individuals previously excluded from the cultural dialogue. In the educational context, this means advancing proposals for curriculum changes involving new canons, including excluded voices and cultures, and sometimes new programs like African-American or Mexican-American studies.

Multiculturalism elicited intense cultural wars as conservatives defended Western culture, with its canons of great (mostly) European white males, against the multicultural offensive. In opposition to multiculturalism, conservatives thus (re)affirm monoculturalism leading to intense battles over education and culture wars that are still raging.[1] Yet there are a variety of discourses of multiculturalism in the U.S. today, including liberal versions for whom multiculturalism serves as did previous ideologies of tolerance and humanism to cover over differences and inequalities, as opposed to more radical versions who would use the concept to restructure education and society, exactly as conservatives fear. Yet here too there are tensions between nationalist groups and advocates of identity politics who use it to advance their own particular agenda, as opposed to those who support a politics of alliance and solidarity and call for fundamental social restructuring. Appiah criticizes the version of multiculturalism which calls for separatism and which loudly trumpets the superiority of one's specific culture as "illiberal multiculturalism" (1997: 30ff).

Hence, there are a variety of discourses of multiculturalism in the U.S. today, including liberal versions for whom multiculturalism covers differences and inequalities – as did previous liberal ideologies of tolerance and humanism. By contrast, more radical versions of multiculturalism would use the concept to restructure education and society, precisely as conservatives fear. Yet here, too, there are tensions between advocates of identity politics who use it to advance their specific interest groups, as opposed to those who support a politics of alliance and solidarity and call for fundamental social restructuring. Some would use the term as a cover for liberal notions of tolerance and humanism, contrasted to those who want to reconstruct our conceptions of human beings, such as Katsiaficas and Kiros (1998), who propose multiculturalism as a "concrete universal" which resists Western ethnocentrism and sees humanity as constructed through differences and hybridities which makes possible new modes of identity and solidarities.

While some pedagogues adopted the term "critical multiculturalism" to distinguish it from a socially affirmative liberal version, Giroux proposes the term "insurgent multiculturalism" to denote the efforts of oppositional and previously excluded groups contesting their exclusion and marginalization (2018). In *The Postmodern Adventure* (2001), Steven Best and I propose the concept of "critical, progressive, and activist multiculturalism" to signify that we need a multiculturalism that transcends the liberal pluralist version and assimilates the moments of activism and oppositionalism involved in the concepts proposed by hooks and West (1994), Appiah (1994), Giroux (1994), and Katsiaficas and Kiros (1998).

There are thus diverse strands of multiculturalism ranging from liberal and centrist versions, which replicate melting pot ideologies that celebrate the existing society as egalitarian and open to all, to more radical interpretations, which affirm the value of diversity and inclusion, while stressing the need for oppressed groups to struggle against institutionalized forms of hierarchy and domination. This "insurgent" multiculturalism responds to 1960s activism and demands for acceptance of otherness and difference combined with an appreciation of marginal, minority, or different ideas, people, and practices. It articulates the 1960s belief that individuals of diverse races and styles could live together in peace and harmony and that tolerance, cooperation, and community were positive values upon which a more democratic and egalitarian social order could be founded. Insurgent multiculturalism is often advocated by precisely those individuals who have been excluded from modern culture and society because of their gender, race, or class positions. The critical moment involves constantly reflecting on one's presuppositions, criticizing conventional and conservative forms, and deploying multiculturalism as a lever for radical social and cultural transformation.

Thus progressive critical multiculturalism requires appreciating otherness and differences, which demands understanding other individuals different from one's own groups' experiences, cultures, and histories. This entails the active education of each person in the history and culture of others, as well as our shared history. Some universities have pursued this goal in recent years by advancing a multicultural education program that critiques Western civilization courses, the "Great Books" program, and teaches courses in non-Western cultures and cultures of color, as well as critical presentations of one's own culture and history. Although standard Western civilization courses are valuable in teaching literacy skills and offering an introduction to influential figures and texts, they often reinforce elitist values and ignorance of nonwhite and non-Western cultures. Critical multiculturalism, therefore, wants to expand the curricula to include voices, perspectives, and groups excluded from the mainstream and canons of "Western civilization."

Thus, whereas traditional, modern curricula focused and centered on the West and dominant white male authors, a critical multiculturalist curriculum is less ethnocentric, more decentered, and open to voices and cultures excluded from the modern canon. Yet it should be emphasized that, with few exceptions, the attempts to create a new "canon" have been those of supplementing, not replacing, the standard works of Plato, Shakespeare, or Bach. I know no professors or students who want to jettison Western culture like Mao's Red Guard armies of destruction. However, this is the false impression generated by conservative critics of multicultural education.

Critical multiculturalism also involves grasping the contradictory nature of a multicultural reality where our identities are overdetermined and multiple. Identity politics often suppresses differences within their group, for instance, ignoring gender, class, or race distinctions in favor of a fixed, essentialist, and simple unitary identity – black, white, Christian, or another reductive identity. Critical multiculturalism, by contrast, recognizes that we all have multiple identities that should be affirmed and celebrated. Rather than reducing identity to one fetishized term (be it gender, race, sexual preference, or other differences), we should recognize that each of us is defined by a multiplicity of differentiations and should see ourselves as complex and overdetermined in our identities that are, as Kimberly Crenshaw (1989) has argued, intersectional.

This involves accepting and affirming hybridity, as people from different ethnicities, races, classes, and regions intermix and produce new generations of hybrid individuals and identities like Barack Obama and Kamala Harris.[2] Becoming a unique individual in today's world thus requires developing complex identities that affirm multiple determinations of our being, aiming at developing a many-sided human being, as the young Karl Marx envisaged (Tucker 1978, pp. 66–132).

Whereas traditional education often teaches conformity to mainstream values and identities, radical pedagogy aims at a process of self-constitution and a multi-dimensional identity. A self-constituting individual can select and evaluate ideas, values, modes of behavior, cultural forms, institutions, and social practices in a critical and discriminatory mode to make them their own and engage in self-discovery and self-development. Education, then, provides the tools, the abilities, and the knowledge to create a self-constituting individual capable of thinking and making choices for oneself and capable of getting along with other people, respecting and appreciating differences, and able to reach consensus on the common good, settling arguments, and to resolve differences amiably, or to accept and live with differences that must be accepted and respected. The twofold challenge of education in a democratic and multicultural society is thus to produce self-constituting and democratic social selves.

Accordingly, in the following sections, I will address what is involved in multicultural education and what sorts of literacy are necessary to produce a healthy, diverse, and vibrant multicultural society and democratic, self-governing, and empowered selves. In the next section, I will argue that multiple critical media and digital literacies are necessary to produce individuals capable of developing critical consciousness and self-empowerment in a digital and media culture, in order to meet the challenges of a technological and multicultural society in a creative, democratic, and empowering fashion.

Critical Media Literacies, Multiculturalism, and the Challenges of Contemporary Education

Many educators and theorists recognize the ubiquity of media culture in contemporary society, the growing trends toward multicultural education, and the need for critical media literacy that addresses the issue of multicultural differences. There is expanding recognition that media representations help construct our images and understanding of the world and that education must meet the dual challenges of teaching critical media and digital literacy in a multicultural society and sensitizing students and publics to the inequities and injustices of a society based on gender, race, and class inequalities and discrimination. Recent critical studies see how broadcasting and digital media are exacerbating these inequalities, and how media education and the production of alternative media can promote a healthy multiculturalism of diversity and a more robust democracy (see Kellner and Share 2019).

Multicultural education is partly a response to dealing creatively with growing diversity, facilitating "strategies for sharing, understanding, and enjoying" our proliferating cultural multiplicities and differences (Carson in Carson and Friedman 1995: 87f). Hence, a radical pedagogy should develop educational practices promoting multicultural understanding, empowering students, and strengthening education for contemporary and forthcoming challenges. Since cultural differences are constructed at the level of meaning and significance through the mediation of media and cultural representations, students and citizens must become aware of the ways that culture constructs a system of social differences and identities, with hierarchies, exclusions, defamations, and sometimes legitimation of the dominant social groups' power and domination. A critical multicultural education will thus make teachers and students sensitive to the politics of representation, to how media audiences' images of race, gender, sexuality, and cultural differences are in part generated by cultural representations, how damaging stereotyping presents harmful cultural images, and the need for a diversity of representations to capture the cultural wealth of contemporary America.

For instance, a society riven with modes of division and oppression organized around the axes of race, gender, class, sexuality, and other factors of identities and differences, establishes hierarchies that make some identity markers dominant and others subordinate. As bell hooks has argued (1990), we are in a White Male Supremacist and Classist Patriarchal and Heterosexual society in which straight, wealthy White Men are dominant, and people of color and working people, women, and LGBQT+ people are subordinate. These divisions and axes of oppression are learned at home, in school, through the media, and in everyday life, and consequently create societies and social relations divided into those who are dominant and those who are subordinate.

Yet families, schools, the media, and other organizations can also be used to teach positive multicultural understanding and education. Through cultivating the skills of critical media literacy (CML), teachers can discover how to use media to promote multicultural education and to teach the study of media critically through the lenses of the politics of representation. Multicultural education can promote genuine diversity and expand the curriculum if one is prepared to breach certain disciplinary boundaries and to teach and affirm multicultural diversity. Indeed, it is crucial for groups excluded from mainstream education to learn about their heritage and for dominant groups to explore the experiences and voices of minority and excluded groups.

Moreover, while it is essential and valuable to study cultures and voices excluded from traditional canons, the Great Books of Western Civilization may have as much importance to teach all students as excluded representatives of minority groups whom multiculturalists want, often with good reason, to include in the curriculum. Thus, Friedman convincingly argues that: "Western culture, despite its myriad faults, remains a crucial influence on American political, intellectual and social thought and, as such, should play an important role in classrooms" (in Carson and Friedman 1995: 3).

Few advocates of multicultural education call for jettisoning the traditional canon and altogether replacing the classics with a new multicultural fare. Genuine multicultural education requires expanding, not contracting, the curricula, broadening and enriching the field of education, not impoverishing it. Critical multiculturalism also involves, as Friedman stresses (1995), including white ethnic groups in the multicultural spectrum and searching out those shared values and ideals that cut across racial and cultural boundaries. Thus, multicultural education can help us understand our history and culture and move toward producing a more diverse and inclusive democratic society.

Yet education and all media of communication can (and often do!) construct models of multicultural difference, privileging some groups while denigrating others. Grasping the construction of difference and hierarchy in all texts requires learning how different texts and media are constructed, how they communicate and metacommunicate, and how they influence their audiences. Textual and semiotic analysis of print and media artifacts helps to reveal their codes and conventions, values and ideologies, and thus their meanings and messages (see Kellner 1995; 2nd revised edition 2020). In particular, critical cultural studies should analyze representations of class, gender, race, ethnicity, sexual preference, and other identity markers in the texts of media and other forms of culture, as well as attend to national, regional, and other cultural differences, how they are articulated in cultural representations, and how these differences among audiences create different readings and receptions of cultural texts.[3]

The argument for developing critical media literacy as part of formal educational training is that the media themselves are a form of cultural pedagogy and, thus, must be countered by a critical media pedagogy that dissects how media communicate and affect their audiences and how students and citizens can gain skills to analyze the media critically. Indeed, the ubiquity of media culture in contemporary society and our bombardment through all kind of print, broadcasting, digital and all forms of media produce a more general argument for critical media literacy as a response to media overload and manipulation, requiring the necessary skills to decode its meanings and message.

CML involves knowledge of how media work, construct meanings, serve as a form of cultural pedagogy, and function in everyday life (Kellner and Share 2019). A media literate person is skillful in analyzing media codes and conventions, able to criticize media stereotypes, values, and ideologies, and thus literate in reading media critically. Thus, critical media literacy empowers people to use media intelligently, discriminate and evaluate media content, dissect media forms critically, and investigate media effects and uses.

Critical media literacy is necessary since media culture strongly influences our view of the world, imparting knowledge of geography, technology and the environment, political and social events, how the economy works, and what is currently happening in our society and around the world. Media entertainment is also a form of cultural pedagogy, teaching dominant values, ways of thought and behavior, style and fashion, and providing resources for constituting individual identities (Kellner 1995; 2020). The media are both crucial sources of knowledge and information and sources of entertainment and leisure activity. They are our storytellers and entertainers and are incredibly influential since we often need to be made aware that media narratives and spectacles are a form of education, imparting cultural knowledge and values and shaping how we see and live our social worlds.

Consequently, CML is an integral part of multicultural education since many people's conceptions of gender, sexuality, race, ethnicity, and class are constituted in part by the media, which are often crucial in determining how people view social groups and reality, conceive of gender roles of masculinity and femininity, and distinguish between good and evil, right and wrong, attitudes and behavior. Since the media also provide role models and conceptions of proper and improper conduct and crucial cultural and political information, they are a necessary form of pedagogy and socialization. Thus, a media literate person can read, understand, evaluate, discriminate, and criticize media materials and produce media artifacts to use media as means of expression and communication.

Sometimes "the media" are lumped into one homogeneous category. Still, it is important to discern that there are many media of communication and forms of cultural pedagogy, ranging from print media such as books, newspapers, and magazines to film, radio, television, popular music, photography, advertising, and many other multimedia cultural forms, including video and computer games, computer culture, and social media. Thus, critical media literacy requires traditional print literacy skills as well as visual and aural literacy and the ability to analyze narratives, spectacles, and a wide range of cultural forms. CML involves reading images critically, interpreting sounds, and seeing how media texts produce meaning in multiple ways. Since media are a central part of our cultural experience from childhood to the grave, training in critical media literacy should begin early in life and continue into adulthood, as new technologies are constantly creating new media and new genres, while technical innovations, aesthetic forms, and conventions are continually emerging.

It is the challenge of education and educators to devise strategies to teach CML while using media materials to contribute to advancing multicultural education. Against McLuhan, who claims that the younger generation is naturally media literate (1964), I argue that developing critical media literacy requires cultivating explicit cultural pedagogy strategies and media education models. CML involves making unconscious and pre-reflective understanding conscious and reflective, drawing on individuals' learned abilities to interact with media. All people in a media culture such as ours are in some ways media literate, they can read and interpret the multitude of cultural forms with which they daily interact, but their media literacy is often unconscious and unreflective, requiring the cultivation of cognitive skills of analysis, interpretation, and critique. Moreover, as many media literacy students and teachers have discovered, most individuals who cultivate CML competencies reach new levels of media enjoyment and understanding due to their abilities to apply critical skills to reading media which discloses new dimensions, connections, and meanings.

Yet, within educational circles, there is a debate over what constitutes the field of media pedagogy, with different agendas and programs. A traditionalist "protectionist" approach would attempt to "inoculate" young people against the effects of media addiction and manipulation by cultivating a taste for book literacy, high culture, and the values of truth, beauty, and justice, denigrating all forms of media and computer culture. Neil Postman exemplifies this approach in his books *Amusing Ourselves to Death* (2005) and *Technopoly* (1992). A "critical media literacy" movement, by contrast, attempts to teach students to read, analyze, and decode media texts in a fashion parallel to the cultivation of print literacy. Media arts education, in turn, prepares students to appreciate media's aesthetic qualities and use various media technologies as tools of self-expression and creation. Critical media literacy (CML) builds on these approaches, analyzing media culture as products of social production and struggle, while teaching students to be critical of media representations and discourses, but also stressing the importance of learning to use the media as modes of self-expression and social activism (Kellner and Share 2019).

CML not only teaches students to learn from media, resist media manipulation, and empower themselves vis-a-vis the media, but it is concerned with developing skills that will empower citizens and make them more motivated and competent participants in social life. Critical media literacy is thus tied to the project of radical democracy and is concerned with developing skills that will enhance democratization and participation. CML takes a comprehensive approach that teaches critical skills at understanding and interpreting media, and how to use media as instruments of social change. Communication technologies are becoming increasingly accessible to young people and average citizens, and they should be used to promote education, democratic self-expression, and social progress. Thus, technologies that could help produce the end of participatory democracy by transforming politics into media spectacles and the battle of images and turning spectators into cultural zombies could also be used to help invigorate democratic debate and participation.

Indeed, teaching critical media literacy should be a participatory, collaborative project. Students are often more media savvy, knowledgeable, and immersed in media culture than their teachers, and thus can contribute to the educational process by sharing their ideas, perceptions, and insights. On the other hand, critical discussion, debate, and analysis should be encouraged, with teachers bringing their critical perspectives to student readings of all media material. Since media culture is often part and parcel of a student's identity and rich cultural experience, teachers must be sensitive in criticizing artifacts, and perceptions students hold dear. Yet, an atmosphere of critical respect for difference and inquiry into the nature and effects of media culture should be encouraged.

Another complexity in developing critical media pedagogy results from the fact that, in a sense, it is not a pedagogy in the traditional sense with firmly established principles, a canon of texts, and tried-and-true teaching procedures. Critical media pedagogy is in its infancy, just beginning to produce results, and is thus more open and experimental than established print-oriented pedagogy. Moreover, the material of media culture is so polymorphous, multivalent, and polysemic that it requires sensitivity to different readings, interpretations, and perceptions of the complex images, scenes, narratives, meanings, and messages of media culture, which in its ways is as complex and challenging to decipher as book culture critically.

I have downplayed hostility toward media education and the media in some educational and political circles. Educational traditionalists conceive of literacy in more limited print-media paradigms and, as I suggested above, often adopt a "protectionist" approach when they address the issue of the media, warning students against corruption or urging that they limit media use to "educational" materials. Yet many teachers at all levels, from kindergarten to University, have discovered that judiciously used media material can be valuable in various instructional tasks, helping make the complex subject matter accessible and engaging. Media cannot substitute for print material and classroom teaching and should be seen as a supplement to traditional materials rather than a magic panacea for the failures of traditional education. Moreover, as I argue in the next section, traditional print literacy and competencies are more critical than ever in our new high-tech societies.

It is also highly instructive to teach students at all levels to engage critically in popular media materials, including the most familiar film, television, music, and other forms of media culture. Yet, one must avoid an uncritical media populism emerging within specific British and North American cultural studies sectors. In a review of *Rethinking Media Literacy* (McLaren, Hammer, Sholle, and Reilly 1995), for instance, Jon Lewis attacked what he saw as the overly critical postures of the contributors to this volume, arguing: "If the point of a critical media literacy is to meet students halfway – to begin to take seriously what they take seriously, to read what they read, to watch what they watch -teachers must learn to love pop culture" (1996: 26). Note the authoritarian injunction that "teachers must learn to love popular culture" (italics are Lewis'), followed by an attack on more critical approaches to media literacy.

Teaching critical media literacy, however, involves occupying a site above the dichotomy of fandom and censor. One can teach how media culture provides significant statements or insights about the social world, positive visions of gender, race, and class, or complex aesthetic structures and practices, thus putting a positive spin on how it can significantly contribute to education. Yet one should also indicate how media culture can promote sexism, racism, ethnocentrism, homophobia, other forms of prejudice, misinformation, problematic ideologies, and questionable values. A more dialectical approach to media literacy engages students' interests and concerns.

As suggested above, it should involve a collaborative process between teachers and students since students are deeply absorbed in media culture and may know more about some of its artifacts and domains than their teachers. Consequently, they should be encouraged to speak, discuss, and intervene in teaching and learning. This is not to say that media literacy training should romanticize student views. That may be superficial, mistaken, uninformed, and full of various problematical biases. Yet exercises in critical media literacy can often productively involve intense student participation in a mutual learning process where teachers and students learn critical media literacy skills and competencies together.

It is also a mistake to institute a top-down program of CML imposed from above on teachers, with fixed texts, curricula, and prescribed materials. Diverse teachers and students will have very different interests and concerns, naturally emphasize different subject matter, and choose examples relevant to their and their students' interests. Courses in critical media literacy should thus be flexible enough to enable teachers and students to constitute curricula to engage material and topics of current concern and address their interests. Crucially, educators should discern that we are amid one of the most intense technological revolutions in history and must learn to adapt new computer technologies to education, as I suggest in the following section. This requires the development of digital and multiple critical literacies.

Digital Technologies, Multiple Literacies, and Postmodern Pedagogy: The New Frontier

The studies on multicultural education and critical media literacy that I have examined must also engage digital technology and culture, and how the Internet, social media, new digital technologies, and cultural forms dramatically transform the circulation of information, images, and various modes of culture. And so in this concluding section that is engaging education as we move through the 21st century, I want to argue that students should learn new forms of critical computer literacy (CCL) that involve both how to use computer culture to do research and gather information, as well as to perceive it as a cultural terrain which contains texts, spectacles, games, forums of political communication (and misinformation!), and debate in an emergent landscape of interactive multimedia.

Moreover, digital culture is a discursive and political location where individuals can intervene, engage in discussion groups and collaborative research projects, create websites, and produce new multimedia for cultural dissemination. Digital culture and technologies enable individuals to actively participate in cultural production, ranging from discussing public issues to creating their own cultural forms. However, to take part in this culture requires not only accelerated forms of traditional modes of print literacy which are often restricted to the growing elite of students who are privileged to attend adequate and superior public and private schools but new forms of techno-literacies as well, thus posing significant challenges to education.

It is indeed a salient fact of the present age that digital culture is proliferating, so we must begin teaching critical computer and digital literacies early on. Critical computer literacy (CCL), however, itself needs to be theorized. Often computer literacy is synonymous with the technical ability to use computers, master existing programs, and maybe engage in some programming oneself. I want, however, to suggest expanding the conception of computer literacy from using computer programs and hardware to developing, in addition, more sophisticated abilities in traditional reading and writing, as well as the capability to critically dissect cultural forms taught as part of CML, CCL, and new forms of multiple literacies.

Thus, on this conception, genuine critical computer literacy involves not just technical knowledge and skills, but refined reading, writing, and communicating ability that involves heightened capacities for critically analyzing, interpreting, and processing print, image, sound, and multimedia material. CCL involves intensified abilities to read, scan texts and information, put together in meaningful patterns mosaics of knowledge, search for new sources of digitally-mediated information,[4] develop meanings and significance, contextualize and evaluate, and discuss and articulate one's views.

Thus, CCL involves technical abilities concerning developing basic typing skills, using digital programs and devices, accessing information, and using digital technologies for various purposes ranging from verbal communication to artistic expression. There are many implosions between media and digital culture as audio and video material becomes part of the Internet, social and multimedia development, and digital technologies become part and parcel of the home, school, and workplace.

Therefore, the skills of decoding images, sounds, and spectacles learned in critical media literacy training can also be valuable as part of CCL. Furthermore, print literacy takes on increasing importance in the digital world as one needs to critically scrutinize and scroll tremendous amounts of information, putting new emphasis on developing reading and writing abilities. Indeed, Internet discussion groups, chat rooms, email, and various digital forums require writing skills. A new emphasis on the importance of clarity and precision is emerging as communications proliferate. In this context of information saturation, it becomes an ethical imperative not to contribute to cultural and information overload and to communicate one's thoughts and feelings concisely.

The expansion of computers, digital devices, and sources of information over the years requires the cultivation of critical information and news literacies as part of CCL. More and more people are getting their news and information from digital sources that requires a critical digital literacy that can discern good information sources from bogus ones, that can distinguish between information and disinformation, and that can discern the differences between various types of information sources ranging from news to scholarly sources of digital resources. Digital news literacy requires knowledge of how we get our news and information about the world and what constitute reliable and unreliable sources of information ranging from print and broadcast news to digital information sources.

In the world of broadcast news in the United States, there were traditionally three major radio and then television networks (ABC, CBS, and NBC) where largely presented centrist news broadcasts that were pro-U.S. democracy and foreign policy and pro-capitalism, reproducing the interests of the networks' owners, board of directors, and newsroom producers and broadcasters (see Kellner 1990). With the rise of cable television and the Internet multiple news and information sources dramatically multiplied. The cable news networks presented Fox News with an increasingly Republican and rightwing new bias while the MS-NBC cable news network was increasing pro-Democratic party and left liberal. CNN tried to maintain a centrist position but increasingly has been losing viewers as the U.S. public becomes more polarized.

Thus broadcasting news literacy in the U.S. can handily present studies of biases of the major news networks, although there are constant wars over disinformation, biases, and outright lies on broadcasting news, requiring critical news and information literacies to distinguish information from disinformation, and truth form lies. News literacy is thus a contested terrain torn by the competing politics of major broadcasting networks and thus requires critical scrutiny and increased focus on critical news literacy.[5]

Critical digital literacy (CDL) and the digitalization of all major news sources ranging from print and broadcasting media to Internet and always-expanding social media sources requires serious study of all the major forms of news and information on digital media ranging from news and information to scholarly sources. Traditional studies of newspapers and print media and their biases thus become part of CDL, as do studies of broadcasting media, social, media and other digital sites. This has led to specialized studies of newspapers, broadcasting media, and social media sources which become literally a lifetime enterprise for those of us who want to access the best news and information and scholarly sources and to avoid misinformation, propaganda, and anti-democratic sources.

A good citizen today must thus have the ability to process the multiple sources of print, broadcasting, and digital information to which we are presented with in an increasingly complex and contested info-sphere. In a certain sense, digital devices and digitalization are becoming the technological equivalent of Hegel's Absolute Idea, able to absorb everything into its form and medium. Digital devices are now not only repositories of text and print-based data, but also contain a wealth of images, multimedia sights and sounds, and interactive environments that, like the media, are a form of education that require a critical pedagogy of electronic, digitized culture and communication. From this conception, CCL is like a Hegelian synthesis of print, and visual literacy, technical skills, and media literacies brought together at a new and higher stage. While Postman and others produce a simplistic Manichean dichotomy between print and visual and media literacy, we need to learn to think dialectically, to read text and image, to decipher sight and sound, and to develop forms of critical digital literacies adequate to meet the exigencies of an increasingly high-tech society.

Thus, a radical pedagogy today requires developing critical forms of print, media, and computer literacy, which are crucial in the new technoculture of the present and fast-approaching future. Whereas modern pedagogy tended to be specialized, fragmented, and differentiated and was focused on print culture, contemporary pedagogy involves developing multiple literacies and critically analyzing, dissecting, and engaging a multiplicity of cultural forms, some of which are the products of new technologies and require developing new literacies to engage the new cultural forms and media.

Contemporary culture is thus marked by a proliferation of cultural machines which generate a panoply of print, sound, environmental, and diverse aesthetic artifacts within which we wander, trying to navigate this forest of words, images, sounds and spectacles. This requires developing new critical multimedia literacy to scan, interact with, traverse, and organize proliferating multimedia educational environments. Critical multimedia literacy involves not just reading but interacting, clicking, and moving from one field to another if one is engaged in a hypertext environment such as one finds on the Internet, video games, or, increasing, personal digital devices. Activity in digital culture involves capturing, downloading, saving, organizing, and reconfiguring material relevant to one's own projects; and responding verbally or adding one's material if it is a site that invites participation and sharing resources.

In addition to the linear cognitive skills needed for the traditional reading of print material, critical multimedia literacy requires reading hypertexts that are often multidimensional, requiring connecting images, graphics, texts, and sometimes audio-video material. It also involves connecting the complex and multilayered cyberworld and its connection with the real world. Moreover, Alan and Carmen Luke reminds us: "Since all meaning is situated relationally – that is, connected and cross-referenced to other media and genres, and to related meanings in other cultural contexts – a critical literacy relies on broad-based notions of intertextuality" (2000: 10).

Thus, one must learn to read multimedia forms that are themselves overlapping and interrelated, switching from text to graphics to video to audio, decoding, in turn, sight, sound, and text. In a global information environment, this also may involve switching from sites from one country to another requiring contextual understanding and literacy that can read and interact with people and sites from different cultures. As the Lukes puts it: "[N]ew [forms of] virtual communication are emerging, which require an intertextual understanding of how meanings shift across media, genres, and cultural frames of reference. Whether one 'visits' the Louvre online, joins an international newsgroup of parents of Downs Syndrome children, or visits the site of an agricultural college in Georgia, cross-cultural understanding and `netiquette' is increasingly crucial for participating effectively in global communications" (Luke and Luke 2000: 10).

In addition, critical multimedia literacy should be contextual; it requires thematizing the background and power relations of cultural forms (i.e., including analysis of the political economy of the media and technology, of how corporate organizations control production and dissemination, of how political groups may circulate propaganda and misinformation, while all media sources display some point of view and bias. An activist use of media should explore how oppositional and alternative media and uses are possible, as well as the context and power relations of the specific media use in question (i.e., the differences between television watching in the classroom, at home with one's family, with one's friends or alone; or the differences between computer use for research, data organization, email, or playing games, and so on). Critical multimedia literacy also envisages new modes of collaborative work on research projects or websites, new forms of student/teacher participation and interaction, and new pedagogical uses for the emergent technologies which may often appear exotic in the present, but which will become increasingly commonplace in the future and will force a rethinking of education.

And so we need to learn how to read and deploy these new multimedia environments and interact with these fascinating and seductive cultural forms whose massive impact on our lives we have only started to understand. Indeed, education should attend to the new multimedia culture and teach how to read and interact with the latest digital and multimedia environment as part of new forms of multiple critical literacies. Such an effort would be part of a radical pedagogy that attempts to critically empower individuals to analyze and criticize the emerging technoculture and participate in its cultural forums and sites.

In addition to the critical media literacy, print literacy, computer literacy, and multimedia literacy discussed above, multiple literacies involve, as outlined in the previous chapter, cultural literacy, social literacy, and ecoliteracy. Since a multicultural society is the context of education in the contemporary moment, new forms of social interaction and cultural awareness are needed that appreciate differences, multiplicity, and diversity. Therefore, expanded social and cultural literacy is needed to appreciate diverse groups' cultural heritage, histories, and contributions. Thus, whereas one can agree with E.D. Hirsch (1987) that we need to be literate in our shared cultural heritage, we also need to become culturally literate in hitherto invisible cultures, as Henry Louis Gates and his colleagues have been arguing in their proposals for multicultural education (1996).

Social literacy should also be taught throughout the educational systems, focusing on relating and getting along with various individuals, negotiating differences, resolving conflicts, and communicating and socially interacting in diverse situations. Social literacy also involves ethical training in values and norms, delineating proper and improper individual and social values. It also requires knowledge of contemporary societies and thus overlaps with social and natural science training. Indeed, given the tremendous role of science and technology in the modern world, given the threats to the environment, and the need to preserve and enhance the natural as well as social and cultural worlds, it is scandalous how illiterate the entire society is concerning science, nature, and even our bodies. An ecoliteracy should thus appropriately teach competency in interpreting and interacting with our natural environment, ranging from our bodies to natural habitats like forests and deserts.[6]

The challenge for education today is thus to promote multiple critical literacies to empower students and citizens to use emerging technologies and digital devices to enhance their lives and to create a better culture and society based on respect for multicultural differences and aiming at fuller democratic participation for individuals and groups excluded from wealth and power in the previous modern society. A democratic and multicultural postmodernity would thus involve the creation of a more egalitarian and just society, in which more individuals and groups were empowered to participate. The great danger facing us is that the continuous development and proliferatin of new technologies will increase the current inequalities based on class, gender, and racial divisions. So far, the privileged groups have had more direct and immediate access to the new technologies. It is, therefore, a challenge of education today to provide access to the new technologies and the literacies needed for competence to overcome some of the divisions and inequalities that have plagued contemporary societies during the modern age.

Yet, there is also the danger that youth will become immersed in a brave new world of high-tech experience and lose their social connectedness and ability to interpersonally communicate and relate concretely to other people and the natural world. Statistics suggest that more and more youth sectors can access cyberspace and that college students with Internet accounts are spending more and more time in the new realm of technological experience.[7] The media themselves, however, have been generating a moral panic concerning allegedly growing dangers in cyberspace with lurid stories of young boys and girls lured into dangerous sex or running away from home, endless accounts of how pornography on the Internet and social media is proliferating, and the publicizing of calls for increasing control, censorship, and surveillance of communication – usually by politicians who are computer illiterate. The solution, however, is not to ban access to new technologies, but to teach students and citizens how to use these technologies for productive and creative rather than problematical ends.

To be sure, there are dangers in cyberspace and elsewhere. Still, the threats to adolescents are significantly higher through the danger of family violence and abuse than seduction by strangers on the Internet. And while there is a flourishing trade in pornography on the Internet, this material has become increasingly available in various venues, from video stores to the newspaper stand, so it seems unfair to demonize the Internet. Further, attempts at Internet censorship are part of the attack on youth, which would circumscribe their rights to obtain entertainment and information and create their subcultures. Consequently, devices like the V-chip that would exclude sex and violence on television, or block computer access to objectionable material, are more an expression of adult hysteria and moral panic than genuine dangers to youth which certainly exist, but much more strikingly in the real world than in the sphere of hyperreality.

Throughout this century, there has been a demonization of new media and forms of media culture, ranging from comic books to film to popular music to television and now to the Internet. As Henry Jenkins argues (1997), this demonization is supported by an assumption of the innocence of childhood, that children are merely passive receptacles, easily seduced by cultural images, and in need of protection from nefarious and harmful cultural content. Further, Jenkins contends (1997: 30f) that the myth of "childhood innocence" strips children of active agency, of being capable of any thoughts of their own, of having the ability to decode and process media materials themselves. Of course, children need media education, they need to be involved in an active learning process concerning their culture. Still, censorship and vilification of media do not help young people become enthusiastic critics and participants in their culture.

Accordingly, Jon Katz (1996) has argued for children's "cyber-rights," arguing that our youth's access to Internet cyberculture and media culture, in general, is necessary for their participation in the larger culture and their education and development. Mastery of the culture can be the difference between economic success and hardship. The Internet allows participation in many dimensions of social and cultural life and the cultivation of technical skills to help children later in life.

Therefore, it is necessary to divest ourselves of myths of childhood innocence and the passivity of children's media consumption, positing instead the possibility of active and creative use of media material in which media education is seen as part of youth's self-development and constitution. Accordingly, Henry Jenkins proposes "a new kind of radical media education based on the assumption that children are active participants within popular culture rather than passive victims. We need to help our children become more critically reflective about the media they use and the popular culture they embrace. Yet, we can only achieve this by recognizing and respecting their existing investments, skills, and knowledge as media users. Ultimately, our goals must be not to protect our children but to empower them" (1997: 31).

Thus, rather than demonizing and rejecting out-of-hand new technologies, we should see how they can be used constructively for positive ends. Indeed, in studying the kaleidoscopic array of discourses which characterize the new technologies, I am somewhat bemused by the extent to whether they expose either a technophilic discourse that presents new technologies as our salvation that will solve all our problems or they embody a technophobic discourse that sees technology as our damnation, demonizing it as the primary source of all our problems (Kellner 2021). Similar, one-sided, and contrasting discourses greeted the introduction of other new technologies this century, often hysterically. To some extent, this was historically the case with film, radio, TV, and now digital and social media.

Film, for instance, was celebrated by early theorists as providing a new documentary depiction of reality, even redemption of reality, a new art form, new modes of mass education and entertainment – as well as demonized for promoting sexual promiscuity, juvenile delinquency and crime, violence, and copious other forms of immorality and evils. Its demonization led in the United States to a Production Code that rigorously regulated the content of Hollywood films from 1934 until the 1950s and 1960s – no open-mouthed kissing was permitted, crime could not pay, drug use or attacks on religion could not be portrayed, and a censorship office rigorously surveyed all films to make sure that no subversive or illicit content emerged (Kellner 2010).

Similar extreme hopes and fears were projected onto radio, television, and computers. Whenever there are new technologies, people project fantasies, fears, hopes, and dreams onto them. This has been happening over the past decades with computers, the Internet, social media and new multimedia technologies. It is striking that if one looks at the literature on new technologies, especially the Internet and now social media, it is either highly celebratory and technophilic or sharply derogatory and technophobic. A critical theory of technology, however, and radical pedagogy, should avoid either demonizing or deifying the emergent technologies and should develop pedagogies that will help us use the technologies to enhance education, and life and to criticize the limitations and limitations false promises made on their behalf by technophiles and the promoters of the Newest and Next Great Thing.

Indeed, there is no doubt that the cyberspace of digital worlds contains as much banality and stupidity as real life, and one can waste much time on any number of useless activities. Yet compared to the bleak and violent urban worlds portrayed in rap music and youth films like *Kids* (1995), the technological worlds are havens of information, entertainment, interaction, and connection where youth can gain valuable skills, knowledge, and power necessary to survive the postmodern adventure.

Youth can create new, more multiple, flexible selves in cyberspace and new subcultures and communities. Indeed, it is exciting to cruise the digital world and discover how many interesting websites young people and others have established, often containing valuable educational material. There is, of course, the danger that corporate and commercial interests will come to colonize the Internet. Still, there will likely continue to be spaces where individuals can empower themselves and create their communities and identities. A central challenge for youth (and others) is to learn to use digital technologies and devices for positive cultural and political projects rather than just entertainment and passive consumption.

Reflecting on the growing social importance of digital devices and the continuous growth of the cyberworld makes it clear that it is of essential importance for youth today to gain various kinds of critical techno-literacies to empower themselves for the emerging new cybersociety (this is true of teachers and adults as well). To survive in a postmodern world, individuals of all ages need to gain skills in media and computer literacy to enable ourselves to negotiate the overload of media images and spectacles; we all need to learn technological skills to use emergent media and digital technologies to subsist in the new high-tech economy and to form our own cultures and communities, as well as new forms of multiple critical literacies to traverse the cultural, social, and natural worlds in which we exist.

It is, therefore, essential for the future of democracy to make sure that youth of all classes, races, genders, and regions gain access to emergent and expanding digital technologies, and receive training in critical media and digital literacy skills to provide the opportunities to enter the high-tech job market and society of the future, while also attempting prevent an exacerbation of class, gender, and race inequalities. And while multiple forms of critical literacies will be necessary, traditional print literacy skills are even more important in a cyberage of word-processing, information gathering, and omnipresent digital communication. Moreover, what I am calling multiple critical literacies should involve training in philosophy, ethics, value thinking, and the humanities which are necessary now more than ever. How new digital devices and cultures will be used depends on the overall education of youth and the skills and interests they bring to the new technologies, which can be used to critically analyze educational and valuable cultural material or pornography and the banal wares of cybershopping malls.

Thus, the concept of multiple critical literacies and the postmodern pedagogy that I envisage would argue that it is not a question of either/or, e.g., either print literacy or multimedia literacy, either the classical curriculum or a new curriculum, but it is rather a question of both/and that preserves the best from classical literacy education, that enhances the emphasis on print literacy, but that also develops new literacies to engage the latest technologies.

Cyberlife is just one dimension of experience, and one still needs to learn to interact in the "real world" of school, jobs, relationships, politics, and other people. Youth – indeed, all of us! – need to learn to interact in many dimensions of social reality and to gain a multiplicity of literacy and skills that will enable us to create identities, relationships, and communities that will nurture and develop our entire spectrum of potentialities and satisfy a wide array of needs. Our lives are more multidimensional than ever, and part of the postmodern adventure is learning to live in a variety of social spaces and to adapt to intense change and transformation. Education too must meet these challenges, and both utilize new technologies to promote education and to devise strategies in which new technologies can be deployed to create a more democratic and egalitarian multicultural society.

Notes

1 See, in Chapter 1, the discussion of Florida Republican Governor Ron DeSantis's attempts to prevent schools from teaching a College Board-approved advanced placement (AP) course in African American studies.
2 The election of Barack Obama as President in the 2008 and 2012 Presidential Election highlights the growing number of hybrid identities in an emigrant society such as the United States where marriage is open to people of multiple racial, ethnic, religious, and other identities, and has both highlighted the significance of the growing number of hybrid identities and generated a debate about hybridity, post-racial identities, and the reaction against it and

debates about the terms. See the contrasting arguments in the book edited by Parks and Hughey (2011) and the book by Marotta (2011).
3 For more on how a critical cultural studies can contribute to multicultural education and the teaching of critical media and digital literacies, see Chapter 3 below on "Key Components of a Critical Cultural Studies."
4 By "search for new sources of digitally-mediated information," I am referring to discovering and researching new digital sources of information which are regularly appearing at public, University, and other data bases and digital sources. This also involves critical digital and informational literacies which I discuss above.
5 For an important effort on news literacy, see the Center for News Literacy at the Stony Brook University School of Journalism at the studies by Ashley (2019) and Fleming (xx).
6 On ecoliteracy, see the discussion in Chapter 1 and Kahn 2010.
7 The *New York Times* informs us: "On average, daily screen use went up among tweens (ages 8 to 12) to five hours and 33 minutes from four hours and 44 minutes, and to eight hours and 39 minutes from seven hours and 22 minutes for teens (ages 13 to 18)." See Melinda Wenner Moyer, "Kids as Young as 8 Are Using Social Media More Than Ever, Study Finds. The report highlights a 17 percent increase in screen use among teens and tweens in the last two years – more than in the four years prior," *New York Times*, March 24, 2022 at <https://www.nytimes.com/2022/03/24/well/family/child-social-media-use.html> (accessed June 20, 2024).

References

Appiah, K. Anthony (1994). "Identity, authenticity, survival: multicultural societies and social reproduction", in Taylor, Charles and Gutmann, Amy (eds.), *Multiculturalism: Examining the Politics of Recognition*. Princeton, New Jersey: Princeton University Press, pp. 149–164 .
Best, S. and Kellner, D. (2001). *The Postmodern Adventure. Science, Technology, and Cultural Studies at the Third Millennium*. New York and London: Guilford and Routledge.
Crenshaw, K. (1989). "Demarginalizing the Intersection of Race and Sex: A Black Feminist Critique of Antidiscrimination Doctrine, Feminist Theory and Antiracist Politics," *University of Chicago Legal Forum*, Volume 1989, Issue 2, Article 8 at <https://chicagounbound.uchicago.edu/cgi/viewcontent.cgi?article=1052&context=uclf> (accessed March 8, 2023).
Carson, D. and Friedman, L. (1995). (eds.), *Shared Differences, Multicultural Media and Practical Pedagogy*. Chicago: University of Illinois Press.
hooks, bell (1984). *Feminist Theory: From Margin to Center*. Boston: South End Press.
Kellner, D. (1990). *Television and the Crisis of Democracy*. Boulder, Col.: Westview Press.
Kellner, D. (1995 [2nd revised edition 2020]). *Media Culture. Cultural Studies, Identity and Politics Between the Modern and the Postmodern*. London and New York: Routledge.
Kellner, D. (2010). *Cinema Wars: Hollywood Film and Politics in the Bush/Cheney Era*. Malden, Mass. and UK: Blackwell.
Kellner, D. (2021). *Technology and Democracy: Toward a Critical Theory of Digital Technologies, Technopolitics, and Technocapitalism*. Springer Publications.
Kellner, D. and Share, J. (2019). *The Critical Media Literacy Guide: Engaging Media and Transforming Education*. Rotterdam, The Netherlands: Brill-Sense Publishers.

Lewis, J. (1996). "Practice What You Teach," *Afterimage*, 25: 4.
Luke, A. and Luke, C. (2000). "A Situated Perspective on Cultural Globalization", in: *Globalization and Education*, edited by N. Burbules and C. Torres. London and New York: Routledge, pp. 275–298.
Marotta, V. (2011). *Hybrid identities in a globalised world*," Researchgate, at <www.researchgate.net/publication/305348952_Hybrid_identities_in_a_globalised_world> (accessed April 9, 2023).
McLaren, P., Hammer, R., Sholle, D. and Reilly, S. (1995). *Rethinking Media Literacy*. New York: Peter Lang.
Parks, G. and Hughey, M. (eds.). (2011). *The Obamas and a (Post) Racial America*. Oxford, UK: Oxford University Press.
Postman, N. (2005). *Amusing Ourselves to Death: Public Discourse in the Age of Show Business*. Penguin Books.
Postman, N. (1993). *Technopoly: The Surrender of Culture to Technology*. New York: Vintage Books.
Tucker, R. (ed.). (1978). *The Marx-Engels Reader*. New York: Norton.

· 3 ·

KEY COMPONENTS OF CRITICAL CULTURAL STUDIES

In this chapter, I will discuss the potential contributions of a cultural studies perspective to media critique and literacy. From the 1980s to the present, cultural studies have emerged as a set of approaches to studying culture, society, and politics. The project was inaugurated by the University of Birmingham Centre for Contemporary Cultural Studies in the 1960s, which developed various critical methods for the analysis, interpretation, and criticism of cultural artifacts. Through a set of internal debates and responses to social struggles and movements from the 1960s to the present, cultural studies became global. It focused on the interplay of representations and ideologies of class, gender, sexuality, race, ethnicity, and nationality in cultural texts, including media culture.[1]

British cultural studies were among the first group to study the effects of newspapers, radio, television, film, advertising, and other popular cultural forms on audiences.[2] They also focused on how various audiences interpreted and used media culture differently, analyzing the factors that made different audiences respond in contrasting ways to various media texts and use media in their personal and social lives in a multiplicity of ways.

Through studies of youth subcultures, British cultural studies demonstrated how culture came to constitute distinct forms of identity and group membership for young people. In cultural studies, media culture provides the materials for constructing views of the world, behavior, and even identities. Those who uncritically follow the dictates of media culture tend to "mainstream" themselves, conforming to the dominant fashion, values, and behavior. Yet cultural studies are also interested in how subcultural groups and individuals resist dominant forms of culture and identity, creating their style and identities. Those who obey ruling dress and fashion codes, behavior, and political ideologies thus produce their identities as members of specific social groupings within contemporary U.S. culture, such as White, middle-class conservative American men who go to work in suits and ties, and thus produce identities as corporate male members of the business class. By contrast, persons who identify with subcultures, like African-American and Latino or LGBTQ+ subcultures, look and act differently from those in the mainstream and thus create oppositional identities, defining themselves against standard white mainstream conservative models.

Cultural studies insist that culture must be studied within the social relations and system through which culture is produced and consumed. Thus, the study of culture is intimately bound up with the study of media, society, politics, and economics. Cultural studies show how media culture articulates the era's dominant values, political ideologies, and social developments and novelties. It conceives U.S. culture and society as a contested terrain with various groups and ideologies struggling for dominance (Kellner 1995 and [2020]). Television, film, music, and other popular cultural forms are thus often liberal or conservative – or occasionally express more radical or oppositional views, and can thus be contradictory and ambiguous in their meanings and messages.

Cultural studies are valuable because they provide methods and tools that enable individuals to read and interpret culture critically. Earlier mainstream academic approaches to culture tended to be primarily literary and elitist, dismissing media culture as banal, trashy, and unworthy of serious attention. By contrast, the project of cultural studies avoids cutting the field of culture into high and low or popular against the elite. Such distinctions are difficult to maintain and generally serve as a front for normative aesthetic valuations and, often, a political program (i.e., either dismissing mass culture for high culture/art or celebrating what is deemed "popular" while scorning "elitist" high culture).

Critical cultural studies open the way toward more differentiated political, rather than aesthetic, valuations of cultural artifacts in which one attempts to distinguish vital and oppositional from conformist and conservative moments in a cultural artifact. For instance, studies of Hollywood film show how essential 1960s films promoted the views of radicals and the counterculture and how film in the 1970s was a battleground between liberal and conservative positions (Kellner & Ryan, 1988); late 1970s films, however, tended toward conservative positions that helped elect Ronald Reagan and films and TV shows during the Reagan as president often featured strong male conservative heroes and narratives. Interestingly, during the Bush-Cheney era, films were released that repeatedly criticized the administration's military and conservative policies, like the documentaries of Michael Moore. At the same time, African American actor Will Smith was the top-grossing U.S. actor during the Bush/Cheney era, and Denzel Washington won two Academy Awards. He played a wide range of characters, while Morgan Freeman played a president, corporate executive, crime figure, and even God (Kellner 2010), attesting that the U.S. public was ready to see African Americans in major positions in all areas of society, anticipating the presidency of Barack Obama, demonstrating that cultural texts can have an anticipatory dimension as well as serving as conservative celebrations of the status quo.

From the beginning, British cultural studies were highly political. They focused on the potential for resistance in oppositional subcultures, first valorizing the possibility of working-class cultures, then youth subcultures to resist the hegemonic forms of capitalist domination. British cultural studies turned to youth cultures as providing potentially new forms of opposition and social change. Through studies of youth subcultures, British cultural studies demonstrated how culture came to constitute distinct forms of identity and group membership and appraised the oppositional potential of various youth subcultures (see Hebdige 1979).

Cultural studies focused on how subcultural groups resist dominant forms of culture and identity, creating their own style and identities. Individuals who conform to dominant dress and fashion codes, behavior, and political ideologies thus produce their identities within mainstream groups as members of specific social groupings (such as white, middle-class conservative Americans). Individuals who identify with subcultures, like punk culture or black nationalist subcultures, look and act differently from those in the mainstream and thus create oppositional identities, defining themselves against standard models.

There is thus an intrinsically critical and political dimension to the project of cultural studies that distinguishes it from objectivist and apolitical academic approaches to the study of culture and society. British cultural studies, for example, analyzed culture historically in the context of its societal origins and effects. It situated culture within a theory of social production and reproduction, specifying how cultural forms served to further social domination or enable people to resist and struggle against power. It analyzed society as hierarchical and antagonistic social relations characterized by the oppression of subordinate class, gender, race, ethnicity, and national strata.

Employing the Italian sociologist Antonio Gramsci's model of hegemony and counterhegemony (1971), cultural studies seek to analyze "hegemonic," or ruling, social and cultural forces of domination and to seek counterhegemonic forces of resistance and struggle. On this model, as suggested above, during the Reagan and Trump conservative regimes, one could analyze how dominant examples of media culture would either reproduce their conservative politics or present figures, narratives, and discourses that would oppose the hegemonic conservative ideologies of the ruling Republican regimes. Similarly, during the Obama and Biden presidencies, one would see how liberal media positively presented liberal and progressive ideals while conservative media attacked them.

The cultural studies project is also aimed at social transformation and attempts to specify forces of domination and resistance to aid the process of political struggle and emancipation from oppression and domination. For cultural studies, the concept of *ideology* is of central importance, for dominant ideologies serve to reproduce social relations of domination and subordination.[3] Ideologies of class, for instance, celebrate upper-class life and denigrate the working class. Ideologies of gender promote sexist representations of women, oppressive ideologies of sexuality promote homophobia, and ideologies of race use racist expressions of people of color and various minority groups. Ideologies make inequalities and subordination appear natural and just, thus inducing consent to relations of domination.

Cultural studies see contemporary societies as structured by opposing groups who have competing political ideologies (liberal, conservative, radical, etc.) and specify what, if any, ideologies are operative in each cultural artifact (which could involve, of course, the specification of ambiguities and ideological contradictions). In this chapter, I will provide some examples of how different ideologies are operative in media and cultural texts and accordingly give examples of ideological analysis and critique.

Cultural studies and ideological critique are vital components of radical pedagogy and critical media and digital literacies, so in this chapter, I present what I see as the foundational importance of cultural studies for the radical pedagogy I am developing in these studies. cause of its focus on representations of race, gender, sexuality, and class and its critique of ideologies that promote various forms of oppression, cultural studies lend itself to a multiculturalist program that demonstrates how culture reproduces certain forms of racism, sexism, and biases against members of subordinate classes, social groups, or alternative lifestyles. Multiculturalism affirms the worth of different types of culture and cultural groups, claiming, for instance, that Black, Latino, Asian, Native American, Gay, Bisexual, Lesbian, Transgendered, Queer/Questioning (GBLTQ+), and other oppressed and marginal voices have their validity and importance.

Cultural studies valorize positively strong and realistic representations of these groups while criticizing negative racist, sexist, homophobic, and other biased attacks on these groups and thus become a target of conservative forces that wish to preserve the existing canons of White male, Eurocentric privilege while attacking multiculturalism in cultural wars raging from the 1960s to the present over education, the arts, and the limits of free expression.[4]

Cultural studies thus promote a critical multiculturalist politics and media pedagogy that aims to make people sensitive to how relations of power and domination are "encoded" in cultural texts, such as those of television or film, or how alternative media can be used for oppositional pedagogical or political purposes (Kahn and Kellner 2008; Kellner and Share 2019). Critical cultural studies also specify how people can resist the dominant encoded meanings and produce their own vital and alternative readings and media artifacts, as well as new identities and social relations. Cultural studies can show how media culture can manipulate and indoctrinate its audiences. Thus, they can empower individuals to resist the dominant ideological meanings in media cultural products and produce their meanings. It can also point to moments of resistance and criticism within media culture and thus help promote the development of more critical consciousness.

Thus, Critical cultural studies develop concepts and analyses that will enable readers to dissect contemporary media culture's artifacts analytically and gain power over their cultural environment. By exposing the entire field of culture and media technology to knowledgeable scrutiny, a critical cultural study provides a broad, comprehensive framework to undertake studies of culture, politics, and society for individual empowerment and social and political struggle and transformation. In the following pages, I will indicate some of the chief components of critical cultural studies that I find most helpful in understanding contemporary U.S. society, culture, and politics.

Components of a Critical Cultural Studies

As a theoretical apparatus, critical cultural studies contain a threefold project of analyzing the production and political economy of culture, cultural texts, and the audience reception of those texts and their effects in a concrete socio-historical context. This comprehensive approach avoids too narrowly focusing on one dimension of the project to the exclusion of others. To avoid such limitations, I propose a multiperspectival approach that (a) discusses production and political economy, (b) engages in textual analysis, and (c) studies the reception and use of cultural texts[5].

Since cultural production has been neglected in many modes of recent cultural studies, it is important to stress the importance of analyzing cultural texts within their production and distribution system, often referred to as the political economy of culture.[6] Inserting texts into the system of culture within which they are produced and distributed can help elucidate features and effects of the texts that textual analysis alone might miss or downplay.

This economic factor explains why there are cycles of certain genres and subgenres, sequelmania in the film industry, crossovers of popular films into television series, and a certain homogeneity in products constituted within systems of production marked by relatively rigid generic codes, formulaic conventions, and well-defined ideological boundaries. Some forms of media analysis, however, reduce media texts to the ideologies of their owners and claim that media culture is primarily an ideological apparatus that reproduces the dominant ideologies of the capitalist media corporations that produce them.

While there is some truth in this perspective, to avoid a cultural reductionism that would claim the media corporations that produce media culture reproduce the dominant ideology, I propose a multiperspectival approach that (a) discusses production and political economy, (b) engages in textual analysis, and (c) studies the reception and use of cultural texts[7].

Production and Political Economy

Because it has been neglected in many modes of recent cultural studies, it is essential to stress the importance of analyzing cultural texts within their production and distribution system, often called the political economy of culture.[8] Inserting texts into the system of culture within which they are produced and distributed can help elucidate features and effects of the texts that textual analysis alone might miss or downplay. Rather than being an antithetical approach to culture, political economy can contribute to textual analysis and critique. The system of production often determines what sort of artifacts will be produced, what structural limits there will be as to what can and cannot be said and shown, and what kind of audience effects the text may generate, yet, as I'll argue in the next sections, it is also essential to do textual and audience analysis.

The study of the codes of television, film, or popular music, for instance, is enhanced by studying the formulas and conventions of production. Well-defined rules and conventions structure these cultural forms, and the study of the production of culture can help elucidate the codes in play. Because of the demands of the format of radio or music television, for instance, most popular songs are 3–5 minutes, fitting into the structure of the distribution system. Because of their control by giant corporations oriented primarily toward profit, television production in the United States is dominated by specific genres such as talk and game shows, soap operas, situation comedies, action/adventure series, reality TV, and so on. At the same time, film traditionally has dominant genres of comedy, horror, crime, romance, and other popular forms. This economic factor explains why there are cycles of specific genres and subgenres, sequelmania in the film industry, crossovers of popular films into television series, and a certain homogeneity in products constituted within systems of production marked by rigid generic codes, formulaic conventions, and well-defined ideological boundaries.

Likewise, study of political economy can help determine the limits and range of political and ideological discourses and effects. My analysis of television in the United States, for instance, disclosed that the takeover of the television networks by major transnational corporations and communications conglomerates in the 1980s was part of a "right turn" within U.S. society whereby powerful corporate groups won control of the state and the mainstream media (Kellner 1990). For example, during the 1980s, all three networks were taken over by major corporate conglomerates: ABC was taken over in 1985 by Capital Cities, NBC was taken over by GE, and the Tisch Financial Group took over CBS. Both ABC and NBC sought corporate mergers, and this motivation, along with other benefits derived from Reaganism, might well have influenced them to downplay criticisms of Reagan and to generally support his conservative programs, military adventures, and simulated presidency.

Corporate conglomeratization has intensified further, and today Paramount, Fox, Time Warner, Disney, and other global media conglomerate control ever more domains of the production and distribution of culture (McChesney

2000, 2007). In this global context, one cannot really analyze the role of the media in the Gulf War, for instance, without analyzing the production and political economy of news and information, as well as the actual text of the Gulf War and its reception by its audience (see Kellner 1992). Likewise, the ownership by conservative corporations of dominant media corporations helps explain mainstream media support of the Bush-Cheney administration and their policies, such as the wars in Afghanistan and Iraq (Kellner 2003, 2005).

Looking toward entertainment, one can only fully grasp the Madonna phenomenon by analyzing her marketing strategies, her political environment, her cultural artifacts, and their effects (Kellner 1995; [2021]). Similarly, younger female pop music stars, such as Britney Spears, Beyonce, Taylor Swift, or Lady Gaga, also deploy the tools of the glamor industry and media spectacle to become icons of fashion, beauty, style, and sexuality, as well as purveyors of music who create powerful fan cultures. And in appraising the full social impact of pornography, one needs to be aware of the sex industry and the production process of pornographic films and videos, and not just dwell on the texts themselves and their effects on audiences.

Furthermore, in an era of globalization, one must be aware of the global networks that produce and distribute culture in the interests of profit and corporate hegemony. Yet political economy alone does not hold the key to cultural studies; important as it is, it has limitations as a single approach. Some political economy analyses reduce the meanings and effects of texts to rather circumscribed and reductive ideological functions, arguing that media culture merely reflects the ideology of the ruling economic elite that controls the culture industries and is a vehicle for capitalist ideology. It is true that media culture overwhelmingly supports capitalist values, but it is also a site of intense struggle between different races, classes, gender, and social groups. Thus, to fully grasp the nature and effects of media culture, one needs to develop methods to analyze the full range of the meanings and effects of dominant texts, genres, and spectacles of media culture.

Textual Analysis

The products of media culture require multidimensional close textual readings to analyze their various forms of discourses, ideological positions, narrative strategies, image construction, and effects. There has been a wide range of types of textual criticism of media culture, ranging from quantitative content analysis that dissects the number of, say, episodes of violence in a text to qualitative study that examines images of women, people of color, alternative sexualities, or other groups. Radical cultural studies apply various critical theories to unpack the texts' meanings and explicate how texts function to produce meanings and messages.

Traditionally, the qualitative analysis of texts was the task of formalist literary criticism, which explicates the central meanings, values, symbols, and (sometimes) ideologies in cultural artifacts by attending to the formal properties of imaginative literature texts – such as style, verbal imagery, characterization, narrative structure and point of view, and other formal elements of the artifact. From the 1960s on, however, literary-formalist textual analysis has been enhanced by methods derived from semiotics, a system for investigating the creation of meaning not only in written languages but also in other, nonverbal codes, such as the visual and auditory languages of film and TV, as well as socio-historical readings of cultural texts such as I am producing in this chapter and in other works.

Semiotics analyzes how linguistic and nonlinguistic cultural "signs" form systems of meanings, as when giving someone a rose is interpreted as a sign of love, or getting an A on a college paper is a sign of mastery of the rules of the specific assignment. Semiotic analysis can relate to genre criticism (the study of conventions governing established types of cultural forms, such as soap operas) to reveal how the codes and forms of genres follow particular meanings. Situation comedies, for instance, classically follow a conflict/resolution model that demonstrates how to solve some social issues by correct actions and values and thus provide morality tales of proper and improper behavior. Soap operas, by contrast, proliferate problems and provide messages concerning the endurance and suffering needed to get through life's endless miseries, while generating positive and negative models of social behavior. And advertising shows how commodity solutions solve problems of popularity, acceptance, success, and the like.

A semiotic and genre analysis of *Rambo* films (1982, 1985, 1998, 2008, 2019), for instance, would show how they follow the conventions of the Hollywood genre of the war film that dramatizes conflicts between the United States and its "enemies" (see Kellner 1995). Semiotics describes how the images of the villains are constructed according to the codes of World War II or Cold War movies and how the resolution of the conflict and happy ending follows the traditional Hollywood classical cinema, which portrays the victory of good over evil. Semiotic analysis would also include studying the strictly cinematic and formal elements of a film like Rambo, dissecting how camera angles present

Rambo as a god, or slow-motion images of him gliding through the jungle code him as a force of nature.

Likewise, semiotic analysis of James Cameron's *Avatar* (2009) would reveal how the images in the film present an anti-militarist and pro-ecological agenda. However, the narrative form celebrates a White male savior, replicating more conservative ideologies. *Avatar* also demonstrates how fantasy artifacts can project a wealth of political and ideological meanings, often ambiguous or contradictory. Discussions of *Avatar* have also generated heated debates in the politics of representation concerning how it has represented gender, sexuality, race, the military, the environment, and other dimensions of the film.

The textual analysis of cultural studies thus combines formalist analysis of style and form with a critique of how cultural meanings convey specific ideologies of gender, race, class, sexuality, nation, and other ideological dimensions. Ideological textual analysis should deploy a wide range of methods to fully explicate each dimension and show how they fit into textual systems. Each critical approach focuses on certain features of a text from a specific perspective: The perspective spotlights, or illuminates, some features of a text while ignoring others. Marxist methods tend to focus on class, for instance, while feminist approaches will highlight gender, critical race theory spotlights race and ethnicity, and gay and lesbian theories explicate sexuality.

Various critical methods have their strengths, limitations, optics, and blind spots. Traditionally, Marxian ideology critiques have been strong on class and historical contextualization and weak on formal analysis. At the same time, some versions of orthodox Marxism are highly "reductionist," reducing textual analysis to denunciation of ruling class ideology. Feminism excels in gender analysis and, in some versions, is formally sophisticated, drawing on such methods as psychoanalysis and semiotics. However, some versions are reductive, and early feminism often limited itself to the analysis of images of gender. Psychoanalysis, in turn, calls for the interpretation of unconscious contents and meanings, which can articulate latent meanings in a text, as when Alfred Hitchcock's dream sequences project cinematic symbols that illuminate his characters' dilemmas or when the image of the female character in *Bonnie and Clyde* (1967), framed against the bar of her bed, suggests her sexual frustration, imprisonment in middle-class family life, and need for revolt.

Consequently, I have been arguing for multiperspectival cultural studies that engage the dimensions of production and political economy, textual analysis, and audience reception, in which textual analysis is also multiperspectival, using a variety of critical theories to engage the representations and discourse of class, gender, race, sexuality, and other dimensions of meaning in a text. Cultural texts like films, television, music, and other forms of media culture are polysemic, containing multiple dimensions of meanings, sometimes ambiguous and contradictory. Thus a multiperspectival cultural analysis attempts to spell out the dominant ideological and other meanings in a text and to do a multidimensional reading of discourses and representations of gender, race, class, sexuality, and different dimensions present in specific texts, with the political agenda of criticizing racism, sexism, classism, homophobia, militarism, and other forms of bias and ideological meanings that could promote harassment, prejudice, hate, and violence in today's societies.

Of course, each reading of a text is only one possible reading from one critic's subject position, no matter how multiperspectival, and may or may not be the reading preferred by audiences (which themselves will be significantly different according to their class, race, gender, ethnicity, ideologies, regions, and so on). Because there is a split between textual encoding and audience decoding, there is always the possibility of a multiplicity of readings of any text of media culture (Hall 1980b). There are limits to the openness or polysemic nature of any text, of course, and textual analysis can explicate the parameters of possible readings and delineate perspectives that aim at illuminating the text and its cultural and ideological effects. Such analysis also provides the materials for criticizing misreadings or one-sided and incomplete readings. Yet to further carry through a critical cultural studies analysis, one must also examine how diverse audiences read media texts and attempt to determine what effects they have on audience thought and behavior.

Audience Reception and Use of Media Culture

All texts are subject to multiple readings depending on the perspectives and subject positions of the specific members of an audience. Film or TV viewers of distinct genders, classes, races, nations, regions, sexual preferences, and political ideologies will read texts differently, and cultural studies can illuminate why diverse audiences interpret texts in various, sometimes conflicting, ways. Media culture provides materials for individuals and communities to create identities and meanings, and cultural studies work on audiences detects different potentially empowering uses of cultural forms. It is one of the merits of cultural studies to have focused on audience reception in recent years, and this focus provides one of its major contributions. However, there are also some limitations and problems with the standard cultural studies approaches to the audience.[9]

Ethnographic research is frequently used to determine how texts affect audiences and shape their beliefs and behavior. Ethnographic cultural studies have indicated various ways audiences use appropriate texts, often to empower themselves. For example, teenagers use video games and music television to escape the demands of a disciplinary society. Males use sports as a terrain of fantasy identification, in which they feel empowered as "their" team or star triumphs. Such sports events also generate a form of community, currently being lost in our time's privatized media and consumer culture.

Indeed, fandoms of all sorts, ranging from *Star Trek* fans ("Trekkies") to devotees of *Buffy the Vampire Slayer*, or Pop Stars like Taylor Swift, Lady Gaga, or Beyonce, also form communities that enable people to relate to others who share their interests and hobbies. Some fans, in fact, actively re-create their favorite cultural forms (see examples in Jenkins 1992; Lewis 1992; and Sandvoss 2017). Other studies have shown that audiences can subvert the intentions of the producers or managers of the cultural industries that supply them, as when astute young media users laugh at obvious attempts to hype certain characters, shows, or products (see de Certeau, 1984, for more examples of audiences constructing meaning and engaging in practices in critical and subversive ways).

The emphasis on active audience reception and appropriation, then, has helped cultural studies overcome the previous one-sided textualist orientations to culture and has directed focus on the actual socio-ideological and political effects that texts may have. By combining quantitative and qualitative research, audience reception studies are essential to how people interact with cultural texts.

Yet I see several problems with reception studies as they have been constituted within cultural studies, particularly in the United States. First, there is a danger that class will be downplayed as a significant variable that structures audience decoding and use of cultural texts. Cultural studies in England were susceptible to class and subcultural differences – in the service and reception of cultural texts. Still, I have noted many dissertations, books, and articles in cultural studies in the United States where attention to class has been downplayed or is missing altogether. This is not surprising as neglect of class as a constitutive feature of culture and society is an endemic deficiency in U.S. institutions ranging from K-12 through university studies in most disciplines.

There is also the reverse danger of exaggerating the constitutive force of class and downplaying or ignoring, such other variables as gender or ethnicity.

Janet Staiger (1992) notes that John Fiske, building on Jon Hartley, lists seven "subjectivity positions" that are important in cultural reception – "self, gender, age-group, family, class, nation, ethnicity" – and proposes adding sexual orientation. All these factors, and no doubt more, interact in shaping how audiences receive and use texts and must be considered in studying cultural reception, for audiences decode and use texts according to the specific constituents of their class, race or ethnicity, gender, sexual preferences, and so on.

Furthermore, I would warn against a tendency to romanticize the "active audience" by claiming that all audiences produce their meanings and denying that media culture may have powerful manipulative effects. There is a tendency within the cultural studies tradition of reception research to dichotomize between dominant and oppositional readings (Hall 1980b, a dichotomy that structures much of Fiske's work). "Dominant" readings are those in which audiences' appropriate texts in line with the interests of the dominant culture and the ideological intentions of a text, as when audiences feel pleasure in the restoration of male power, law and order, and social stability at the end of a film such as *Die Hard*, after the hero and representatives of authority eliminate the terrorists who had taken over a high-rise corporate headquarters. An "oppositional" reading, by contrast, celebrates the resistance to this reading in audience appropriation of a text; for example, Fiske (1993) observes resistance to dominant readings when homeless individuals in a shelter cheered the destruction of police and authority figures during repeated viewings of a videotape of *Die Hard*.

Although this can be a helpful distinction, there is a tendency in cultural studies to celebrate resistance per se without distinguishing between types and forms of resistance (a similar problem resides with an indiscriminate celebration of audience pleasure in certain reception studies). For example, resistance to social authority by the homeless, evidenced in their viewing of *Die Hard*, could strengthen brutal masculinist behavior and encourage manifestations of physical violence to solve social problems. Jean-Paul Sartre, Frantz Fanon, and Herbert Marcuse, among others, have argued that violence can be either emancipatory when directed at forces of oppression or reactionary when directed at popular points struggling against oppression. Many feminists, by contrast, or those in the Gandhian tradition, see all violence as forms of brute masculinist behavior, and many people see it as a problematical form of conflict resolution. Therefore, resistance and pleasure cannot be valorized per se as progressive elements of the appropriation of cultural texts. Still, difficult discriminations must be made regarding whether the resistance, oppositional reading, or pleasure in a given experience is progressive or reactionary, emancipatory, or potentially producing hateful or destructive effects.

Thus, while an emphasis on the audience and reception was an excellent correction to the one-sidedness of purely textual analysis or purely political economy approaches to media culture, I believe that in recent years, cultural studies has overemphasized reception and textual analysis while underemphasizing the production of culture and its political economy. This type of cultural studies fetishizes audience reception studies. It neglects both production and textual analysis, thus producing populist celebrations of the text and audience pleasure in its use of cultural artifacts. This approach, taken to an extreme, would lose its critical perspective and would lead to a positive gloss on the audience experience of whatever is being studied. Such studies also might lose sight of the manipulative and conservative effects of certain types of media culture and thus serve the interests of the cultural industries as they are presently constituted.

A new way, in fact, to research media effects is to use the Internet and other digital sources to trace the effects of media artifacts such as *The X-Files, Buffy the Vampire Slayer, American Idol,* and the *Star* Wars and *Avatar* films, or advertisements for corporations such as Nike and McDonalds, through analysis of references to them in the media through Google or other search engines, or searching fan sites on the topic studied. Likewise, there is an expanding terrain of Internet and social media audience research that studies how fans act in listserves or chat rooms devoted to their favorite artifacts of media culture, create their own fansites, or construct artifacts that disclose how they are living out the fantasies and scripts of the culture industries.[10]

Previous studies of the audience and the reception of media privileged ethnographic studies that selected slices of the vast media audiences, usually from the site where researchers lived. Such studies are invariably limited, and broader effects research can indicate how the most popular artifacts of media culture have a wide range of effects. In my book *Media Culture* (Kellner 1995 [2021]), I studied some examples of popular cultural artifacts that influenced behavior in audiences throughout the globe. Examples include groups of kids and adults who imitated Rambo in various forms of asocial behavior and fans of Beavis and Butt-Head who started fires or tortured animals in the modes practiced by the popular MTV cartoon characters. Media effects are complex and controversial, and it is the merit of cultural studies to make their study an important part of its agenda.

Finally, digital media such as Facebook, YouTube, and other social networking sites produce forums for more active audiences and new sites for audience research. Audiences critically discuss or celebrate their preferred artifacts or criticize some characters or episodes, while others have other favorites they promote. Audience and reception studies reveal a contested terrain, as do studies of TV cable news networks like Fox, CNN, and MSNBC, or the texts of TV, film, and popular music entertainment (Kellner 1995 [202]).

Consequently, I advocate cultural studies that are critical, multicultural, and multiperspectval. To avoid the one-sidedness of solely adopting or privileging political economy, textual analysis, or audience and reception studies audiences, I propose that cultural studies itself be multiperspectival, getting at culture from the perspectives of political economy, text analysis, and audience reception, as outlined above. Further textual analysis should use multiple perspectives and critical methods, and audience reception studies should delineate the wide range of subject positions or perspectives through which audiences' appropriate culture.

As discussed above, cultural studies that are critical and multicultural provide comprehensive approaches to culture that can be applied to a wide variety of media artifacts, from advertising and pornography to Beyoncé and the *Avatar* or *Star Trek* films and TV series, from reality TV and *World of Warcraft* to Barbie and Britney Spears. Its comprehensive perspectives encompass political economy, textual analysis, and audience research and provide critical and political perspectives that enable individuals to dissect dominant cultural forms' meanings, messages, and effects.

Thus, Cultural studies is part of a critical media pedagogy that enables individuals to resist media manipulation and increase their freedom and individuality. It can empower people to gain sovereignty over their culture and to be able to struggle for alternative cultures and political change. Cultural studies are thus not just another academic fad but can be part of a struggle for a better society and life.

Thus, a critical cultural study draws on the notion of multiple critical literacies and radical pedagogy that I outlined in the last chapter. As an example of critical cultural studies analysis in the concluding sections of this chapter, I will analyze Donald Trump and the Trump phenomenon, which is dominating the U.S. media as I write this chapter in Spring 2023, and that will no doubt dominate the media and U.S. politics for the foreseeable future.

British cultural studies were inherently political in its origins, beginning in the 1960s with a focus on youth culture and the potential for political and cultural change in the rebellious youth and oppositional political movements of the time. In the 1980s, both the U.S. and the U.K. underwent a conservative turn under the hegemony of the Reagan and Thatcher regimes. Many practitioners of critical cultural studies of the 1980s did analyses of Reaganism and Thatcherism, including myself.[11] Hence, in the following research, I will show how a critical cultural studies provides foundations of a critical media literacy approach by reading and critiquing Donald Trump and the Trump phenomenon.

Donald Trump and the Politics of the Spectacle

One could argue that Donald Trump won the Republican primary contest and then the 2016 U.S. Presidential Election partly because he is the master of **media spectacle**, a concept that I've been developing and applying to U.S. politics and media since the mid-1990s.[12] In this study, I will first discuss Trump's use of media spectacle in his business career, his effort to become a celebrity and reality TV superstar, and his political campaigns. Then, I examine how Trump uses both broadcasting and social media in his U.S. presidential campaign and presidency and deploys a war against the mainstream media to delegitimize criticism or opposition to his presidency. Yet Trump's war against the media has generated a momentous battle in which segments of the media are fighting back against Trump in what must be the most contested media spectacle in modern U.S. political history.

I first developed the concept of media spectacle to describe the critical phenomenon of US media and politics in the mid-1990s. This was the era of the O.J. Simpson murder case and trial, the Clinton sex scandals, and the rise of cable news networks like Fox, CNN, and MSNBC, which inaugurated a 24/7 news cycle and pointed to partisan debate that has dominated US politics and media since then.[13] The 1990s was also when the Internet and social media took off so that anyone could be a political commentator, player, and participant in the spectacle. This phenomenon accelerated as new digital technologies morphed into social media that teenagers, celebrities, politicians, and others wanting to become part of the networked virtual world could access and participate in virtual worlds of their interests and self-images anytime and any place, through their phones, tablets, or other portable digital devices. From the beginning of his rise to celebrity fame, Trump promoted media in a range of print and broadcasting media and then social media, helping to make him a celebrity spectacle with a broad audience.

The scope of the spectacle has thus increased in the past decades with the proliferation of new digital media and social networking like Facebook, YouTube, Twitter, Instagram, and the like that expands the scope and participation of the spectacle. By "media spectacles" I am referring to media constructs that present events that disrupt ordinary and habitual flows of information and which become popular stories that capture the attention of the media and the public and circulate through broadcasting networks, the Internet, social networking, smartphones, and other new media and communication technologies. In a global networked society, media spectacles proliferate instantaneously, become virtual and viral, and in some cases become tools of socio-political transformation. In contrast, other media spectacles become mere moments of media hype and tabloidized sensationalism.

I've argued since 2008 that the key to Barack Obama's success in two presidential elections is that he became a Master of Media spectacle, blending politics and performance in carefully orchestrated media spectacles (Kellner 2009 and 2012). Previously, the model of the mastery of presidential spectacle was Ronald Reagan, who performed his presidency daily in a well-scripted and orchestrated daily spectacle. Reagan was trained as an actor, and every night, Ron and Nancy reportedly practiced his lines for the next day performance like they had done in their Hollywood days. Reagan breezed through the day scripted with a teleprompter and well-orchestrated media events, smiling frequently, and pausing to sound-bite the line of the day.

Trump's biographies reveal that he was driven by a need to compete and win,[14] and entering the highly competitive real estate business in New York in the 1980s, Trump saw the need to use the media and publicity to promote his celebrity and image. It was a time of tabloid culture and media-driven celebrity. Trump even adopted the pseudonym "John Baron" to give the media gossip items that touted his successes in business, with women, and as a rising man about town (Fisher & Hobson, 2016).

In the 2016 presidential election and into his presidency, Donald Trump emerged as a major media spectacle. He has long been a celebrity and master of the spectacle, promoting his buildings and casinos from the 1980s to the present, his reality TV shows, self-promoting events, and his presidential campaign and election. Hence, Trump was empowered and enabled to run for the presidency partly because media spectacle has become a significant force in US politics, helping to determine elections, the mode of government, and, more broadly, the ethos and nature of our culture and political sphere. Consequently, we see how a focus on Trump's use of broadcasting and digital media led to his initial popularity. In the next section, we see how Trump used the spectacle to promote his celebrity and form a political base of followers following him into his political career.

The Apprentice, Twitter and the Summer of Trump

Since Trump's national celebrity derived in part from his role in the reality TV series *The Apprentice*,[15] we need to deploy critical cultural studies perspectives to interrogate this widespread TV phenomenon to help explain the Trump phenomenon. The opening theme music, "For the Love of Money," a 1973 R&B song by The O'Jays, established the capitalist ethos of the competition for the winning contestant to get a job with the Trump organization. Obviously, money is the key to Trump's business and celebrity success. However, there is much controversy over how rich Trump is, and so far he has not released his tax returns to quell rumors that he isn't as rich as he claims, that he does not contribute as much to charity as he has stated, and that many years he had paid little or no taxes (see O'Brien 2016 [2005]).

In the original format of *The Apprentice*, several contestants formed teams to carry out a task dictated by Trump, and each "contest" resulted in a winner and Trump barking "you're fired" to the losers. Curiously, some commentators believe in the 2012 presidential election that Barack Obama beat Mitt Romney handily because he early on characterized Romney as a billionaire who liked to fire people, which is ironic since this is Trump's signature personality trait in his business, reality TV, and now political career, which saw him fire two campaign managers and more advisors by August 2016, and made dramatic firings of key officials a defining feature of his chaotic administration.

The Apprentice's TV Producer Mark Burnett broke into national consciousness with his reality TV show *The Survivor*, a neo-Darwinian epic of alliances, backstabbing, and nastiness, which provides an allegory of how one succeeds in the dog-eat-dog business world in which Donald Trump has thrived, and spectacularly failed as many of the books about him document. Both Burnett and Trump share the neo-Darwinian (a)social ethos of 19th-century ultracompetitive capitalism with some of Donald Trump's famous witticisms proclaiming:

When somebody challenges you unfairly, fight back – be brutal, be tough – don't take it. It is always important to WIN!
I think everyone's a threat to me.
Everyone that's hit me so far has gone down. They've gone down big league.
I want my generals kicking ass.
I would bomb the shit out of them.
You bomb the hell out of the oil. Don't worry about the cities. The cities are terrible.
(Trump in Pogash, 2016, pp. 30, 152, 153)

In any case, *The Apprentice* made Trump a national celebrity who became well-known enough to run for president plausibly. Throughout the 2016 U.S. presidential campaign against Hillary Clinton, Trump used his celebrity to gain media time and attention. In addition to his campaign's ability to manipulate broadcast media, Trump has long been a heavy user of Twitter and tweets out his messages daily and night. Indeed, Trump may be the first major Twitter presidential candidate, and indeed he has been the politician using it most aggressively and frequently into his presidency and beyond.

Twitter was launched in 2006, but I don't recall it being used significantly in the 2008 election. However, Obama used Facebook, and his campaign bragged that he had over a million "Friends" and deployed Facebook as part of his daily campaign apparatus. I don't recall, however, previous Presidential candidates using Twitter in a big way like Donald Trump, although today most politicians have accounts and deploy it in their daily "messaging." In the next section, I accordingly interrogate Trump's use of Twitter and social media and will highlight its' asocial and problematic aspects.

Twitter, (A)social Media, and Trump

Twitter is a perfect vehicle for Trump as you can use its 140-character framework for attacking, bragging, and getting out simple messages or posts that engage receivers who feel they are in the know and involved in TrumpWorld when they get pinged and receive his tweets. When asked at an August 26, 2015, Iowa event why he uses Twitter so much, he replied that it was easy, only took a few seconds, and that he could attack his media critics when he "wasn't treated fairly." Trump has also used Instagram – an online mobile photo-sharing, video-sharing, and social networking service that enables its users to take pictures and videos and share them on various social networking platforms, such as Facebook, Twitter, Tumblr, and Flickr.

Twitter is perfect for General Trump, who can blast out his opinions and order his followers what to think. It enables businessmen and Politician Trump to define his brand and mobilize those who wish to consume or support it. Trump's Twitter gratifies the need for Narcissist Trump to be noticed and recognized as a Master of Communication who can bind his warriors into an online community. Twitter enables the Pundit-in-Chief to opine, rant, attack, and proclaim on all and sundry subjects and to subject TrumpWorld to the indoctrination of their Fearless Leader.

Hence, Trump has mastered social media as well as dominating television and old media through his orchestration of media events as spectacles and his daily Twitter Feed. In Trump's presidential campaign kickoff speech on June 16, 2015, when he announced he was running for President, Trump and his trophy wife Melania dramatically ascended down the stairway at Trump Towers, and the Donald strode up to a gaggle of microphones and dominated media attention for days with his drama. The opening speech of his campaign made a typically inflammatory remark that held in thrall news cycles for days when he stated: "The U.S. has become a dumping ground for everybody else's problems. [Applause] Thank you. It's true, and these are the best and the finest. When Mexico sends its people, they're not sending their best. They're not sending you. They're not sending you. They're sending people that have lots of problems, and they're bringing those problems with us. They're bringing drugs. They're bringing crime. They're rapists. And some, I assume, are good people."

This comment ignited a firestorm of controversy and a preview of Things to Come concerning vile racism, xenophobia, Islamophobia, and the other hallmarks of Trump's Cacophony of Hate. Debate over Trump's assault on undocumented immigrants would come to dominate daily news cycles of the Republican primaries and would continue to play out in the general election in Fall 2016.

In the lead-up to the first Republican primary debate in Fall of 2015, Donald Trump got most of the media time, and his daily campaign appearances and the Republican primary debates became media spectacle dominated by Trump. Every day that Trump had a campaign event, the cable news networks would hype the event with crawlers on the bottom of the TV screen proclaiming, "Waiting for Trump," with airtime on cable TV dominated by speculation on what he would talk about. Trump's speeches were usually broadcast live, often in their entirety, a boon of free TV time that no candidate of either party was awarded. After the Trump event, the rest of the day, the pundits would dissect what he had said and his standing vis-à-vis the other Republican candidates.

If Trump had no campaign event planned, he would fire off a round of Tweets against his opponents on his highly active Twitter account – which then would be featured on network cable news discussions and social media.

Hence, Trump's orchestration of media spectacle and a compliant mainstream media was a crucial factor in thrusting Trump ever further into the front-runner status in the Republican primaries and winning for him the overwhelming amount of media attention and eventually the Republican nomination. The first major quantitative study released notes that from mid-June 2015 after Trump announced he was running through mid-July, Trump was in 46% of the news media coverage of the Republican field, based on Google news hits; he also got 60% of Google news searches (Somiya 2015), and I will bet that later academic studies will show how he dominated all media from newspapers to television to Twitter and new media to social networking during the Republican primaries and then during the general election.

During the primary campaign, Trump bragged about how one prominent media insider told him that it was the "Summer of Trump" and that it was amazing how he utterly dominated news coverage. I think Trump also correctly explained why he was getting all the media attention: "RATINGS," he explained, "it's ratings, the people love me, they want to see me, so they watch TV when I'm on." And I do think it is ratings that leads the profit-oriented television networks to follow Trump's events and give him live TV control of the audience almost exclusively.

From the beginning of his business career into his presidency, Trump has been particularly assiduous in branding the Trump name and selling himself as a businessman, a celebrity, and in Election 2016, as a presidential candidate (see Klein 2017). Indeed, Trump's presidential campaign represents an obscene branding of a con man and fake celebrity billionaire into a political candidate whose campaign was run on bombast, dominating daily the mediascape, and gaining the attention of voters/consumers. Trump is highly skilled at orchestrating political theater, his theatrics are sometimes entertaining, and, as I noted earlier, his candidacy represents another step in the merger between entertainment, celebrity, and politics(here, Ronald Reagan played a key role, our first actor President). Yet Trump is arguably the first major candidate to pursue politics as entertainment, and thus to collapse the distinction between entertainment, news, and politics, so that the 2016 presidential election and then the Trump presidency can be seen as a form of infotainment and TV reality show.

The Trump Presidency, Authoritarian Populism, and Covid

Much has been made of Donald Trump's character and whether he is fit to be president of the United States. In the following analysis, I want to suggest that the theories of Erich Fromm and his fellow German-Jewish refugees known as the "Frankfurt School" help provide an analysis of authoritarian populism that helps explicate Trump's character, his appeal to his followers, and in general the Trump phenomenon.[16]

Erich Fromm was a German Jewish intellectual and psychoanalyst who was affiliated with the Frankfurt School, a group of German Jews and progressives who left Hitler's Germany in the early 1930s and settled in the United States, developing critical theories of fascism, contemporary capitalism, and Soviet Marxism from a theoretical standpoint that combines Marx, Freud, Weber, Nietzsche and other radical theorists and critics of Western civilization.[17] Fromm was the group's Freud expert affiliated with the Frankfurt Psychoanalytic Institute in Germany and was a practicing analyst in Germany and then the United States. After breaking with the Frankfurt school in the late-1930s, Fromm became a best-selling author and radical social critic in the United States.

Fromm was a strong critic of Hitler and German fascism, and I believe that his significant books and some key ideas help explain the character, presidential campaign, and supporters of Donald Trump. Hence, in this discussion, I develop a Frommian analysis of Trump and his followers and take on the issue of Trump's authoritarian populism and how Trump manipulated his base in winning the election and into his presidency and beyond. This project begins with Fromm's *Escape from Freedom* (1940), which explains how individuals submitted to oppressive and irrational regimes in modernity and how Germans surrendered to Hitler and fascism. *Escape* combines historical, economic, political, ideological, and socio-psychological analysis, as is typical of the best multidimensional work of Fromm and the Frankfurt School and provides a model that we can apply to analyzing Trump and our current political situation.

Indeed, Trump is not Hitler, and his initial followers during the 2016 election were not technically fascists,[18]. However, we can use **authoritarian populism** or **neo-fascism** to explain Trump and his supporters in the lead-up to the 2016 election and into his presidency.[19] Authoritarian movements ranging from German and Italian fascism to Franco's Spain to Latin American and other dictatorships throughout the world center on an authoritarian leader and followers who submit to their leadership and demands. I argue that Donald Trump is an authoritarian leader who has mobilized an authoritarian populist movement that follows his leadership. Arguably, Trump started as an authoritarian populist in the traditions of Ronald Reagan and Margaret Thatcher. Like Reagan, Trump came out of the entertainment industry and was a celebrity as he announced his candidacy in the summer of 2015 thanks in part to his television celebrity as every mainstream media outlet touted his announcing his candidacy. Trump does not share the conservative ideology of Reagan and Thatcher. However, he shares their electoral strategy of taking a populist pose claiming to represent the people against the political establishment.

Yet Trump lacks Reagan's disciplined skills as a performer and Thatcher's "Iron Lady" self-discipline and political rationality. Instead, Trump shoots from the lip and cannot resist insults, attacks, impolitic language, and rants against those who dare to criticize him. While Trump did not initially have a party apparatus or ideology like the Nazis, parallels to Nazism appeared clear to me the summer of Trump's presidential run at his August 21, 2015, Alabama megarally in Mobile, Alabama. I watched all afternoon as the cable news network's broadcast nothing but Trump, hyping up his visit to a stadium where he was expecting 30–40,000 spectators, the biggest rally of the season. Although only 20-some thousand showed up, which was still a "huge" event in the heat of summer before the primaries had even begun in earnest, Trump's flight into Alabama on his own Trump Jet and his rapturous reception by his admirers became the main story of the news cycle, as did many such daily events in what the media called "the summer of Trump."

What I focused on in watching the TV footage of the event was how the networks began showing repeated images of Trump flying in his airplane over and around the stadium before landing, as the media coverage cut away to big images of the Trump Jet every few minutes. This media spectacle reminded me of one of the most potent propaganda films of all time – Leni Riefenstahl's *Triumph of the Will* – a German Nazi propaganda film of 1935. *Triumph* focuses on Hitler flying in an airplane through the clouds, looking out the window at the crowds below, landing, and driving through mass crowds applauding him as he proceeded through the streets of Nuremberg for a mass rally. The crowds along the way and in the stadium greeted Hitler with rapture as he entered the spectacle of a highly touted and orchestrated Nuremberg mass Nazi rally Riefenstahl captured on film.

I do not know if the Trump operatives planned this parallel or if it was just a coincidence. Still, Trump, like Hitler, has organized a fervent mass movement outside the conventional political party apparatuses. The anger and rage that Fromm attributed to Nazi masses in *Escape From Freedom* is also exhibited in Trump's followers, as is the **idolatry** toward their Fuhrer, who arguably see Trump as the **magic helper** who will solve their problems by building a giant wall to keep out the threatening Other, a Fairy Tale scenario that Fromm would have loved to deconstruct.[20]

Like followers of European fascism in the 1930s, Trump's supporters have suffered economic deprivation, political alienation, humiliation, and a variety of hard times, and they appear to be looking for a political savior to help them out with their problems and address their grievances. Trump proposed magical solutions like a wall along the Mexican border that would keep out swarms of immigrants that he claimed are taking away U.S. jobs and committing waves of crime. Trump promised he would create millions of "great" jobs without giving specific plans – a claim refuted by his problematic business record that includes many bankruptcies, hiring of foreign workers to toil on his projects, some of whom he does not pay, and failures to pay many subcontractors who worked on his projects.[21]

Trump thus presents himself as a Superhero who will magically restore the U.S. to greatness, provide jobs and create incredible wealth, and restore the U.S. to its rightful place as the world's Superpower. In this Fairy Tale, the billionaire King will fight and destroy all the Nation's domestic and foreign enemies and Superman will triumph and provide a Happy Ending for the U.S. people.[22]

While Trump plays the role of the *Ubermensch* (Superman or Higher Man) celebrated by the Nazis and embodies their *Fuhrerprincip* (leadership principle), Trump is a very American form of the Superhero and lacks the party apparatus, advanced military forces and disciplined cadres that the Nazis used to seize and hold power. Like other rightwing American populists, Trump bashes the Federal Reserve, the U.S. monetary system, Wall Street hedge fund billionaires, and neoliberal globalization in the same fashion as Hitler attacked German monopoly capitalism. While Hitler ranted against monopoly capitalists, at the same time, he accepted significant donations from German industrialists, as brilliantly illustrated in the famous graphic by John Heartfield "the meaning of the Hitler salute" which showed Hitler with his hand up in the Nazi salute, getting bags of money from German capitalists. (Heartfield images).[23] Just as Hitler denounced allegedly corrupt and weak party politicians in the Weimar Republic, Trump decries all politicians as "idiots," "stupid," or "weak" – some of the would-be strongman's favorite words. Trump even attacks lobbyists and claims he alone is above being corrupted by money since he is self-financing his own campaign (which is not true but seems to impress his followers).[24]

Trump has his roots in an American form of populism that harkens back to figures like Andrew Jackson, Huey Long, George Wallace, Pat Buchanan and, of course, the American carnival barker and snake oil salesman.[25] Like these classical American demagogues, Trump plays on the fears, grievances, and anger of people who feel that the elites have left them behind. Like his authoritarian populist predecessors, Trump also scapegoats targets from Wall Street to a feared mass of immigrants allegedly crossing the Mexican border and pouring into the States, overwhelming and outnumbering a declining White population.[26]

Trump's followers share antecedents in the Know Nothing movement of the 1850s, the Ku Klux Klan movement, which achieved popularity and media in the 1920s, with Donald's father, Fred Trump, arrested at one of its rallies (Kranish/Fischer 2016, pp. 27–28),[27] and the movement that made George Wallace a popular candidate in the 1960s. Like the alienated and angry followers of authoritarian populist movements worldwide, Trump's admirers had suffered under the vicissitudes of capitalism, globalization, and technological revolution. For decades, they have watched their jobs moved overseas, displaced by technological innovation, or lost through unequal economic development amid increasing divisions between rich and poor. With the global economic crisis of 2007–08, many people lost jobs, housing, and savings, and suffered through a slow recovery under the Obama administration. The fact that Obama was the first black president further outraged many who had their racism and prejudices inflamed by eight years of attacks on Obama and the Obama administration by right-wing media and the Republican Party.

Indeed, Donald Trump was one of the most assiduous promotors of the "birther" myth, erroneously claiming that Barack Obama was born in Africa and was thus not eligible to serve as President of the United States (D'Antonio 2015, pp. 282ff.).[28] In the 2008 presidential election, Trump made a big show of insisting that Obama show his birth certificate to prove he was born in the U.S. Although the Obama campaign provided photocopies of the original birth certificate in Hawaii and notices of his birth in Honolulu newspapers at the time, Trump kept insisting they were frauds and many of his followers continue to this day to believe the myth that Obama was not born in the USA.[29]

Yet unlike classic dictators who are highly disciplined with a fixed ideology and party apparatus, Trump is chaotic and undisciplined, viciously attacking whoever dares criticize him in his daily Twitter feed or speeches, thus dominating the daily news cycles with his outrageous attacks on Mexicans, Muslims, and immigrants, or politicians of both parties who dare to criticize him. Trump effectively used the broadcast media and social media to play the powerful demagogue who preys on his followers' rage, alienation, and fears. Indeed, by March 2016, media companies estimated that Trump received far more media coverage than his Republican Party contenders, and by June, *MarketWatch* estimated that he had received $3 billion worth of free media coverage.[30] Yet, at his whim, Trump bans news media from his rallies, including *The Washington Post*, if they publish criticisms that he does not like.

Like followers of European fascism, Trump's authoritarian populist supporters are driven by rage: they are angry at the political establishment and system, the media, and economic and other elites. They are eager to support an anti-establishment candidate who claims to be an outsider (which is only partly true as Trump has been a capitalist real estate industry member for decades, following his father, and has other businesses as well, many of which have failed).[31] Trump provokes his troops rage with classic authoritarian propaganda techniques like the Big Lie when he repeats over and over that immigrants are pouring across the border and committing crime, that all his primary opponents, the media, and Hillary Clinton are "big liars," and that he, Donald Trump is the only one telling the truth – the biggest lie of all.[32]

Trump's anti-immigrant and racist rhetoric, his Islamophobia, and his xenophobic nationalism play into a violent racist tradition in the U.S. and activates atavistic fears of other races and anger among his white followers. Like European fascism, Trump draws on restorative nostalgia and promises to "Make America Great Again." Thus, to mobilize his followers, Trump arguably manipulates racism and nationalism and plays to the vile side of the American psyche and the long tradition of nationalism, America First-ism, and xenophobia, wanting to keep minorities and people of color outside of the country and "in their place."

Gun rights fanatics were one of Trump's strong core constituencies and never had a candidate (who previously had no visible connection to gun culture) that so rabidly defended gun rights, attacking Clinton and the Democrats who were allegedly dead-set on taking guns away from men who had little else to cling to.[33] Trump also played on the fears, grievances, and resentments of evangelicals who feared that in a secular culture their religious rights would be curtailed,[34] and nationalists who believed the nation was in decline and resented as well liberals who allegedly pushed civil rights agendas that favored people of color.

An article in *The New Yorker* by Evan Osmos describes Trump's followers as "The Fearful and the Frustrated" with the subtitle: "Donald Trump's nationalist coalition takes shape – for now." (Osmos 2015) The reporter has been following Trump's campaign and interviewing his followers and the article reveals that Trump has not only attracted Tea Party followers, but also white nationalists with journals like *The Daily Stormer* "who urged white men to 'vote for the first time in our lives for the one man who actually reps our interests.'" Osmos interviews all over the country other members of far right neo-Nazi, white supremacist, and ultra nationalist groups and concludes:

> From the pantheon of great demagogues, Trump has plucked some best practices – William Jennings Bryan's bombast, Huey Long's wit, Father Charles Coughlin's mastery of the airwaves – but historians are at pains to find the perfect analogue, because so much of Trump's recipe is specific to the present. Celebrities had little place in U.S. politics until the 1920 Presidential election, when Al Jolson and other stars from the fledgling film industry endorsed Warren Harding. Two decades ago, Americans were less focused on paid-for politicians, so Ross Perot, a self-funded billionaire candidate, did not derive the same benefit as Trump from the perception of independence." (Osmos 2015)

Like fascists and authoritarian populists, Trump thus presents himself as a Superhero leader who can step from the outside and solve the problems that Washington and its politicians have created. In the form of **authoritarian idolatry** described by Fromm,[35] his followers appear to believe that Trump alone can stop the decline of the United States and make it "great" again. Over and over, Trump supporters claim that he is the only one who talks about issues like immigration, problems with Washington and politics, and the role of money in politics. Trump promotes himself as the tough guy who can stand up to the Russians and Chinese and to "America's enemies." In the Republican primaries, he presented himself as "the most militarist" guy in the field. He promised to build up the US military and to destroy ISIS and America's enemies, restoring the U.S. to its superpower status, which he says was lost by the Obama administration. Trump embodies the figure of the excess of masculinity that Jackson Katz describes as a key motif in recent U.S. presidential elections (see Katz 2016). With his bragging, chest-pounding, and hyper-macho posturing, Trump promises to restore White Male Power and authority that will restore America to its greatness.

Macho Superman Trump will make "America Great Again" and vanquish all its enemies. Indeed, "Make America Great Again" is perhaps the defining motif of Trump's presidency – a slogan he puts on his baseball caps that he hands out or sells to his supporters. The baseball hat makes it appear that Trump is an ordinary fellow and links him to his followers as one of them, a clever self-presentation for an American authoritarian populist. Sporting a baseball cap on the campaign trail is especially ironic, given that Trump appears to have borrowed this fashion from award-winning, progressive documentary filmmaker Michael Moore, perhaps the anti-Trump in the U.S. political imaginary.

Further, in his speech at the 2016 Republican convention, the shouting red-faced, orange-haired demagogue presented himself as the "voice of the forgotten men and women" – a Depression era phrase of the Roosevelt administration which Trump inflects toward his white constituency who believes they have been forgotten and passed over in favor of the rich, minorities, and liberals. In the speeches, Trump uses the discourse of national crisis also deployed by classic fascist and authoritarian regimes to describe the situation in the U.S. and the need for a savior to solve all the problems. In contrast to the Nazis, however, Trump tells his followers that it's his deal-making skills as a supercapitalist billionaire which credentials him to be the President, and he induces his followers to believe he will make a "great deal" for them and "Make America Great Again."

The slogan "Make America Great Again" refers for some of Trump's supporters to a time where White Males ruled and women, people of color, and others knew their place. It was a time of militarism where U.S. military power was believed to position America as the ruler of the world – although as the ambiguous Cold War and U.S. military defeats in Vietnam and the uncontrollable spaces of Iraq and Afghanistan, this era of American greatness was essentially a myth. Yet the slogan is vague enough that Trump's followers can create a fantasy of a "great" past and dream that Trump will resurrect it – a fantasy conceit nourished by many authoritarian leaders in the 20th century.

Trump is replicating this phenomenon of authoritarian populism, and his campaign exhibits in many ways the submission to the leader and the cause found in classic authoritarian movements. Yet Trump also embodies trends toward celebrity politics and the implosion of politics and entertainment, which is becoming an increasingly important feature of U.S. politics. Further, Trump is a master of PR and promoting his image and would even call up journalists pretending to be a PR agents to get gossip items planted about him in newspapers (see Note 5). More disturbing is the oft-played footage of Trump mimicking a *New York Times* reporter with a disability (see CNN 2015). Indeed, there is a sinister side to Trump and a cartoonish and creepy side.

Trump is thus an authoritarian populist, and his campaign replicates in some ways the submission to the leader and the cause found in classic authoritarian movements. In some ways, however, it is Mussolini, rather than Hitler, who Trump most resembles. Hitler was deadly serious, restrained, and repressed, while Trump is comical, completely unrestrained, and arguably unhinged.[36] Curiously, on February 28, 2016, Trump used his Twitter feed to post a quote attributed to Mussolini, which compared the Italian dictator to Trump. In an interview on NBC's "Meet the Press," that morning said: "It's a very good quote," apparently not bothered by being associated with Mussolini (Habermann 2016). There were also news clips that showed Trump speaking, chin jutting out in Mussolini-like fashion, and making faces and performing gestures that seemed to mimic characteristics associated with Mussolini (Media Matters 2015).[37]

Like Mussolini, Trump has a buffoonish side which his mobocracy finds entertaining but which turns off more serious folks. Trump is the embodiment of trends toward celebrity politics and the implosion of politics and entertainment, which is becoming an increasingly important feature of U.S. politics.[38] Further, Trump is a master of PR and promoting his image, and would even call up journalists pretending to be a PR agent to get gossip items planted about him in newspapers.[39] More disturbing is the oft-played footage of Trump attacking people of color, women, and government members, often in violent and threatening forms. Indeed, there is a disturbing side to Trump, and in the conclusion, I draw on Frankfurt School thinkers Erich Fromm and Herbert Marcuse to comment on Trump's at-once banal and sinister aspects and personality type.

Trump's Downfall, the Indictment, and the Revenge of the Spectacle

From March 2020 through the 2020 election and into the 2020s, the COVID-19 Pandemic has been a daily media spectacle that has dominated the news and people's lives despite Trump's daily antics of distraction, diversion, and denial. Many of us that have been on lockdown throughout the pandemic are angry at Trump and his enablers for not properly dealing with the pandemic, while millions of families have suffered medical crises and deaths from the pandemic and lost jobs, businesses, and lives because of its deadliness. While the mainstream broadcasting media and social media circulate Trump's lies and evasions, they also broadcast the spectacle of daily mass death at the hands of the COVID-19 virus.[40]

By late February, 2021 there were more deaths from COVID-19 every day in the U.S. than died in the terror attacks of 9/11/2001 or the Pearl Harbor attack that propelled the U.S. into World War II.[41] This spectacle of horror, will be forever associated with Donald Trump's failed presidency. While his mastery of media spectacle and social media propelled his rise to power, the same technologies that won and sustained his presidency are helping bring about his downfall, confirming that these forces can also destroy those who rise and triumph via media technology and spectacle. However, I suspect Donald Trump will have an afterlife via media spectacle that will continue to the end of his days and beyond.

Having read a stack of books and countless articles on Trump and followed the Trump spectacle closely since he announced for presidency in 2015, I see Donald J. Trump as a paragon of what Herbert Marcuse called "one-dimensional man." (Marcuse 1964) Trump's one-dimension is his gigantic ego that must be fed with unlimited amounts of adulation, money, power, and attention (an account in Fromm's analysis of Trump that I cite above).[42] Trump's ego extends to his family, whom he undoubtedly sees as extensions of himself or part of his business enterprise (which they literally are). Trump seems to have no lifelong friends, no interests or hobbies beyond his business and now political enterprise, no interest in culture or ideas beyond those he can exploit in his business or political campaign, and, as biographers have noted, he does not seem to be burdened with selfhood that involves depth, self-reflection, or self-awareness, let alone self-criticism, beyond an overwhelming sense of self-importance and entitlement, now aggravated by narcissistic resentment after losing the election, failing to overthrow the election in the January 6, 2021 insurrection he promoted, and is now experiencing as he faces one indictment after another in Washington D.C., New York, Georgia, and via Special Prosecutor Jack Smith.

Indeed, Trump's resentment mushroomed during 2023 as prosecutions were pursued in New York City and for his problematic business enterprise and payoffs for adulterous sexual adventures that led to hush-money payoffs, a sordid part of his first indictment by Alvin Bragg,[43] with possible indictments coming in Georgia for his attempt to overturn the ballot in that closely fought swing state in the 2020 election, through the Justice Department and Special Counsel Jack Smith for his role in the January 6, 2021 insurrection, that I noted above, and in his stealing government documents deemed a national security risk after losing the 2020 election which he illegally took with him to his fantasy castle Mar-a-Lago and other of his residences, many of which were found and subjected him to illegally stealing documents of national security importance.[44]

Thus Trump has faced a multiplicity of Federal indictments, including illegally possessing national security documents in Mar-a-Lago and must recently was indicated in early August by Special Counsel Jack Smith on several federal counts relating to his January 6 insurrection, which, along with other indictments, will keep Trump subject to trial court throughout the 2024 Primary Season and, if he wins, during his presidency – an unprecented situation in U.S. politics.

The news of Trump's indictment created a media spectacle as the cable news network's brought on legal and political experts to debate the indictment, and the national print and digital media intensely analyzed and discussed the unfolding consequences of Trump's criminal prosecution.[45] The usual partisan response exploded with Democrats and Trump opponents elated but worried about potential upheavals around the indictment, while some Republicans remained quiet, whereas others attacked the prosecutor and the indictment.

A highly volatile, highly contested, and dangerous political environment had emerged with the ferocious debate and once again concerning Trump's fate in the wall-to-wall 24/7 presentation of media reports, debates, and opinion pieces. The Trump Indictment Spectacle demonstrated once again the central role of print, broadcasting, and social media in U.S. politics and society. The burning need for critical media and digital literacy to access the most reliable information sources, to appraise the biases of mainstream media of all sorts, and to become an informed citizen ready to take one's role in the political issues and struggles of the time. Once again, the importance of education for democracy that Dewey stressed comes to the fore, and the need for a critical theory of society that Marcuse helped develop becomes apparent to make sense of the day's social and political struggles and upheavals.

In this chapter, I have been arguing for the importance of critical cultural studies to help us understand the phenomenon of Donald Trump and his mob by analyzing the media spectacle, discourses, media images, and actions occurring throughout the media spectrum and the info-sphere. We now live in a technologically mediated ecosphere that requires us to become aware (woke!), critical, and engaged in confronting the major socio-political-cultural issues of the day, such as the Donald Trump phenomenon. The struggles against autocracy and democracy have their worldwide resonances and analogs in battles against autocratic leaders and movements throughout the world in the global cultural wars and battle for a democratic future that we are now engaged in.

In the U.S., by Summer 2023, uncharted political waters were inundating the ecosphere of media and information/disinformation, saturating the public. Just before the March 30 indictment, Trump warned via his social media feed, unaptly named Truth Social, of "death and destruction if he was indicated, called N.Y. Prosecutor Alvin Bragg "an animal" and "degenerate," controlled by the radical left and George Soros. Trump's tirades against Alvin Bragg and Democratic Party and progressive supporter George Soros reveals the racist and anti-Semitic roots of Trump's attack on Democracy as if it were blacks and Jews (i.e., George Soros, the right's favored figure for the Jewish conspiracy behind the Left), who were leading the charge and prosecutions against Trump.

The increasingly violent and growing fascist nature of Trump's assault against the Judiciary and constitutional division of powers was revealed in a picture Trump released on "Truth Social" portraying Trump with a baseball bat aligned at Bragg's head, giving a message to his followers to assault Bragg and the New York Judiciary. During the same outburst, Trump posted that there would be "death and destruction" if Trump were to be indicted, which generated death threats against the N.Y. prosecutor who was indicting him while attempting to promote a violent response by the Trump Gang, as Trump presented his indictment as a "witch hunt" and "political prosecution" by the media, legal and political system (as Trump and his supporters saw it).[46]

A few days after this outburst, Trump held a campaign rally at Waco, Texas on March 25.[47] Trump was speaking at the Thirtieth Anniversary of a federal raid on the apocalyptic doomsday Branch Davidian sect who turned Waco into a symbol of anti-government attacks on religious and gun freedoms. Cult leader David Koresh had organized a compound outside Waco with him as the Prophet and many young female members as his wives. Loading the compound with an arsenal of guns, Koresh preached Holy War and prophesized the End Times. The end of Koresh's cult did come when Federal Agents raided the compound because of alleged sexual abuse of women and children and dangers to the community from a violent religious cult armed and loaded for a fight. The compound caught on fire during the raid. At least 84 cult members, including many women and children, and four Federal Agents were killed.

After that, Waco became a symbol of Federal evil for the anti-Government movement and a key influence on the burgeoning right-wing militia movement and mass killings. One observer of the Waco conflagration, Timothy McVeigh, bombed the Federal Building in Oklahoma City on the Waco Anniversary on

April 19, 1995. The anti-Government militia movement ran with bombings, mass shootings, and anti-government violence. In contrast, groups like the Proud Boys and Oath Keepers, who had been part of Trump's movement participating in the January 6, 2021, insurrection, convened and listened to Donald Trump at Waco attacking his indictment and calling his troops to organize and respond, promising them again, "I am your retribution" (and Fuhrer!).

Indeed, just as Trump embraced the American Nazis in their Charlottesville March on August 11–12, 2017, to terrorize blacks and the University of Virginia, he was now Supreme Leader of the most violent rightwing groups who had been central in the January 6th insurrection, and whom he was mobilizing to strike again to try to block his prosecution or to get retribution for Trump. Hence, "retribution" became a central theme in Trump's unhinged social media messages and rallies like the Waco spectacle. Trump promised that he would get retribution for himself and his crazed followers when he regained the presidency. These followers also included the foot soldiers of Trump's MAGA movement and extreme right, with Pastor Charles Pace proclaiming during Trump's rally in Waco that "Donald Trump is the anointed of God... He is the battering ram that God is using to bring down the Deep State of Babylon."[48]

Republican candidates for the Presidency, such as Florida Governor Ron DeSantis, "said on Twitter that Florida will not work with New York on extradition requests in case one is necessary for the newly indicted former president...'Florida will not assist in an extradition request given the questionable circumstances at issue" with Manhattan District Attorney Alvin Bragg (D) and his "political agenda," DeSantis said." Trump's former Vice-President Mike Pence blabbered on CNN that the indictment was "outrage" and a "political prosecution" that was unconstitutional and was lectured by helpful CNN hosts and legal experts on the law and constitution. On the far right, news of Trump's indictment evoked "threatening rhetoric and calls for violence from a pro-Trump extremist forum that hosted much of the planning for the attack on the U.S. Capitol on Jan. 6, 2021. Users called for civil war and '1776 round 2.' They envisioned a "real insurrection" – an apparent reference to the Capitol attack – and instructed each other, 'Form organized militias.' Their fury was mainly directed against Alvin Bragg (D), the Manhattan district attorney, with one writing under a photo of the prosecutor, 'There once was a time when he would have been lynched for much less.' Another vowed, this cannot go unpunished. The DA needs to pay dearly.'"[49]

As noted, the New York criminal indictment were the first of many indictments that have been leveled at Trump for much more severe crimes against the Republic and U.S. democracy. Yet the crazed and violent response of Trump and his followers to what can be seen as a significant volley of the Trump Criminal Wars of 2023 which culminated in Trump tweeting after his August Federal Indictments by Jack Smith, that "If you are Coming for me, I am Coming for you." This call to ballte portends a period of uncertainty in which struggles for the fate of U.S. democracy will be at stake.

Whatever happens in the Trump Indictments and the wild media spectacles they are sure to produce, Trump has been an unmitigated disaster for the U.S. and the world. His one-dimensional narcissism and aggressive pursuit of self-interest are accompanied by a gloomy, pessimistic view of the world encapsulated in the philosophical vision that: "Man is the most vicious of all animals, and life is a series of battles ending in victory or defeat. You just can't let people make a sucker out of you." (Kranish/Fischer 2016, p. 94)[50] Winning is all for one-dimensional Trump, the only purpose of life, the only thing worth pursuing, and the organizing principle of Donald's existence. To win, Trump will do anything, raising the specter of what would an unhinged Trump do with nuclear weapons under his control were he to regain the presidency and what destruction might his unrestrained Ego and uncontrollable Id unleash upon the world if Trump is threatened in any way as it now appears he is. It is also worrisome to contemplate that Trump has developed a large following through his demagoguery and that his increasingly fascistic behavior and following constitutes a clear and present danger to U.S. democracy and global peace and well-being.

It is also clear that Trump is now the Biggest Loser, a self-image that he cannot sustain and that will drive him to dangerous and unpredictable responses. Trump lost the U.S. Presidency to Joe Biden in 2000; he failed in his attempt to overthrow the election with the January 6, 2021 Insurrection, which caused five deaths and the imprisonment of multitudes of his supporters; his chosen candidates for the Senate mostly went down to defeat in the 2022 midterms causing the Democrats to be the Senate Majority Party; and his 2023 indictment(s) are causing unprecedented turmoil with unpredictable consequences that have thrown U.S. democracy into crisis.

Critical social theory, cultural studies, and radical pedagogy need to engage these momentous events surrounding Trump and other struggles against autocracy and dictatorship throughout the world. As I am arguing, a critical theory of society and radical pedagogy provide indispensable tools of critical media and digital literacies, socio-historical contextualization, and political engagement that are crucial to the future of democracy, a project that I will spell out further in future chapters.[51]

Notes

1 My book *Media Culture* (Kellner 1995 [2020]) bringing together studies of U.S. film, television, popular music, advertising, and other forms of media culture helped introduce British Cultural Studies to the U.S., while I and others created North American versions. Many scholars, in the U.S. and throughout the Americas, were introduced to British Cultural Studies at a conference, "Marxism and the Interpretation of Culture," held at the University of Illinois, Urbana, July 1983. Conference papers were collected in a book edited by Grossberg, Nelson, Triechler 1992.
2 For more information on British cultural studies, see Hall 1980b; Johnson 1986/87; Fiske 1986; O'Conner 1989; Turner 1990; Grossberg 1989; Agger 1992; During 1992, 1998; Kellner 1995; and Durham and Kellner 2000. I might note that the Frankfurt School also provided much material for a critical cultural studies in their works on mass culture from the 1930s through the present; on the relation between the Frankfurt School and British cultural studies, see Kellner 1997.
3 On the concept of ideology, see Kellner 1978 and 1979; the Centre for Contemporary Cultural Studies, 1980; Kellner and Ryan 1988; and Thompson 1990.
4 A recent and telling example of conservative attacks on progressive representations of culture emerged in Florida Governor Ron DeSantos's attack on Disney – one of the most powerful corporations in his state – because of a lesbian character in a Disney cartoon. Conservative cultural warriors in the present are always on the look-out for "woke" representations of gender, race, or sexuality in the media so these can launch a crusade against it (and get their unwoke followers to fork out money to support the crusades that enable cash contributions for their re-election funds (or deep pockets).
5 This model was adumbrated in Hall 1980a and Johnson 1986/87 and guided much of the early Birmingham work. Around the mid-1980s, however, some in the Birmingham group began to increasingly neglect the production and political economy of culture and focused largely on audience studies.
6 The term *political economy* calls attention to the fact that the production and distribution of culture take place within a specific economic system, constituted by relations between the state and economy. For instance, in the United States, a capitalist economy dictates that cultural production is governed by laws of the market, but the democratic imperatives of the system mean that there is some regulation of culture by the state. There are often tensions within a given society concerning how many activities should be governed by the imperatives of the market, or economics, alone and how much state regulation or intervention is desirable, to ensure a wider diversity of broadcast programming, for instance, or the prohibition of phenomena agreed to be harmful, such as cigarette advertising or pornography (see Kellner 1990; McChesney 2007 and 2013).
7 See Ien Ang, *Living Room Wars: Rethinking Media Audiences.* London and New York: Routledge, 2006.

8 Influential Cultural studies that have focused on audience reception include Brunsdon and Morley (1978), Radway (1983), Ang (1985, 1996), Morley (1986), Fiske (1989a, 1989b), Jenkins (1992), and Lewis (1992). On "fandom," see Gray, Sandvoss, and Harrington, (eds.) (2007).
9 See Ien Ang, Living Room Wars: Rethinking Media Audiences. London and New York: Routledge, 2006.
10 See, for example, an article on popular social media sites that include fan forums, by Sorav Jain Thinker in Chief. "40 Most Popular Social Networking Sites of the World," *Social Media Today*, October 6, 2012 at <https://www.socialmediatoday.com/content/40-most-popular-social-networking-sites-world> (accessed March 29, 2023).
11 For analyses of Thatcherism from a critical cultural studies perspective, see Hall 2021. On Reaganism, see Grossberg 1988 and Kellner 1990.
12 On my concept of media spectacle, see Kellner 2001, 2003a, 2003b, 2005, 2008, 2012, 2016, and 2017. This article draws upon and updates my two Trump books Kellner 2016 and 2017.
13 I provide accounts of the O.J. Simpson Trial and the Clinton sex/impeachment scandal in the mid-1990s in Kellner 2003b; engage the stolen election of 2000 in the Bush/Gore presidential campaign in Kellner 2001; and describe the 9/11 terrorist attacks and their aftermath in *From 9/11 to Terror War* in Kellner 2003a.
14 See D'Antonio (2015), Blair (2000) and Kranish & Fisher (2016). Blair's chapter on "Born to Compete," (p. 223) documents Trump's competitiveness and drive for success at an early age.
15 Trump's book *The Art of the Deal*, co-written with Tony Schwartz (2005 [1987]), helped introduce him to a national audience and is a key source of the Trump mythology; see Blair 2000, pp. 380ff.
16 This Frommian analysis of Trump was first presented as "Fromm and the Counterrevolutionary Character: Frommian Reflections on Donald Trump" in a conference "The (in)sane society: Remembering Erich Fromm and the Frankfurt School," CUNY, New York, April 1, 2016. On the Frankfurt School, see the histories by Martin Jay, *The Dialectical Imagination: A History of the Frankfurt School and the Institute of Social Research, 1923–1950*. Berkeley, Cal.: University of California Press (March 5, 1996), and Rolf Wiggershaus, *The Frankfurt School: Its History, Theories, and Political Significance*. Cambridge: Mass.: The MIT Press, 1995. On the Frankfurt School social theory, see Douglas Kellner, *Critical Theory, Marxism, and Modernity*. Cambridge, UK and Baltimore, Md.: Polity Press and John Hopkins University Press, 1989.
17 On Fromm, see Daniel Burston, *The Legacy of Erich Fromm*. Cambridge, Mass: Harvard University Press, 1991; Rainer Funk, *Erich Fromm: His Life and Ideas*. Translators Ian Portman, Manuela Kunkel. New York: Continuum International Publishing Group, 2003; Lawrence J. Friedman, *The Lives of Erich Fromm: Love's Prophet*. New York: Columbia University Press, 2013.
18 Parenthetically, there were enough media comparisons between Trump and Hitler and fascism for Trump to say with some perhaps genuine perplexity "I'm not Hitler! I don't like the guy!" See Sam Sanders, "Trump Champions The 'Silent Majority,' But What Does That Mean In 2016?" *NPR*, January 22, 2016 at <http://www.npr.org/2016/01/22/463884201/trump-champions-the-silent-majority-but-what-does-that-mean-in-2016> (accessed on July 20, 2016). At this time, Trump was asking his followers to raise their hands if they would

vote for him as President, and the simultaneous raised hands going up looked like a mob of Hitler salutes! And there is a story out there that Trump keeps a book of Hitler's writings by his bedside; see O'Brien, op. cit., p. 200; the story originates from a *UPI* report, August 9, 1990, cited in O'Brien, op. cit., p. 260.

19 Carl Bernstein started calling Trump a neo-fascist and an American-brand fascist on CNN on June 19, 2016. See Tom Boggioni, "Carl Bernstein: Donald Trump is a 'pathological liar' and America's first 'neofascist' nominee," *Rawstory*, June 19, 2016 at <http://www.rawstory.com/2016/06/carl-bernstein-donald-trump-is-a-pathological-liar-and-americas-first-neofascist-nominee/>(accessed on July 20, 2016). In an article by Adam Gopnik, "Being Honest About Trump, *The New Yorker*, July 14, 2016 at <http://www.newyorker.com/news/daily-comment/being-honest-about-trump> (accessed on July 20, 2016), Gopnik comments: "It is the essence of fascism to have no single fixed form – an attenuated form of nationalism in its basic nature, it naturally takes on the colors and practices of each nation it infects. In Italy, it is bombastic and neoclassical in form; in Spain, Catholic and religious; in Germany, violent and romantic. It took forms still crazier and more feverishly sinister, if one can imagine, in Romania, whereas under Oswald Mosley, in England, its manner was predictably paternalistic and aristocratic. It is no surprise that the American face of fascism would take on the forms of celebrity television and the casino greeter's come-on, since that is as much our symbolic scene as nostalgic re-creations of Roman splendors once were Italy's." Op. cit. My take on this is Trump's movement began modeled on authoritarian populism of Latin American and other dictators and gradually morphed into full-blown fascism with the January 6, 2021 insurrection in which Trump led his followers to occupy the Capitol to block the legitimate transfer of power, which led to his impeachment and a series of local, state, and federal investigations ongoing as I write in Spring-Summer 2023. These investigation led to a first indictment in New York City where Trump surrendered to a New York Court on an indictment of 42 cases of felony charges, leading Defendant Trump to give-himself up and plead "Not guilty" on April 4, 2023, to the 42 felony charges, forcing the Defendant to stand trial later in the year; so far Trump and his supporters' media response to his indictment, and further forthcoming indictments, is a full-on fascist attack on the local, state and federal U.S. Judiciary that are investigating and potentially indicating him. Trump carried out a verbally explosive attacks on the African-American New York prosecutor and Georgia state prosecutor, with strong racist and proto-fascist underpinnings as I describe below.

20 The notion of "the magic helper" to whom the follower submits to the authoritarian leader in the hopes that their problems will be solved is found in Erich Fromm's *Escape from Freedom*, op. cit., pp. 174–178; on "authoritarian idolatry," see *Sane Society*, op. cit. p. 237f. *Escape from Freedom* not only critiqued Nazi ideology, the party apparatus, the concept of the Fuhrer, and the psychology of Nazi mass followers of Hitler, but Fromm also analyzed fairy tales and magical thinking in National Socialism, a theme he expanded in later writings like *The Forgotten Language: An Introduction to the Understanding of Dreams, Fairy Tales and Myths*. New York: Random House, 1988.

21 On Trump's business failures, see Wayne Barrett, *Trump: The Greatest Show on Earth: The Deals, the Downfall, the Reinvention*. New York: Regan Books, 2016 (revision of 1992 book *Trump: The Deals and the Downfall*); O'Brien, *op. cit.*; D'Antonio, *op. cit.*; David Cay Johnston, *The Making of Donald Trump*. New York: Melville House; and Kranish and Fisher,

Trump Revealed, op. cit. See also and "The Art of the Bad Deal. Donald Trump's Business Flops, Explained," *Newsweek*, August 8, 2018: 24–33,

22 On the centrality of the role of a Superhero in U.S. culture and politics, see Robert Jewett and John Lawrence, *The American Monomyth*. New York: Anchor, 1977 and Robert Jewett and John Lawrence, *The Myth of the American Superhero*. Grand Rapids, Michigan: Wm. B. Eerdmans Publishing Company, 2002. Trump's campaign follows this model of the redemptive Hero who will slay America's enemies and return the Kingdom to peace and prosperity, and he has been playing the martyred hero trying to regain his lost people and redeem and get retribution for his followers, words and tropes Trump is actually using as I write this analysis in Spring 2023.

23 See the Heartfield images at <https://www.google.com/search?q=John+Heartfield:+the+meaning+of+the+Hitler+salute&biw=1600&bih=1028&tbm=isch&tbo=u&source=univ&sa=X&ved=0ahUKEwjt4KvV-N7LAhVM6WMKHUPABGMQsAQIJg> (accessed March 22, 2016).

24 After bragging how his campaign was self-funded during the Republican primaries, Trump released a statement showing that much of the money he spent was paid into his own companies; see Nicholas Confessore and Sarah Cohen, "Donald Trump's Campaign, Billed as Self-Funded, Risks Little of His Fortune." *The New York Times*, February, 5, 2016 at <http://www.nytimes.com/2016/02/06/us/politics/donald-trumps-campaign-billed-as-self-funded-risks-little-of-his-fortune.html?_r=0> (accessed July 29, 2016). During the Fall Presidential election, Trump was forced to court donors and raise funds, thus undercutting his claims to be the only self-financing candidate.

25 Famous Showman P.T. Barnum proclaimed that there is a sucker born every minute, and Trump's suckers continued to fund him through his failed presidency and two impeachments, through the January 6, 2021 insurrection, and into his initial indictment on 42 felony charges. On how individuals join authoritarian movements and see the Leader as representing their grievances and solving their problems, see Lauren Langman and George Lundskow, "Escape From Modernity: Authoritarianism and the Quest for the Golden Age," Paper delivered at "The Psychodynamics of Self & Society," Eighth Annual ASA Mini-Conference, Seattle, August 18, 2016.

26 Trump's vision of Latin American immigrants pouring over the border into the U.S. is a fantasy, as studies have shown that more Mexicans are returning to Mexico after working in the U.S. than coming into the country, illegal or not; see Ana Gonzalez-Barrera, "More Mexicans Leaving Than Coming to the U.S. Net Loss of 140,000 from 2009 to 2014; Family Reunification Top Reason for Return." November 19, 2015 at <http://www.pewhispanic.org/2015/11/19/more-mexicans-leaving-than-coming-to-the-u-s/> (accessed September 3, 2016).

27 Kranish and Fisher, op. cit., pp. 27–28. It was not clear from police and media reports whether Fred Trump was marching with the Klan or was just part of the crowd that got involved in a melee with the police.

28 On the birther myth, see Michael D'Antonio, *Never Enough. Donald Trump and the Pursuit of Success*. New York: Thomas Dunne Books, 2015, pp. 283ff.

29 Public Policy Polling reports that a "new poll finds that Trump is benefiting from a GOP electorate that thinks Barack Obama is a Muslim and was born in another country, and that immigrant children should be deported. 66% of Trump's supporters believe that

Obama is a Muslim to just 12% that grant he's a Christian. 61% think Obama was not born in the United States to only 21% who accept that he was. And 63% want to amend the Constitution to eliminate birthright citizenship, to only 20% who want to keep things the way they are." *Public Policy Polling.* "Trump Supporters Think Obama is A Muslim Born in Another Country," September 01, 2015 at <http://www.publicpolicypolling.com/main/2015/08/trump-supporters-think-obama-is-a-muslim-born-in-another-country.html> (accessed August 3, 2016).

30 Nicholas Confessore and Karen Yourish, "$2 Billion Worth of Free Media for Donald Trump," *The New York Times*, March 15, 2016 at <http://www.nytimes.com/2016/03/16/upshot/measuring-donald-trumps-mammoth-advantage-in-free-media.html?_r=0> (accessed August 6, 2016)and Robert Schroeder, "Trump has gotten nearly $3 billion in 'free' advertising." *Marketwatch*, May 6, 2016.

31 On Trump's business failures, see Note 16 above.

32 At the Republican convention, Trump insisted that "you won't hear any lies here," For documentation of Trump's Big and little lies, see Hank Berrien, "Lyin' Donald: 101 Of Trump's Greatest Lies," *Dailywire*, April 11, 2016 at <https://x.com/cher/status/762749541674160128> (accessed August 8, 2016). Trump continued lying through his presidency and constructed his biggest Big Lie after losing to Joe Biden in the 2020 election, when he argued the election was stolen, a lie that prompted his followers to invade the Capitol on January 6, 2021 to try to block the legitimate transfer of power to Biden; see the January 6th Report at <https://www.govinfo.gov/collection/january-6th-committee-final-report?path=/GPO/January%206th%20Committee%20Final%20Report%20and%20Supporting%20Materials%20Collection> (accessed March 30, 2023). Trump continues telling the Big Lie about the alleged "Steal" to this day.

33 On Trump's appeal to gun owners, see Daniel Hayes, "Donald Trump Takes Aim," *The New York Times*, August 20, 2016 at <http://www.nytimes.com/2016/08/21/opinion/campaign-stops/donald-trump-takes-aim.html?_r=0> (accessed August 24, 2016).

34 In an article subtitled "How the Christian right came to support a thrice-married adulterer," see Daniel K. Williams "Why Values Voters Value Donald Trump," *The New York Times*, August 20, 2016 at <http://www.nytimes.com/2016/08/21/opinion/sunday/why-values-voters-value-donald-trump.html> (accessed August 24, 2016).

35 On Fromm and "authoritarian idolatry," see *Sane Society*, op. cit. p. 237f.

36 In a classic example of Freudian projection, over the weekend of August 6–7, 2016, Trump accused Hillary Clinton of being unbalanced, coming unhinged, and being mentally unstable, previously the charges being deployed against Trump which I discuss below using Fromm's categories. See Jose A. DelReal, "Trump, in series of scathing personal attacks, questions Clinton's mental health," *Washington Post*, Aug. 7, 2016 at <https://www.washingtonpost.com/news/post-politics/wp/2016/08/06/trump-in-series-of-scathing-personal-attacks-questions-clintons-mental-health/> (accessed August 10, 2016). In a speech in West Bend, Wisconsin, on August 16, 2016, Trump called Clinton a "bigot," a charge frequently tossed at him.

37 Media Matters Staff, "Ted Koppel Compares Donald Trump To Benito Mussolini. Koppel: Trump And Mussolini Both 'Say Very Little In Terms Of Substance, But The Manner In Which They Say It Gets The Crowds Excited,'" *Media Matters*, December 16, 2015

at <http://mediamatters.org/video/2015/12/16/ted-koppel-compares-donald-trump-to-benito-muss/207564> (accessed August 9, 2016).

38 For my take on celebrity politics and the implosion of entertainment and politics in U.S. society, see Douglas Kellner, "Barack Obama, Media Spectacle, and Celebrity Politics" in *A Companion to Celebrity*, Edited by P. David Marshall and Sean Redmond. Malden, MA and Oxford, UK: Wiley-Blackwell, 2015: 114–134. See also Mark Wheeler, *Celebrity Politics*. Cambridge, UK: Polity, 2013.

39 Marc Fisher, Will Hobson, "Donald Trump 'pretends to be his own spokesman to boast about himself.' Some reporters found the calls disturbing or even creepy; others thought they were just examples of Trump being playful." *The Independent*, May 13, 2016 at <http://www.independent.co.uk/news/world/americas/us-elections/donald-trump-pretends-to-be-his-own-spokesman-to-boast-about-himself-a7027991.html> (accessed August 9, 2016).

40 For Trump's lies and evasions on Covid-19 which broke out during his presidency, see Kim Bellware "Coronavirus: An epidemic of misinformation," *Washington Post*, February 13, 2020 at <https://www.washingtonpost.com/podcasts/post-reports/coronavirus-an-epidemic-of-misinformation/> (accessed June 17, 2021).

41 Summer Lin, "Daily COVID deaths in US likely to exceed 9/11 death toll for months, CDC director says." *Miami Herald,* December 11, 2020 at <https://www.miamiherald.com/news/coronavirus/article247775935.html> (accessed December 15, 2020).

42 On Trump's malignant narcissism, see also "Donald Trump as Authoritarian Populist: A Frommian Analysis," *Logos*, Summer 2016: Vol 15, nos. 2–3 at <http://logosjournal.com/2016/kellner-2/> (accessed September 12, 2016).

43 During the afternoon when I was finishing this chapter and ready to send it to my editor late afternoon on March 30, 2023, the dramatic news flashed over broadcasting media, Internet news sources, and social media – TRUMP INDICTED – the headlines that appeared the next morning on my *New York Times* and *Los Angeles Times* which I subscribe to. The rest of the evening Cable News brought out their legal and political experts and discussed the first criminal indictment of a sitting president in U.S. history, and perhaps the first of several criminal indictments as the Attorney General of Georgia examines Trump for criminal violation of state election laws, and Special Counsel Jack Smith investigates trump for a variety of criminal violations of Federal Laws ranging from his role in inciting the January 6, 2021 insurrection to stealing classified documents from the U.S. Government as he was leaving the White House after his decisive defeat by Joe Biden.

44 On Special Counsel Jack Smith, see the Wikipedia entry at https://en.wikipedia.org/wiki/Jack_Smith_(lawyer) (accessed August 12, 2024).

45 Peter Baker, "A President Faces Prosecution, and a Democracy Is Tested. For more than two centuries, American presidents were effectively shielded from indictment. But the case against former President Donald J. Trump breaks that taboo and sets a new precedent," *The New York Times*, March 31, 2023, p. A1; Perry Stein, "Trump is indicted in N.Y. Here's what it means and what happens next," *Washington Post*, March 30, 2023, p. A1; Stephanie K. Baer, David Mack, and Paige Skinner, "Donald Trump has become the first president

in US history to face criminal charges," *Buzzfeed News*, March 31, 2023 at <https://www.buzzfeednews.com/article/skbaer/donald-trump-charged-indicted-stormy-daniels?utm_source=Sailthru&utm_medium=email&utm_campaign=03/31/2023%20Incoming%20newsletter&utm_term=News%20confirmed%20list> (accessed March 31, 2023). The most amusing account the Day of Trump's Indictment was a report that a gasp was heard on Fox News as Donald Trump's indictment was announced, a sound-byte that was immediately recycled and may be laughed at for days to come.

46 See Lee Brown and Steven Nelson, "Trump posts disturbing baseball bat photo with Alvin Bragg, threatens 'death and destruction,'" *New York Post*," March 24, 2023 at <https://nypost.com/2023/03/24/trump-shares-pic-holding-baseball-bat-near-das-head/> (accessed on March 31, 2023).

47 See Charles Homans, "A Trump Rally, a Right-Wing Cause and the Enduring Legacy of Waco," *New York Times*, March 24, 2023 at <https://www.nytimes.com/2023/03/24/us/politics/donald-trump-waco-branch-davidians.html> (accessed March 31, 2023). I discuss the Waco Branch Davidian spectacle and the subsequent Oklahoma City bombings, mass shootings, and rightwing movements that see Waco as a Holy Site in the extreme right's Gun Wars and Religious Freedom Wars in Best and Kellner 2001 and Kellner 2008.

48 "Trump 'Went to Waco to Bring Back Visions' of Cult Leader David Koresh, Democratic Rep. Says. A Branch Davidian pastor also said that the former president was 'making a statement' with his choice of rally location." *Rolling Sone*, March 26, 2023 at <https://www.rollingstone.com/politics/politics-news/trump-waco-rally-david-koresh-cult-1234703923/> (accessed April 3, 2023).

49 Isaac Stanley-Becker, "Calls for violence come from pro-Trump extremist website," *Washington Post*, March 31, 2023 at <https://www.washingtonpost.com/politics/2023/03/31/trump-indictment-new-york-news-updates/> (accessed March 31, 2023). For an instructive catalogue of the MAGA Republican response to Trump's indictment that echo Trump's own latest phrases like "witch hunt" and "political prosecution" parroted again and again by the Repugs, and other tart examples of recent Republican "crazy talk" in response to Trump's indictment, see Dana Milbank, "The GOP response to Trump is one hell of an indictment," *Washington Post*, March 31, 2023 at <https://www.washingtonpost.com/opinions/2023/03/31/house-gop-debates-public-urination/> (accessed March 31, 2023).

50 Donald J. Trump cited in Kranisch and Fisher, *op. cit.*, p. 94.

51 While I will address these crises of democracy in the chapters to follow, I want to highlight Chapter 8 where I lay out the crucial contributions of Herbert Marcuse and Paolo Freire to critical social theory and radical pedagogy, after having presented the resources of a critical cultural studies for educating students and citizens to engage in the struggles for democracy and social justice in the present and future, and argued throughout the book for the need for a radical pedagogy to help reconstruct education for the Battles of Democracy and provide essential tools like critical media and digital literacies that are provided in few schools of Education in the U.S. today, leading to the crisis and poverty of schools of education that I will address in the Epilogue.

References

Agger, B. (1992). *Cultural Studies*. London: Falmer.
Ang, I. (1985). *Watching Dallas*. New York: Metheun.
Ang, I. (1996). *Living Room Wars: Rethinking Media Audiences for a Postmodern World*. London: Routledge.
Barrett, Wayne. (2016). *Trump: The Greatest Show on Earth: The Deals, the Downfall, the Reinvention*. New York: Regan Books.
Bellware, Kim. (2020). "Coronavirus: An Epidemic of Misinformation," *Washington Post*, February 13, 2020 at <https://www.washingtonpost.com/podcasts/post-reports/coronavirus-an-epidemic-of-misinformation/> (accessed June 17, 2021).
Blair, Gwenda. (2000). *The Trumps*. New York: Simon and Schuster.
Boggioni, Tom. (2016). "Carl Bernstein: Donald Trump is a 'Pathological Liar' and America's First 'Neofascist' Nominee," *Rawstory* <http://www.rawstory.com/2016/06/carl-bernstein-donald-trump-is-a-pathological-liar-and-americas-first-neofascist-nominee/> (accessed on July 20, 2016).
Brunsdon, C. and Morley, D. (1978). *Everyday Television: "Nationwide."* London: British Film Institute.
Centre for Contemporary Cultural Studies. (1980). *On Ideology*. London: Hutchinson.
de Certeau, M. (1984). *The Practice of Everyday Life*. Berkeley: University of California Press
Crenshaw, K. W. (1991). Mapping the Margins: Intersectionality, Identity Politics, and Violence against Women of Color. *Stanford Law Review*, 43(6): 1241–1299.
Durham, M. G. and Kellner, D. (eds.). (2012). *Media and Cultural Studies: Key Works* (Rev. 2nd ed.). Malden, MA: Blackwell.
During, S. (1992, 1998). *Cultural Studies*. London: Routledge.
Fiske, J. (1986). "British Cultural Studies and Television." In R. C. Allen (ed.), *Channels of Discourse* (pp. 254–289). Chapel Hill: University of North Carolina Press.
Fiske, J. (1989a). *Reading the Popular*. Boston: Unwin Hyman.
Fiske, J. (1989b). *Understanding Popular Culture*. Boston: Unwin Hyman.
Fiske, J. (1993). *Power Play. Power Works*. London: Verso.
Friedman, Lawrence J. (2013). *The Lives of Erich Fromm: Love's Prophet*. New York: Columbia University Press.
Fromm, Erich. (1988). *The Forgotten Language: An Introduction to the Understanding of Dreams, Fairy Tales and Myths*. New York: Random House.
Fromm, Erich. (1991 [1941]). *Escape from Freedom*. New York: Holt Paperbacks.
Funk, Rainer. (2003). *Erich Fromm: His Life and Ideas*. Translators Ian Portman, Manuela Kunkel. New York: Continuum International Publishing Group.
Gopnik, Adam. (2016). "Being Honest About Trump." *The New Yorker*. at <http://www.newyorker.com/news/daily-comment/being-honest-about-trump> (accessed on July 20, 2016).
Gramsci, A. (1971). *Selections from the Prison Notebooks of Antonio Gramsci*. Q. Hoare and G. Nowell Smith (eds). New York: International Publishers.
Gray, J., Sandvoss, C. and Harrington, C. L. (eds.). (2007). *Fandom: Identities and Communities in a Mediated World*. New York: NYU Press

Grossberg, L. (1988). "Rockin' with Reagan, or the Mainstreaming of Postmodernity," *Cultural Critique*, No. 10, "Popular Narrative, Popular Images," (Autumn, 1988), pp. 123–149.

Grossberg, L. (1989). "The Formations of Cultural Studies: An American in Birmingham." *Strategies*, 22, 114–149.

Grossberg, L., Nelson, C. and Treichler, P. (1992). *Cultural Studies*. New York: Routledge.

Hall, S. (1980a). "Cultural Studies and the Centre: Some Problematics and Problems." In S. Hall, D. Hobson, A. Lowe, and P. Willis (eds.), *Culture, Media, Language: Working Papers in Cultural Studies, 1972–79* (pp. 15–47). London: Hutchinson.

Hall, S. (1980b). Encoding/decoding. In S. Hall, D. Hobson, A. Lowe, and P. Willis (eds.), *Culture, Media, Language: Working Papers in Cultural Studies, 1972–79* (pp. 128–138). London: Hutchinson.

Hall, S. (2021) *The Hard Road to Renewal*. London: Verso.

Hammer, R. and Kellner, D. (2009). *Media/cultural Studies: Critical Approaches*. New York: Peter Lang.

Hebdige, D. (1979). *Subculture: The Meaning of Style*. London: Metheun.

Jenkins, H. (1992). *Textual Poachers*. New York: Routledge.

Johnson, R. (1986–1987). "What is Cultural Studies Anyway?" *Social Text*, 16: 38–80.

Kahn, R. and Kellner, D. (2008). "Technopolitics, Blogs, and Emergent Media Ecologies: A Critical/Reconstructive Approach,' in *Small Tech. The Culture of Digital Tools*, edited by Byron Hawk, David M. Rider, and Ollie Oviedo. Minneapolis: University of Minnesota Press: 22–37.

Kellner, D. (1978, November–December). "Ideology, Marxism, and Advanced Capitalism." *Socialist Review*, 42: 37–65.

Kellner, D. (1979, May–June). TV, Ideology, and Emancipatory Popular Culture. *Socialist Review*, 45: 13–53.

Kellner, D. (1990). *Television and the Crisis of Democracy*. Boulder, CO: Westview.

Kellner, D. (1992). *The Persian Gulf TV War*. Boulder, CO: Westview.

Kellner, D. (1995 and 2020). Media Culture: Cultural Studies, Identity, and Politics between the Modern and the Postmodern. Second Edition (completely revised). London: Routledge.

Kellner, D. (1997). "Critical Theory and British Cultural Studies: The Missed Articulation." In J. McGuigan (ed.), *Cultural Methodologies* (pp. 12–41). London: Sage.

Kellner, D. (2001). *Grand Theft 2000*. Lanham, MD: Rowman & Littlefield.

Kellner, D. (2003). *From September 11 to Terror War: The Dangers of the Bush Legacy*. Lanham, MD: Rowman & Littlefield.

Kellner, D. (2005). *Media Spectacle and the Crisis of Democracy*. Boulder, CO: Paradigm.

Kellner, D. (2009). "Barack Obama and Celebrity Spectacle." *International Journal of Communication*, 3: 1–20.

Kellner, D. (2010). *Cinema Wars: Hollywood Film and Politics in the Bush/Cheney Era*. Malden, MA: Blackwell.

Kellner, D. (2016). *American Nightmare: Donald Trump, Media Spectacle, and Authoritarian Populism*. Rotterdam, The Netherlands: Sense Publishers, 2016.

Kellner, D. (2017). *The American Horror Show: Election 2016 and the Ascent of Donald J. Trump.* Rotterdam, The Netherlands: Sense Publishers.
Kellner, D. and Ryan, M. (1988). *Camera Politica: The Politics and Ideology of Contemporary Hollywood Film.* Bloomington: Indiana University Press.
Kellner, D. and Share, J. (2019) *The Critical Media Literacy Guide: Engaging Media and Transforming Education.* Rotterdam, The Netherlands: Brill-Sense Publishers.
Lewis, L. A. (1992). *Adoring Audience: Fan Culture and Popular Media.* New York: Routledge.
McChesney, R. (2000). *Rich Media, Poor Democracy: Communications Politics in Dubious Times.* New York: New Press.
McChesney, R. (2007). *Communication Revolution: Critical Junctures and the Future of Media.* New York: New Press.
McChesney, R. (2013). Digital Disconnect: How Capitalism is Turning the Internet Against Democracy. New York: The New Press.
O'Brien, Timothy L. (2016 [2005]). *TrumpNation: The Art of Being the Donald.* New York: Grand Central Publishing.
O'Connor, A. (1989, December). "The Problem of American Cultural Studies." *Critical Studies in Mass Communication,* pp. 405–413.
O'Donnell, John and Rutherford, James. (1991). *Trumped!: The Inside Story of the Real Donald Trump-His Cunning Rise and Spectacular Fall.* New York: Simon and Schuster.
Olorunnipa, T. et al. (2020). "Drug Promoted by Trump as Coronavirus 'Game Changer' Increasingly Linked to Deaths." *Washington Post.* May 15, 2020 at <https://www.washingtonpost.com/politics/drug-promoted-by-trump-as-coronavirus-game-changer-increasingly-linked-to-deaths/2020/05/15/85d024fe-96bd-11ea-9f5e-56d8239bf9ad_story.html> (accessed May 31, 2023).
Osmos, Evan. (2015). "The Fearful and the Frustrated: Donald Trump's Nationalist Coalition Takes Shape – For Now" *The New Yorker* at <http://www.newyorker.com/magazine/2015/08/31/the-fearful-and-the-frustrated> (accessed July 22, 2016).
Pogash, Carol. (2016). *Quotations from Chairman Trump,* edited by. New York: Rosetta Books.
Radway, J. (1983). *Reading the Romance.* Chapel Hill: University of North Carolina Press.
Sandvoss, C. (ed.). (2017; second edition). *Fandom.* New York: NYU Press.
Staiger, J. (1992). "Film, Reception, and Cultural Studies." *Centennial Review,* 26(1): 89–104.
Thompson, J. (1990). *Ideology and Modern Culture.* Cambridge, UK: Polity Press and Stanford University Press.
Turner, G. (1990). *British Cultural Studies: An Introduction.* New York and London: Routledge.

· 4 ·

SCHOOL SHOOTINGS, CRISES OF MASCULINITIES, AND CHALLENGES TO EDUCATION

With the brutal massacre of children and administrators at the Sandy Hook Elementary School in Connecticut on December 12, 2012, school shootings received an intense media focus that continues to the present. However, as I shall argue, there has not been sufficient action to protect us from gun violence in schools and society. As President Obama declared in his speech the night of the Sandy Hook tragedy with tears in his eyes: "As a country, we have been through this too many times. Whether it's an elementary school in Newtown, or a shopping mall in Oregon, a temple in Wisconsin, a movie theater in Aurora, or a street corner in Chicago – these neighborhoods are our neighborhoods, and these children are our children." And then, with a resolute look, Obama declared: "And we're going to have to come together and take meaningful action to prevent more tragedies like this, regardless of the politics."[1]

School shootings attract maximum media attention and shooters, craving publicity, and the public eye, gravitate toward schools, which may be why the Sandy Hook shooter chose an elementary school, whose pupils are the most innocent and vulnerable, and whose slaughter would gain maximum media attention. Perhaps for the first time in decades, serious discussions emerged after the Sandy Hook slaughter concerning the need for gun control in an out-of-control gun culture *and* for better mental health care in a society in which mentally disturbed young teenagers and men have been producing an epidemic of mass murder. In the media frenzy in the face of mass shootings, we need to better understand that we face a crisis of masculinity in the country, and that young, alienated males are increasingly turning to guns and murder to construct their identities and resolve their personal crises, resulting in a wave of mass school shootings.[2]

Since school shootings are one of the most frequent and debated site of mass killings in the U.S. today, it is necessary for educators to seriously address this problem and help suggest solutions to make our schools and society safer. In my book *Guys and Guns Amok: Domestic Terrorism and School Shootings from the Oklahoma City Bombings to the Virginia Tech Massacre* (Kellner 2008), I have argued that there are many causes to the rise of school violence and events like the Columbine and Virginia Tech school shootings. Complex historical events like the Iraq invasion or the Virginia Tech and Columbine shootings require a multiperspectivist vision and interpretation of key factors that constitute the constellation from which events can be interpreted, explained, and better understood.

Thus, addressing the causes of problems like societal violence and school shootings involves a range of apparently disparate things such as critique of male socialization and construction of ultramasculine male identities, the prevalence of gun culture and militarism, and a media culture that promotes violence and retribution, while circulating and sensationalizing media spectacle and a culture of celebrity. Such a constellation helps construct the identities, values, and behavior that allows inciting men to use violence to resolve their masculinity crises by creating an ultramasculine identity and media spectacle, producing guys and guns amok.

Accordingly, solutions that I suggest to the problems of school violence and shootings in *Guys and Guns Amok* range from more robust and rational gun laws to better school and workplace security with stronger mental health institutions and better communication between legal, medical, and school administrations, to the reconstruction of masculinity and the reconstruction of education for democracy. In addition, we must consider examining better ways of addressing crime and violence than prisons and capital punishment, draconian measures aimed increasingly today at youth and people of color. Today our schools are like prisons, while in a better society, schools would become centers of learning and self-developing, while prisons could also be centers of learning, rehabilitation, and job-training and not punitive and dangerous schools for crime and violence.

To grasp the magnitude of societal violence and school shootings require a critical theory of society focusing on problems of the present age. Escalating violence in schools and other sectors of society today in the United States is a national scandal and a serious social problem. A UC Davis report in 2019 said there were "about 39,707 deaths from firearms in the U.S." that year and "There are approximately 115,000 non-fatal firearm injuries in the U.S. each year."[3] Moreover, of the 105,000 gun shops in the U.S., only about 1% are the origins of 60% of the guns seized in crimes. As David Olinger notes: "Collectively, U.S. citizens are the most heavily armed in the world. Americans own about 250 million rifles, shotguns, and handguns, nearly one per person and at least one-third of the guns in the world..."[4]

The U.S. has an out-of-control gun culture making it possible to buy weapons ranging from small but deadly pistols to weapons of mass destruction like the AK-47 assault rifle used in many recent mass killings. Texas has among the weakest gun laws in the country, allowing 18-year-olds to walk into gun stores and walk out with an arsenal of weapons and ammunition, as did the Uvalde Killer.[5] Further, the U.S. has explosive crises of masculinity, whereas troubled young men immerse themselves in gun culture and act out their anxieties, anger, and rage in a deadly fashion.

In this chapter, I will suggest some proposals to deal with the escalating problem of social violence and school shootings. I argue that the explosion of school shootings is rooted in crises of masculinities and out-of-control gun culture. I argue for the need to address male rage and crises of masculinity and the need for gun safety reform to engage the issue of mass school shootings and to militate for safer schools and a more non-violent culture that reduces the number of murderous military-grade firearms. I also argue for a critical theory and radical pedagogy that seriously addresses the levels of mental health, rational gun control, and enhanced school and public safety to confront and reduce the wave of school and mass shootings in the U.S. and elsewhere in the 21st century.

Beyond the Culture of Male Violence and Rage

Dealing with problems of school and societal violence will require the reconstruction of male identities and critique of masculinist socialization and identities. Unfortunately, the media and gang culture in some areas, mushrooming gun cultures, sports, and military culture, produce ultramacho men as an ideal, producing societal problems from violence against women to gang murder (see Katz 2006). As Jackson Katz urges, young men must renounce these ideals and behavior and construct alternative notions of masculinity. As Katz concludes, reconstructing masculinity and overcoming aggressive and violent macho behavior and values provides "a vision of manhood that does not depend on putting down others to lift itself. When a man stands up for social justice, non-violence, and basic human rights – for women as much as for men – he is acting in the best traditions of our civilization. That makes him not only a better man but a better human being" (2006, p. 270).

Major sources of violence in U.S. society include cultures of violence caused by poverty; masculinist military, sports, and gun culture; ultramasculine behavior in the corporate and political world; high school bullying and fighting; general societal violence reproduced by media and in the family and everyday life, and in prisons, which are schools for violence. In any of these cases, ultraviolent masculinity can explode and produce societal violence, and until we have new conceptions of what it means to be a man that highlights intelligence, independence, sensitivity, and the renunciation of bullying and violence, societal violence and mass shootings will no doubt increase.

Sports culture, for instance, is a significant part of the construction of American masculinity that can take violent forms. In most of the high school shootings of the 1990s, jocks tormented young teenage boys who took revenge by asserting hyperviolent masculinity and went on shooting rampages. Larkin (2007: 205ff) provides a detailed analysis of "Football and Toxic High School Environments," focusing on Columbine. He describes how sports played a primary role in the school environment, how jocks were celebrities, and how they systematically abused outsiders and marginals like Columbine shooters Eric Harris and Dylan Klebold.

The "pattern of sports domination of high schools," Larkin suggests, "is apparently the norm in America" (206). Larkin notes how football "has become incorporated into a hyper-masculinized subculture that emphasizes physical aggression, domination, sexism, and the celebration of victory. He notes that more "than in any other sport, defeat in football is associated with being physically dominated and humiliated" (208). Further, it is associated with militarism, as George Carlin, among others, has noted in his comedy routine:

> In football the object is for the quarterback, also known as the field general, to be on target with his aerial assault, riddling the defense by hitting his receivers with deadly accuracy in spite of the blitz, even if he has to use the shotgun. With short bullet passes and long bombs, he marches his troops into enemy territory, balancing this

aerial assault with a sustained ground attack that punches holes in the forward wall of the enemy's defensive line.

In baseball the object is to go home! And to be safe! (Carlin, cited in Larkin 208).

Larkin argues that football culture has "corrupted many high schools," including Columbine, where "the culture of hypermasculinity reigned supreme" (209). Hence, Larkin concludes, "If we wish to reduce violence in high schools, we have to de-emphasize the power of sports and change the culture of hypermasculinity. Football players cannot be lords of the hallways, bullying their peers with impunity, sometimes encouraged by coaches with adolescent mentalities" (210).

Hypermasculinity in sports is often a cauldron of homophobia and many of the school shooters were taunted about their sexuality and responded ultimately with an extreme affirmation of compensatory violence. Yet hypermasculinity is found throughout sports, military, gun, gang, and other male subcultures, as well as the corporate and political world, often starting in the family with male socialization by the father, and is reproduced and validated constantly in films, television programs, and other forms of media culture.

There have been, however, educational interventions that address hypermasculinity, violence against women, homophobia, and which provide alternatives to a hegemonic violent masculinity. For example, since 1993 author and activist Jackson Katz and his colleagues have been implementing the Mentors in Violence Prevention (MVP) program, which trains high school, college and professional athletes and other student leaders to speak out and oppose violence against women, gay-bashing, and other forms of domestic and sexual violence. Featuring interactive workshops and training sessions in single-sex and mixed-gender settings, as well as public lectures, MVP has been expanded throughout North America to deal with men's violence in many arenas, from the corporation to politics, police and intelligence agencies, and other institutional arenas where men's violence is a problem.[6]

This is not to say that masculinity per se, or the traits associated with it, are all bad. There are times when being strong, independent, self-reliant, and even aggressive can serve positive goals and resist oppression and injustice. A post-gendered human being would share traits now associated with women and men, so that women could exhibit the traits listed above and men could be more loving, caring, emotional, vulnerable, and other traits associated with women. Gender itself should be deconstructed and while we should fight gender oppression and inequality there are reasons to question fixed gender roles in a more emancipated and democratic world in which individuals create their own personalities and lives out of the potential found traditionally in male and female socially ascribed attributes.

Obviously, media culture is full of violence and of my case studies in Chapter 3 in *Guys and Guns Amok* of violent masculinity, Timothy McVeigh, the two Columbine shooters, and many other school shooters were allegedly deeply influenced by violent media culture. Yet, while media images of violence and specific books, films, TV shows, video and digital games, or artifacts of media culture may provide scripts for violent masculinity that young men act out. Hence, it is the broader culture of militarism, gun culture, extreme sports, ultraviolent video and computer games, subcultures of bullying and violence, and the rewarding of ultramasculinity in the corporate and political worlds that are major factors in constructing of major forms of violent masculinities. Media culture itself obviously contributes to this ideal of macho masculinity but masculinity itself is a contested terrain between different conceptions of masculinity and femininity, and between liberal, conservative, and more radical representations and discourses (Knights & Pullen, 2019).

After dramatic school shootings and incidents of youth violence, there are usually attempts to scapegoat media culture. After the Virginia Tech shootings, the Federal Communication Commission (FCC) issued a report in late April 2007 on "violent television programming and its impact on children" that calls for expanding governmental oversight on broadcast television, but also extending content regulation to cable and satellite channels for the first time and banning some shows from time-slots where children might be watching. FCC Commissioner Jonathan S. Adelstein, who was in favor of the measures, did not hesitate to evoke the Virginia Tech shootings: "particularly in sight of the spasm of unconscionable violence at Virginia Tech, but just as importantly in light of the excessive violent crime that daily affects our nation, there is a basis for appropriate federal action to curb violence in the media."[7]

In the wake of the school shootings after Columbine, fierce criticism and scapegoating of media and youth culture erupted and has continued to the present. I want to avoid, however, the extremes of demonizing media and youth culture contrasted to asserting that it is mere entertainment without serious social influence. There is no question but that the media nurture fantasies and influence behavior, sometimes sick and vile ones, and to survive in our culture requires that we can critically analyze and dissect media culture and not let it gain power over us. Critical media literacy empowers individuals over media so that they can produce critical and analytical distance from media messages and images. This empowers individuals against media manipulation and avoids letting the most destructive images of media gain power over one. It also enables more critical, healthy, and active relations with our culture. Media culture will not disappear, and it is simply a question of how we will deal with it and if we can develop and implement an adequate pedagogy of critical media literacy to empower our youth.

Yet to address problems of societal violence it requires, as I have been arguing, a reconstruction of education and society, and what Herbert Marcuse referred to as "a revolution in values" and a "new sensibility."[8] The revolution in values involves breaking with values of competition, aggression, greed, and self-interest and cultivating values of equality, peace, harmony, and community. Such a revolution of values "would also make for a new morality, for new relations between the sexes and generations, for a new relation between man and nature" (2001: 198). Harbingers of the revolution in values, Marcuse argued, are found in "a widespread rebellion against the domineering values, of virility, heroism and force, invoking the images of society which may bring about the end of violence" (ibid.).

The "new sensibility" in turn would cultivate needs for beauty, love, connections with nature and other people, and more democratic and egalitarian social relations. Marcuse believes that without a change in the sensibility, there can be no real social change, and that education, art, and the humanities can help cultivate the conditions for a new sensibility. Underlying the theory of the new sensibility is a concept of the active role of the senses in the constitution of experience that rejects the Kantian and other philosophical devaluations of the senses as passive, merely receptive. For Marcuse, our senses are shaped and molded by society, yet constitute in turn our primary experience of the world and provide both imagination and reason with its material. He believes that the senses are currently socially constrained and mutilated and argues that only an emancipation of the senses and a new sensibility can produce liberating social change.

Ultimately, addressing the problem of societal violence requires a democratic reconstruction of education and society, new pedagogical practices, new social relations, values, and forms of learning. In the following section, I want to sketch out aspects of a democratic reconstruction grounded in key ideas of John Dewey, Paulo Freire, Ivan Illich, and Herbert Marcuse.

Youth and the Crisis of Education

To begin, we need to recognize a systemic crisis of education in the United States in which there is a disconnect between youth's lives and what they are taught in school. Already in 1964, Marshall McLuhan recognized the discrepancy between kids raised on a fast-paced and multimodal media culture and the linear, book and test-oriented education of the time, where kids sit in a classroom all day. Since then, there has been a proliferation of new media and technologies, but education has been retreating to ever more conservative and pedantic goals, most egregiously during the Bush era and its phony "No Child Left Behind" program which is really a front for "teaching for testing." In this policy, strongly resisted by many states and local school districts, incredible amounts of time are wasted preparing students for tests and teachers, and schools are basically rated according to their test results.[9]

As I have been arguing, digital technologies and cultural forms are dramatically transforming the circulation of information, images, and various modes of culture, and the younger generation needs to gain multifaceted technological skills to survive in the high-tech information society. In this situation, students should learn both how to use media and computer culture to do research and gather information, as well as to perceive it as a cultural terrain which contains texts, spectacles, games, and interactive media which require a form of critical computer literacy. Youth subcultural forms range from 'zines or websites that feature an ever-expanding range of video, music, or multimedia texts to sites of political information and organization.[10]

Moreover, since the 1999 Seattle anti-corporate globalization demonstrations, youth have been using digital technologies and social media to inform and debate each other, organize oppositional movements, and generate alternative forms of politics and culture.[11] Consequently, at present, critical digital literacies involve not merely technical skills and knowledge, but the ability to scan information, to interact with a variety of cultural forms and groups, and to intervene in a creative manner within the emergent digital and political culture.

Whereas youth is excluded for the most part from production in the dominant media culture, digital and multimedia culture is a discursive and political location in which youth can intervene, producing their own websites and personal pages, engaging in discussion groups, linking with others who share their interests, generating digital multimedia for cultural dissemination and a diversity of cultural and political projects. Digital cultures enable individuals to actively participate in the production of culture, ranging from discussion of public issues to creation of their own cultural forms, enabling those who had been previously excluded from cultural production and mainstream politics to participate in the creation of culture and socio-political activism.

After using digital and social media to successfully organize a wide range of anti-corporate globalization demonstrations in Seattle, Washington, Prague, Toronto, and elsewhere, young people played an active role in organizing massive demonstrations against the Bush administration threats against Iraq, creating the basis for an oppositional anti-war and peace movement as the Bush administration threatens an era of perpetual war in the new millennium. Obviously, it is youth that fights and dies in wars that often primarily serve the interests of corrupt economic and political elites. Today's youth is becoming aware that its survival is at stake and that thus it is necessary to become informed and organized on the crucial issues of war, peace, and the future of democracy and the global economy.

Youth were also an important factor in helping elect Barack Obama to two terms as President and strongly opposed the regime of Donald Trump and helped prevent his re-election (Kellner 2020). In addition, youth groups over the past several decades have been organizing to save endangered species, to fight genetically engineered food, to debate cloning and stem cell research, to advance animal rights, to join struggles over environmental causes like climate change and global warming, and to work for creating a healthier diet and alternative medical systems, as well as militating for stronger school and gun safety issues. Digital and social media have become a virtual treasury of alternative information and cultural forms with young people playing key roles in developing the technology and oppositional culture and using it for creative pedagogical and political purposes.

Youth, Social and Digital Media, and School Shootings

Youth has also been subject to an epidemic of school shootings and have been active participants in efforts to reform the out-of-control gun culture and to implement reasonable reforms in gun safety laws. After the wave of school shootings since Columbine, the need for gun control in an out-of-control gun culture *and* for better mental health care in a society in which mentally disturbed young teenagers and men have been producing an epidemic of mass murder. Yet despite the immensity of the tragedy, Republicans, the gun lobbies, and merchants of death have prevented gun safety legislation, and the slaughter continued into the 2020s without significant gun safety laws to protect students, teachers, and citizens from mass shootings.

For instance, the school massacre in Uvalde, Texas, carried out by a young 18-year-old assailant in May 2022, was the 27th school shooting in the U.S. in 2022, according to a report by National Public Radio (NPR 2022). The source reports that 19 students and two teachers were killed. Many more were injured, making the massacre in Uvalde the deadliest shooting at an elementary school since the Sandy Hook massacre ten years previously and the most lethal at any school since a gunman killed seventeen people at Marjory Stoneman Douglas High School in Parkland, Florida, in 2018. The massacre provides yet another black mark on the U.S. social and political system that has witnessed hundreds of school shootings since the Columbine shooting in a culture marked by guys and guns amok (Kellner 2008).

While the cable news networks, news media, and internet commentators provided minute-by-minute coverage of the Uvalde massacre and continued to carefully follow it in days after, as new shocking information continued to come out, liberal politicians quickly joined the pro-gun reform camp calling for immediate action, or like the NRA controlled Republicans evaded the issue. On the day of the shooting on May 24, Senator Chris Murphy (D-Conn.) called on his colleagues to pass gun legislation in a stirring spontaneous and impassioned speech. Sen. Murphy, a Democrat from Connecticut who represented Sandy Hook in the terrible school shooting there, once held a 15-hour filibuster on the Senate floor on the need for stricter U.S. gun laws and pleaded with his colleagues to find a way to put politics aside and work together to stop the carnage of mass shootings.

President Joe Biden came on live TV and said he is "sick and tired" of continued mass shootings in the US and access to military-style weapons for youth. "When in God's name will we do what needs to be done to, not completely stop, but fundamentally change the amount of carnage that goes on in this country." he said. "To state the obvious, I'm sick and tired; I'm, what continues to go on."[12]

Biden had been the point person for the Obama administration to pass gun reform measures, and every time there was a mass shooting, Biden would lead the Democratic Party troops into the fray to try to push through gun reform. But Mitch McConnell, the Republican Senate Majority leader who has blocked any legislation whatsoever that would annoy his NRA pay-masters, continued his nefarious role during the Trump and the Biden Administrations of being the point man for blocking gun reform, winning him admission into the top ranks of Republican Hall of Shame.

There is indeed little hope that Biden will be able to pass any meaningful gun control during the present legislative session, controlled by a Republican Congress, raising hopes that in the coming 2024 U.S. Presidential and Congressional Elections, pro-gun reform advocates will be able to win enough seats to pass meaningful reform, as gun reform measures and women's reproductive rights that are under attack by a hard-right and very Trumpy Supreme Court are critical issues of public debates that should be significant factors in the 2024 Elections.

I also have hope that youth will continue to mobilize around a gun safety movement led by activists such as David Hogg, a survivor of the Parkland 2018 school shooting in Florida. Hogg has continued to be a critic of the out-of-control gun culture and activist for change, responding after every shooting with efforts to organize youth and others into a reform movement. After Uvalde, Hogg tweeted: "No parent should drop their kid off at school and then need a DNA test to ID which child is their child because they have been blown to pieces by an AR 15."[13]

Hogg was referring to the gruesome scenes at Uvalde and other local hospitals after the shootings, where attempts were made to identify murdered students and where worried parents gave their DNA to help identify if their children were among the victim – a truly horrific scene, but one that plays out after every mass shooting. These episodes received significant media coverage, but we should not forget the thousands of victims of gun violence and keep in our minds the horrors of the Sandy Hook and Uvalde massacres to demand and militate for action on gun reform. A media and political consensus seems to be emerging that banning violent assault weapons, which had been put in place in 1994 under the Clinton Administration but left to expire during the Bush-Cheney administration of 2004, should be reinstated. There were also demands that more rigorous background checks be passed to keep guns out of the hands of young male would-be assassins and a federal law forbidding gun sales to youth from 18 to 21, as is the case in many states and local laws. Further, there were reports that the Department of Justice was investigating the police response to the Uvalde shooting.

After the Uvalde shooting, media focus seemed more intense than other school shootings in recent memory. The outrage by politicians and the public raises hope that action will be taken this time. In the past, President Biden has tried, as noted above, many times to pass reasonable gun reform, and it is hoped that this time the country and Congress will rise to the occasion. Alternative sites of information and discussion on every conceivable topic can be found on the Internet, including important issues like human rights or environmental education that are often neglected in public schools.

Radical Pedagogy and Gun Safety

Challenges to education today thus require a radical pedagogy to confront crucial issues of the present, such as school shootings and gun safety laws. Since people get information about guns, shootings, and other acts of violence from the media and digital culture, developing critical forms of print, media, digital, and multiple forms of technoliteracies are crucial in the technoculture of the present and fast-approaching future. Such an effort would be linked to a revitalized radical pedagogy that attempts to empower individuals to analyze and criticize the emerging technoculture and participate in producing its cultural and political forums and sites. More than ever, we need philosophical reflection on the ends and purposes of education and educational technology and on what we are doing and trying to achieve with it in our educational practices and institutions. In this situation, it may be instructive to return to John Dewey and see the connections between education, technology, and democracy, the need for the reconstruction of education and society, and the value of experimental pedagogy to seek solutions to education problems in the present day.

A progressive reconstruction of education will urge that it be done in the interests of democratization, ensuring access to information and communication technologies for all, thereby helping to overcome the so-called digital divide and divisions of the haves and have-nots so that education is placed in the service of democracy and social justice (Dewey 1997 [1916]; Freire (1972, 1978) in light of Ivan Illich's (1970, 1971, 1973) critiques of the limitations and challenges of education in postindustrial societies.[14] Yet, we should be more aware than Dewey, Freire, and Illich of the obduracy of the divisions of class, gender, and race, and so work self-consciously for multicultural democracy and education. This task suggests that we valorize difference, cultural specificity, equality, and shared universal Deweyean values such as freedom, equality, individualism, and participation.

Hence, a significant challenge for education today is thus to promote computer and media literacy to empower students and citizens to use a wide range of technologies to enhance their lives and create a better culture and society. This involves developing Internet projects that articulate significant cultural and political struggles in the contemporary world, developing pedagogies whereby students work together transmitting their technical knowledge to other students and their teachers, and teachers and students work together in developing relevant educational material, projects, and pedagogies in the experimental Deweyean and Freirean mode.

For instance, students interested in school safety and gun reforms can develop sites of information documenting gun violence in the schools and the ease with which one can buy guns from the internet, guns show, or off the streets. Chat forums can debate the pros and cons of gun safety and the importance of specific reform measures, like background checks. Youth can and has been involved in the struggles for gun reform, with David Hogg and other students subjected to school shootings traveling the country militating for gun reform and school safety laws to be passed. In addition, families of Sandy Hook and other school shootings have organized groups for rational gun control. They are active on the community, state, and federal levels arguing for gun safety education and law reform.

Teachers and students, then, need to develop new pedagogies and modes of learning for disseminating information about gun safety and other issues of immediate concern and use all the tools of the technoculture to inform, organize, and militate for gun reform and safer school environments. This should involve the democratization and reconstruction of education, as was envisaged by Dewey, Freire, Illich, and Marcuse, in which education is seen as a dialogical, democratizing, and experimental practice.

New information technologies acting along the lines of Illich's conceptions of "webs of learning" and "tools for conviviality" (1971, 1973) encourage the experimental and collaborative projects proposed by Dewey and can also involve the more dialogical and non-authoritarian relations between students and teachers that Freire envisaged. In this respect, the re-visioning of education consists of the recognition that teachers can learn from students and that students are often ahead of their teachers in various technological literacies and technical abilities. Many of us have learned much about computers, digital media, and technologies from our students. We should also recognize the extent to which young people helped invent the Internet and have grown up in a culture where they may have readily cultivated technological skills from an early age.[15] Peer-to-peer communication among young people is thus often a highly sophisticated development, and democratic pedagogies should build upon and enhance these resources and practices.

One of the challenges of contemporary education is to overcome the separation between students' experiences, subjectivities, and interests rooted in the new multimedia technoculture and the classroom situations grounded in print culture, traditional learning methods, and disciplines (Luke & Luke, 2002). However, the disconnect can be addressed by more actively and collaboratively bringing students into interactive classrooms or learning situations in which they can transmit their skills and knowledge to fellow students and teachers alike. Such a democratic and interactive reconstruction of education thus provides the resources for a democratic social reconstruction and cultivates the new skills and literacies needed for the global media economy. Students and activists can also use these literacies to militate for school safety measures, gun control, and other issues vital to students.

So far, arguments for restructuring education mostly come from the hi-tech and corporate sectors primarily interested in new media and literacies for the workforce and capitalist profit. Yet reconstruction can serve the interests of democratization and the elite corporate few. Following Dewey, we should accordingly militate for education that aims at producing democratic citizens, even as it provides skills for the workplace, social and cultural life. Both Paulo Freire and Ivan Illich saw that a glaring problem with contemporary educational institutions was that they have become fixed in monomodal instruction, with homogenized lesson plans, curricula, and pedagogy, and that they neglect to address challenging political, cultural, and ecological problems, and pressing issues like school safety and gun reform.

The development of convivial tools and radically democratic pedagogies can enable teachers and students to break with these models and engage in Deweyan experimental education and collectively deal with issues of school safety and gun reform. In the Deweyean mode, students should also learn and practice how to be democratic citizens and participate in constructing a safe learning environment.

The reconstruction of education can help to create subjects better able to negotiate the complexities and challenges of emergent modes of everyday life, labor, and culture as contemporary life becomes ever more multi-faceted and dangerous. It is, of course, a scandal that students in the U.S. must deal with the issue of school safety as a crucial issue of survival, as most countries have few if any, school shootings. Indeed, part of the critical pedagogy of school safety and gun control involves a critique of the out-of-control gun culture and the need for dramatic reform of existing gun laws with guns available without background checks on the internet, gun shows, and other unsavory sites life back-street sales of illegal guns that seem to be available everywhere in the United States today.

Supportive, dialogical, and interactive social relations in critical learning situations like school safety and gun control can promote cooperation, democracy, and positive social values and fulfill needs for communication, esteem, and politicized learning. Whereas modern mass education has tended to see life in a linear fashion based on print models and has developed pedagogies, which have divided experience into discrete moments and behavioral bits, critical pedagogies produce skills that enable individuals to navigate better and synthesize the multiple realms and challenges of contemporary life. Deweyean education focused on problem-solving, goal-seeking projects, and the courage to be experimental. At the same time, Freire developed critical problem-posing pedagogies of the oppressed aiming at social justice and progressive social transformation, while Illich offered oppositional conceptions of education and alternatives to oppressive institutions. This critical spirit and vision, which calls for the reconstruction of education and society, can help produce more radicalized pedagogies, school safety, gun reform tools, social and ecological justice, and utopian possibilities for a better world.

A democratic reconstruction of education will involve producing democratic citizens, and empowering the next generation for democracy should be a significant goal of the reconstruction of education in the present age. Moreover, as Freire reminds us (1972 and 1998), critical pedagogy comprises the skills of both reading the word and the world. Hence, multiple literacies include not only media and computer literacies but a diverse range of social and cultural literacies, ranging from ecoliteracy (e.g., understanding the body and environment) to social literacy that provides models of secure and safe communities to economic and financial literacy – as well as to a variety of other competencies that enable us to live well in our social worlds. At its best, education provides the symbolic and cultural capital that empowers people to survive and prosper in an increasingly complex and changing world and the resources to produce a more cooperative, democratic, egalitarian, and just society.

Notes

1 The White House. Office of the Press Secretary, Barack Obama. "Statement by the President on the School Shooting in Newtown," CT, December 14, 2012 at <https://obamawhitehouse.archives.gov/the-press-office/2012/12/14/statement-president-school-shooting-newtown-ct> (accessed March 12, 2023).

2. See my analysis of connections between crises of masculinity, an out-of-control gun culture, and media spectacle in Kellner 2008.
3. Web-based Injury Statistics Query and Reporting System (WISQARS). Centers for Disease Control and Prevention, National Center for Injury Prevention and Control; 2018 at UC Davis <https://health.ucdavis.edu/what-you-can-do/facts.html> (accessed on March 10, 2023).
4. David Olinger, "Living on the Edge, Guns at the Ready," *The Denver Post*, September 30, 2007 at <https://www.denverpost.com/2007/09/30/living-on-edge-guns-at-the-ready/> (accessed on June 20, 2024).
5. Another horrific documentation of school shooting in the US reveals that "More than 300,000 students have experienced gun violence at school since Columbine" *Washington Post* database, compiled by Cox, Rich, Thacker, Muyskens, John and Ulman, Monica 2022. And yet another deeply troubling documentation indicates that as of March 6, 2023, there have been over 100 mass shootings in the United States; see Jacob Knutson, "U.S. surpassed 100 mass shootings in only 64 days," *Axios*, March 7, 2023 at <https://www.axios.com/2023/03/07/us-surpasses-100-mass-shootings-65-days> (accessed March 27, 2023).
6. Information, publications, films, and other material on the Mentors in Violence Program can be found at <https://cultureofrespect.org/program/mentors-in-violence-prevention-mvp/> (accessed March 11, 2023). See also the studies in *Violence Goes to College* edited by Nicoletti, Spencer-Thomas and Bollinger, 2018.
7. Cited in Nick Gillespie, "The FCC's not mommy and daddy," *Los Angeles Times*, May 2, 2007: A23. For my study of the Virginia Tech school shooting, see Kellner 2008 and "Media Spectacle and the 'Massacre at Virginia Tech," in *There is a Shooter on Campus: Tragedy and terror at Virginia Tech*," edited by Ben Agger and Timothy W. Luke. Lanham, MD: Rowman and Littlefied, 2008: 29–54.
8. See Herbert Marcuse, "A Revolution in Values" in Marcuse 2001, and on the new sensibility see my introduction to the volume of collected papers of Marcuse on *Art and Liberation* (2006).
9. This misplaced pedagogy of teaching for testing did not just originate with the Bush administration, but has long been a feature of pedagogically-challenged schools; see Janet Ewell, "Test-takers, not students," *Los Angeles Times*, May 26, 2007: A19. For some compelling criticism of Bush Administration "No Child Left Behind" policies, see the dossier "Correcting Schools," *The Nation*, May 21, 2007: 11–21.
10. See Jones 2002; Kahn and Kellner 2005. Some good sites that exhibit youth voices, participation, and politics include <http://www.moveon.org>; <http://www.raisethefist.com>; <http://www.tao.com> (accessed on May 2, 2007); the youth blog site at <http://www.Bloghop.com/topics.htm?numblogs=14566&cacheid=1044419966.3569> (accessed on May 14, 2007) and the People for the American Way site on Youth Activism and the Young Elected Officials Network (NEO) at <https://www.pfaw.org/young-elected-officials-network/?source=XXWMWXAGK07X00&gclid=CjwKCAjw_YShBhAiEiwAMomsEKby-hZnrnkmqNdF2OSKv229ys6BgiNqFpP00h5kcIaYRFa2zUrjeAhoCZocQAvD_BwE> (accessed March 27, 2023).
11. See Best and Kellner 2001 and Kahn and Kellner 2005. For an overview of the use of digital technology by youth and others for political activism in the contemporary era, see Kellner 2021.

12 Joe Biden "'I am sick and tired of it,' Biden says after Texas school shooting. 'As a nation we have to ask when in God's name are we going to stand up to the gun lobby?' the president said Tuesday evening in remarks at the White House." *NBC News*, May 24, 2022 at <https://www.nbcnews.com/politics/white-house/biden-make-remarks-texas-school-shooting-tuesday-evening-rcna30397> (accessed March 27, 2023).
13 David Hogg on Twitter at <https://twitter.com/davidhogg111/status/1529404174580035584?lang=en> (accessed on March 27, 2023). On Hogg's gun safety activism, see his Wikipedia entry at <https://en.wikipedia.org/wiki/David_Hogg> (accessed on March 27, 2023). On this entry, you can read how Hogg was accused as being a "crisis actor" who had never been a victim of school shooting, and how he was repeatedly the subject of rightwing attacks, including attacks on his life.
14 I address below the importance of John Dewey for radical pedagogy today. On the significance of Freire and Ivan Illich, Richard Kahn and Douglas Kellner, "Paulo Freire and Ivan Illich: technology, politics, and the reconstruction of education," *Policy Futures in Education*, Volume 5, Number 4, 2007: 431–448. On the importance of Herbert Marcuse for philosophy, social critique, and education, see K. Daniel Cho, Douglas Kellner, Tyson E. Lewis, and Clayton Pierce, co-editors, *Marcuse's Challenge to Education*. Lanham, N.J.: Rowman and Littlefield Publishers, 2009, and Douglas Kellner, Tyson E. Lewis and Clayton Pierce. *On Marcuse: Critique, Liberation, and Reschooling in the Radical Pedagogy of Herbert Marcuse*. Rotterdam, the Netherlands: Brill Publishers, 2008.
15 For instance, Mosaic, Netscape and the first browsers were invented by young computer users, as were many of the first Websites, list-serves, chat rooms, and so on. A hacker culture emerged that was initially conceptualized as a reconfiguring and improving of computer systems, related to design, system and use, before the term became synonymous with theft and mischief, such as setting loose worms and viruses. On youth and Internet subcultures, see Kahn & Kellner (2003).

References

Best, Steven and Kellner, Douglas (2001). *The Postmodern Adventure: Science, Technology, and Cultural Studies at the Third Millennium*. New York: Guilford.
Dewey, John (1997 [1916]). *Democracy and Education*. New York: Free Press.
Freire, Paulo (1972). *Pedagogy of the Oppressed*. New York: Herder and Herder.
Freire, Paulo (1998). *A Paulo Freire Reader*. New York: Herder and Herder.
Illich, Ivan (1970). *Deschooling Society*. New York: Marion Boyers Press.
Illich, Ivan (1971). *Celebration of Awareness*. London: Marion Boyars.
Illich, Ivan (1973). *Tools for Conviviality*. New York: Harper and Row.
Jones, Steve (2002). *The Internet Goes to College: How Students Are Living in the Future With Today's Technology*. Pew Internet & American Life Project at <https://www.google.com/books/edition/Internet_Goes_to_College/FBtcMsRcRdwC?hl=en> (accessed May 31, 2023).
Kahn, Richard and Kellner, Douglas (2003). "Internet Subcultures and Oppositional Politics," in *The Post-Subcultures Reader* (Muggleton, David, ed.). Oxford and New York: Berg, 299–314.

Kahn, Richard and Kellner, Douglas (2005). "Oppositional Politics and the Internet: A Critical/Reconstructive Approach," *Cultural Politics*, 1(1): 75–100.
Kahn, Richard and Kellner, Douglas (2006). "Reconstructing Technoliteracy: A Multiple Literacies Approach," in *Defining Technological Literacy*, edited by John R. Dakers. New York and England: Palgrave Macmillan, pp. 253–274.
Katz, Jackson (2006). *The Macho Paradox*. Naperville, Ill.: Sourcebook.
Kellner, Douglas (1995; 2021). *Media Culture*. London and New York: Routledge.
Kellner, Douglas (2004). "Technological Transformation, Multiple Literacies, and the Revisioning of Education." *E-Learning*, 1(1): 9–37.
Kellner, Douglas (2006). "Toward a Critical Theory of Education," *Critical Theory and Critical Pedagogy Today. Toward a New Critical Language in Education*, edited by Ilan Gur-Ze'ev. University of Haifa: Studies in Education,: 49–69.
Kellner, Douglas (2008). Guys and Guns Amok: Domestic Terrorism and School Shootings from the Oklahoma City Bombings to the Virginia Tech Massacre. Boulder, Col.: Paradigm Press, 2008.
Kellner, Douglas and Jeff Share (2007). "Critical Media Literacy, Democracy, and the Reconstruction of Education," *Media literacy. A Reader*, edited by Donald Macedo and Shirley R. Steinberg. New York: Peter Lang, 2007: 3–23.
David Knights and Alison Pullen (2019). "Masculinity: A contested terrain?" *Gender Work and Organization*, 26(10): 1367–1375.
Larkin, Ralph W. (2007). *Comprehending Columbine*. Philadelphia: Temple University Press.
Luke, Allan and Luke, Carmen (2002). "Adolescence Lost/childhood Regained: On Early Intervention and the Emergence of the Techno-subject." *Journal of Early Childhood Literacy*, 1(1): 91–120.
Marcuse, Herbert (2001). *Toward a Critical Theory of Society. Collected Papers of Herbert Marcuse*, Volume 2, edited by Douglas Kellner. London and New York: Routledge.
Marcuse, Herbert (2006 [2001]). *Art and Liberation. Collected Papers of Herbert Marcuse, Volume 4*, edited by Douglas Kellner. London and New York: Routledge.
McLuhan, Marshall (1964). *Understanding Media: The Extensions of Man*. New York: Signet Books.

· 5 ·

DOUGLAS KELLNER, "DANGEROUS NEW DIMENSION TO MASS SHOOTINGS IN AMERICA," INTERVIEW WITH JOANIE HARMAN

Introduction, Joanie Harman: "Trump's vilification of immigrants and a rampant gun culture fuel recent epidemic of mass killings"

In April of 2007, Doug Kellner was on his way to deliver a talk at Virginia Tech when he was notified that the university was closed due to a mass shooting that had just occurred on campus, killing 32 and wounding 17. Kellner, a Distinguished Professor of Education, Gender Studies, and Germanic Languages and a scholar of media and film, was horrified and fascinated.

"I was researching media spectacle at the time," recalls Kellner. "I started reading about [the shooting] ... and thinking about Columbine and other school shootings and the key ideas just hit me," says Kellner. "It's been the same idea for every one of these shootings – that we have an out-of-control gun culture and a crisis of masculinities. These young men who were in crisis... resolved it through these shootings and it became a media spectacle."

Professor Kellner is now examining the newest aspect of mass killings in the Trump era – the role of racism that motivates troubled individuals to kill. He is currently working on a second edition of his 2008 book, *Guys and Guns Amok: Domestic Terrorism and School Shootings from the Oklahoma*

City Bombing to the Virginia Tech Massacre. <https://www.routledge.com/Guys-and-Guns-Amok-Domestic-Terrorism-and-School-Shootings-from-the-Oklahoma/Kellner/p/book/9781594514937> (accessed May 23, 2018).

Kellner is the inaugural George F. Kneller Philosophy of Education Chair in the division of Social Sciences & Comparative Education at UCLA, and a 2003–04 Fellow of the Sudikoff Family Institute for Education & New Media (now the Sudikoff Institute Public Forum <https://sudikoff.gseis.ucla.edu>). He is also the co-author, with TEP faculty advisor Jeff Share, of "The Critical Media Literacy Guide: Engaging Media and Transforming Education," <https://ampersand.gseis.ucla.edu/douglas-kellner-jeff-share-new-book-highlights-need-for-critical-media-literacy-in-schools/> .

Professor Kellner discussed with *Ampersand* the still-prevalent gun culture in the United States, the need for better mental health interventions and regulation of weapons, and the elasticity of the Constitution when it comes to a matter of life or death for those it serves.

Ampersand: What factors of mass killings have changed the most – whether it involves the media, gun control, families, or schools – with recent events?

Douglas Kellner: There is one major thing that has changed in the last two years. All of the previous shootings were rather divorced from sociopolitical factors. In other words, they were mainly individual crises of young men. They could be crises of their family, of their school, or their community.

Most of the mass shootings have been distinguished by the fact that they are somewhat random – that the shooters aren't really targeting any particular people. This is true in most of the mass school shootings, although sometimes the school shooters have a particular individual that's part of the room, and some of the school shooters are anti-women. What they all have in common is their immersion in gun culture, and this has really been accelerated. For example, we saw three [shootings] in the last month [in Summer 2020], in (Gilroy) California, El Paso, and Dayton, Ohio.

The toxicity of gun culture has created a new factor that we have never seen before, that was a major factor in the last few shootings, and that was the election of Donald Trump, and in particular, Trump's rhetoric [on immigrants and his other hate speech]. There haven't been particular racist school shootings before, or so many acts of domestic terrorism in recent years as in the Trump presidency.

The El Paso shooting … was completely different from any of the other acts of domestic terrorism [or] school shootings, because it was targeting

Latinos and immigrants. The shooter made it explicit in the manifesto that he wrote that he was influenced by Trump's anti-immigrant and anti-Mexican sentiments and he targeted them. The shooter drove nine or ten hours from the Dallas area all the way to El Paso. That's a long drive across nothing, just the desert. So, imagine ten hours of driving, thinking about what you're going to do. He had to have some extreme motive and it was fueled by Trump. So, this is my new worry, that there will be others who are likewise motivated.

&: How do you explain an event like this in a state whose overall culture includes a longstanding Latino and Mexican heritage?

Kellner: Again, I think it's Trump. I taught for 25 years at the University of Texas at Austin, and one of the striking things to me was how well Latinos, Anglos, and African Americans got along, at least in Austin and the more progressive metropolitan areas. I don't recall any mass shootings of Latinos by some racist shooter – excluding, of course, racist border shootings against undocumented immigrants. This was from 1973 to the mid-1990s, just before I came to UCLA. So, there's been a big shift.

And the immigrant communities are terrorized. This was clearly an act of terrorism and has terrorized the people of El Paso and immigrants throughout the country. I've seen article after article on how afraid Latinos and immigrants are in certain parts of the country after these shootings.

&: How do the extreme leftist views of the Dayton shooter – who on Twitter, called out the El Paso shooter as a White supremacist and a terrorist – bode badly for those who oppose Trump's views?

Kellner: This is the thing about the larger picture of what's created divisions and increased violence in this country, and that is the divisive nature of Trump's rhetoric. It puts both sides against each other. It creates hate for immigrants and Latinos and liberals and the media in Trump's community. But, you can say that just as strikingly on the other side is the anti-Trump sentiment – I've never seen anything like it. CNN, which was pretty neutral in the presidential election, has been increasingly anti-Trump. I've seen broadcasts where all day, they're attacking Trump. Fox News is just a mouthpiece for Trump's rhetoric and his hate speech, whereas MSNBC is as strongly anti-Trump as Fox is pro-Trump. There really is a division in the country that is extreme and the media has contributed to it.

&: A target in a mass shooting would be an individual in a school or a public place, that has had some relationship with the shooter. Why don't the killers just go after that individual?

Kellner: Well, that's the whole thing with mass shootings – they're a media spectacle. They make the shooter famous, and somehow, they express their societal rage in a way that shootings of targeted individual don't. But, I think that we now have established a tradition of mass shooters. The El Paso shooter was pretty much a copycat, and referred to some previous shooters.

&: Shooters often end up killing themselves or being killed. What is their reward?

Kellner: Martyrdom. Why do these Islamic terrorists kill themselves? They have this notion of martyrdom. Either they're going to go to heaven or become heroes of a certain group.

And copycats – we're now seeing a lot of copycat shooters and what is really disturbing is that White nationalists and other racists might start copy-catting attacks on Latinos or people of color, or immigrant targets. And the White nationalists makes the shootings patriotic and glorify mass shootings of people of color as protecting the White race.

&: How do the internet and other forms of media like video games pose a factor in these acts of mass violence?

Kellner: The media is one of the factors in mass shooting, but it's not necessarily the major determinate. Trump blamed the El Paso shooting on video games and everyone said, this is ridiculous, there is no evidence that it was video games behind mass shootings, because in Japan and Korea, there are more intense video game culture and there are no mass shootings. On the other hand, the Newtown (Connecticut) shooter and quite a few of the other mass shooters were immersed in video game culture. So, I think video game culture probably does contribute to mass shootings, and if I were a parent, I wouldn't let my kids play these games, or would at least monitor and discuss the games with them in the context of mass societal violence.

&: What are some societal changes that need to be made in schools, homes, and society?

Kellner: We have a gun culture like no other country in the world, where it's part of male socialization in some parts of the country. In a lot of cases, rural areas have better gun safety training than in urban areas where there isn't such a developed gun culture. I grew up in Southern California and I never saw a gun. But, I went to high school in Virginia, and I had all these Southern neighbors who were amazed that I never had shot a gun or gone hunting. So, they took me out and I just decided that I didn't like guns or hunting.

The mother of the El Paso shooter actually called the police and told them she was worried that her son has this gun collection and that she was afraid that he was going to do something to hurt himself or other people. And of course, the police didn't do anything about it. What needs to be done is that we need to take these threats of gun violence very, very seriously when there is a report like this. But we need changes in the gun laws as well. This is insane, that we have these assault rifles that anyone can get ... on the internet or at gun shows even without a background check.

There is again serious talk about background checks and red flag warnings, but nobody has done much after the last decades of mass shootings, despite calls for rational gun control. But it is conceivable with the presidential elections and the general elections that if Congress doesn't do anything, some of them could be voted out. I see a possibility that there could be some new gun laws. Few people are against background checks or red flag laws except the NRA and some gun fanatics.

&: How about mental health care and the fact that many kids who are noted to have emotional problems are still mainstreamed into regular classrooms?

Kellner: This is a whole other issue in and of itself. Obviously, it overlaps with the guns. There is a significant degree of mental health disturbance among the shooters, and it's clear that this should be an issue in whether or not people should be allowed to get guns. In other words, if a potential gun buyer has documented mental health issues, they shouldn't be able to purchase guns.

More generally as a society, we really need to take mental health problems more seriously. And this relates to schools in a big way since there have been so many school shootings, often by high school students. In education, we really need to address issues like masculinity, guns, and mental health. If schools see kids acting out and making violent threats, schools need to have resources to address these issues. You have to have mental health professionals in the high schools and individuals who can protect students from potential shooters. There are at present school counselors and psychologists of different sorts, but they really have to have mental health training and be able to deal with potential shooters.

&: How is the fear level that has risen among kids in schools, as well as teachers and families impacting education overall?

There are studies of the growing fear among kids in schools. But it's this last set of shootings where the term terrorism can apply. The last set of shootings – the three this summer [i.e., 2019] – can be labeled as acts of domestic terrorism, and this is the first time I've used the word – *terrorism* – for these shootings. I saw a report on CNN about how kids are afraid to go to school because they are afraid they are going to get shot.

My partner, Rhonda Hammer, was just in a hair salon and there was a teacher telling story after story about how her students are afraid to come to school. There were also some mothers in the salon who said yes, they were afraid to send their kids to school. We've never had a situation where parents and teachers are afraid for their kids because there is such an epidemic of gun violence. One factor they mentioned was that they had been having all these drills about shooting and this absolutely terrifies the kids. And when they see these shootings on television within a week, this just freaks the kids out. Already they're scared during these drills. But then they see the normalizing of three shootings in a week – it terrorizes them.

&: How about the fear that a kid who grows up in this environment of fear would end up enacting mass violence themselves?

Kellner: That's where it's going to end, so this is where we have an urgent need for action. We have to demand of our politicians' new gun laws. It's insane that these assault rifles are allowed. They were banned in the Clinton era. In the 1990s, Bill Clinton banned them, and George W. Bush let the ban expire in 2004, so assault rifles are once again available. The statistics show that gun violence actually went down significantly when assault rifles were illegal. So, these assault rifles seem to have a dangerous, psychological impact on imbalanced young men and there has been a continuous wave of killing with these instruments of death.

&: Do media companies have a responsibility through their products when they contribute to a violent culture?

Kellner: Absolutely, the media is part of the environment that has traditionally glorified guns. The Western is a dominant American genre, but also in crime dramas and detective films, guns are shown as the solution to social problems. Only documentaries show guns as a problem. All of the networks in the last few weeks have had good news reports and some documentaries on gun violence. The media is aware that they have that responsibility and have produced these documentaries and had some good discussions of the problem.

There is another new factor and this goes back to our earlier discussion of the El Paso shootings and the recent spate of shootings. In my analysis, I put a big blame on Trump. I want to put equally big blame on White nationalism, and it's partly because of Trump because he embraced White nationalist groups that supported him. Previously, White nationalism was seen as something out of the American mainstream before Trump, so it wouldn't be covered in the media. It's been there forever, but in terms of normalizing it and in terms of the media reproducing it, this is a new feature. And you have a whole network – *Fox News* – that's trumpeting Trump's racist rhetoric – I didn't intend a pun but it's a good one.

&: How can we look at this from the standpoint of critical media literacy?

Kellner: This is definitely a new challenge for critical media literacy. Jeff Share and I, in our book *The Critical Media Literacy Guide* (2019) have stressed the need to critique violence in the media. We were talking mostly about entertainment – films, TV programs. Now, the new task for critical media literacy is critiquing extremist discourse, which is violent discourse in broadcasting news and on the internet. The internet has become the radicalizing force for a lot of these shooters. Again, this last set of shootings were influenced by right-wing extremism, by hate groups, who find a space to spread their hate and recruit violent people on digital media.

I've always been a libertarian, believing completely in free speech, yet I'm coming to think that these hate sites should be banned. I think it's crazy that the Nazis, the Ku Klux Klan, and other hate groups have sites which glorify racism and gun violence are allowed to promote hate and violence on broadcasting and social media – this is sick and dangerous. We can see the effects of this hate speech and the consequences it has on mass shootings, that we have come to know all too well. We need to take action –NOW!

&: Other nations seem to have better controls over online content that is potentially harmful. How do you draw the line in the United States between freedom of speech and endangering the public?

Kellner: I think human life and survival requires limitations of freedom of speech. If hate speech is endangering human lives and it is known to contribute to mass shootings and acts of violence, it is necessary to seriously deal with this. This has to do with what we were talking about earlier concerning societal violence. People who engage in hate speech that promotes guns violence need help –as do the perpetuators of violence. We need to help them. In addressing the problem of gun violence, you are not abridging freedom of speech – you're helping young people deal with their demons and their problems.

This really puts freedom of speech in a different context. Indeed, we need to rethink this lip-service to freedom of speech as it's not an absolute as some of us once thought it was.

&: What about the Second Amendment?

Kellner: If you look at it, the Second Amendment talked about guns and a well-regulated militia. From the very beginning, there has been the notion of regulation and the Supreme Court has held up all kinds of regulation. So, I don't see the Second Amendment as absolute, just like I don't see the First Amendment as absolute. In both cases, there need to be qualifications in certain contexts. And historically, our notions of both free speech and gun rights have changed.

There's been a debate – I think it was in the 1960s – about hate speech. Some were calling for restrictions on the Nazis and Ku Klux Klan that were calling for violence. For instance, different towns had to deal with Nazis or Klan members coming to rally in their town. There was always freedom of speech and freedom of assembly, but then certain towns said no, this speech is dangerous. Skokie, Illinois had a lot of Holocaust survivors and Jewish people. Having the American Nazis rally in their town was hurtful and traumatic for these people so that was a reason to ban the assembly of groups who have celebrated the holocaust and mass killing of Jewish people. So, there have been qualifications in the past 50–100 years to these absolute [constitutional] rights.

Society is continually growing and evolving, and so our Constitution and the Bill of Rights is changing historical meaning in different eras, and I think most people accept that, except for a few absolutists. In any case, we need to take gun safety and rational gun control much more seriously and act to create a safer and stronger society.

· 6 ·

THE CONFLICTS OF GLOBALIZATION, COSMOPOLITANISM, AND DEMOCRACY

The matrix of technological revolution, globalization, and neo-liberal capital has produced intense change, conflict, and upheaval in society, culture, politics, and education throughout the 21st century. The centrality of globalization and technology in contemporary experience and the need for adequate conceptualizations and responses require critical theory and pedagogy to engage the conjuncture of technology and globalization in the context of neo-liberalism to maintain their relevance in the present age. In this article, I argue that critical educators need to comprehend the effects of globalization and technology on education, work to democratize education, and develop pedagogies adequate to the challenges of an age of neo-liberal capital and corporate education models that we need to contest.

Accordingly, I begin with some comments on globalization, technology, and the reconstruction of education, after which I suggest some pedagogical initiatives to aid in the democratic reconstruction of education in neo-liberalism.

Globalization, Technology, and the Reconstruction of Education

In the face of expanding globalization and digital technologies of information and communication, critical educators need to develop transformative educational strategies to understand and counter the oppressive forces and effects of globalization in conjunction with possibilities for democratization to empower individuals to understand and act effectively in a globalized world, and to struggle for social justice. This requires teaching essential skills such as critical media and digital literacies and helping empower students and citizens to deploy information and communication technologies for progressive purposes. Globalization and information and communication technologies are dominant forces of the present and the future, and it is up to critical educators and activists to illuminate their nature and effects, demonstrate the threats to democracy and freedom, and seize opportunities for progressive education and democratization in the present context.

The project of transforming education will take different forms in different contexts. In the post-industrial or "overdeveloped" countries, individuals need to be empowered to work and act in a hi-tech information economy, and thus should learn skills of critical media and digital literacies to survive in the novel social environment – as I have argued in previous chapters. Traditional crafts of knowledge and critique should also be fostered so that students can name the system, describe it, and grasp its changes and the defining features of the evolving global order. They can learn to engage in critical and oppositional practice in the interests of democratization and progressive transformation. This requires understanding how life can be, of alternatives to the present order, and the necessity of struggle and organization to realize progressive goals. The discourse of hope and praxis must thus supplement languages of knowledge and critique.

The struggle for daily existence is paramount in much of the world, and meeting unmet human and social needs is a high priority. Yet, everywhere, education can provide the competencies and skills to improve one's life to create a better society and a more civilized and developed world. Moreover, as the world becomes a global and networked society, gaining the multiple critical literacies necessary to use a range of technologies becomes vital as media and cyberculture become more ubiquitous and the global economy requires people with ever more sophisticated technical skills.

A critical technology theory maintains that there is democratic potential in information and communication technologies and the possibility for increased domination and the hegemony of capital. While the first generation of computers were large mainframe systems controlled by big government and big business, later generations of "personal computers" and networks created a more decentralized situation in which ever more individuals own their computers and a range of digital technologies and can use them for their own projects and goals. A coming generation of wireless communication could enable areas of the world that do not even have electricity to participate in the communication and information revolution of the emergent global era. This requires, of course, a Marshall Plan for the developing world that would necessitate help in disseminating technologies that would address problems of world hunger, disease, illiteracy, and poverty problems.

Concerning education, the spread and distribution of information and communication technology signify opportunities for research and interaction not previously open to students who still needed to have the privilege of access to significant research libraries or institutions. The Internet opens more information and knowledge to more people than any previous technology and institution in history, despite its many problems and limitations. Moreover, the Internet enables individuals to participate in discussions, circulate their ideas and work, and access material previously closed off from many excluded groups and individuals.

A progressive reconstruction of education that is done in the interests of democratization would demand access to emergent technologies for all, helping to overcome the so-called digital divide and divisions of the "haves" and "have-nots" (see Kellner 2002). Expanding democratic and multicultural reconstruction of education forces educators and citizens to confront the challenge of the digital divide, in which there are divisions between information and technology "haves" and "have nots," just as there are class, gender, and race divisions in every sphere of existing of societies and cultures. Although the latest surveys of the digital divide indicate that the key indicators are class and education and not race and gender, nonetheless, making computers a significant force of democratization in education and society will require substantial investment and programs to ensure that everyone receives the training, literacies, and tools necessary to function in a hi-tech global economy and culture properly.[1]

As a response to globalization and technological revolution, transformations in pedagogy must be as radical as the technological transformations that are taking place. Education should be reconstructed in the light of the importance of citizenship and participation, thus linking, a la Dewey, education and democracy. A public pedagogy involves teaching citizens what is happening in their and other democratic and nondemocratic societies, threats to democracy, and citizenship demands. Training individuals for citizenship involves training in rhetoric, public speaking, and the fundamentals of reading and writing. It also requires cultivating critical tolerance in a multicultural society that affirms respect and tolerance for all while being critical of social institutions and groups that themselves promote fundamentalism and assault tolerance or that use terrorism, militarism, and violence to promote their ends.

Tolerance should be linked with cultural cosmopolitanism that affirms the value of world culture and multi-cultures, and that is not chauvinistic and noncritical toward one's own culture and society. While democratic patriotism can help cultivate respect for the positive features of a culture or society and help create solidarities in times of trouble, blind nationalistic patriotism can lead to submission to aggressive and nondemocratic policies and practices of political manipulation.

Critical citizenship thus involves cultivating abilities to read and critique the text of one's own and other cultures, including political and media discourses, films, television programming, popular music, advertising, and other cultural forms. Thus, a public pedagogy articulates critical cultural studies that require critical educators to rethink the concepts of literacy and the very nature of education in any high-tech and rapidly evolving society. Literacy must be expanded to develop novel forms of cultural and technological literacy, for while the world is undergoing a technological revolution, significant demographic and socio-political changes are occurring in the United States and elsewhere. Emigration patterns have brought diverse peoples into the U.S. in recent decades, and the country is now more racially and ethnically diverse and multicultural than ever before. This creates the challenge of providing people from various races, classes, and backgrounds with the competencies and tools to enable them to succeed and participate in an ever more complex and changing world.

In essays in this volume, I have delineated the **critical multiple literacies** necessary to utilize and deploy information and communication technologies, including an expanded role for essential media and digital literacies and multimedia literacies that provide literacy in reading, researching, and producing in the evolving multimedia world. Yet, radically reconstructing education requires a wide range of other literacies that often must be addressed in the current schooling organization.

Since a multicultural society is the context of education for many in the contemporary moment, innovative forms of social interaction and cultural awareness are needed that appreciate differences, multiplicity, and diversity. Therefore, an expanded **cultural literacy** is required, one that appreciates the cultural heritage, histories, and contributions of diverse groups. Whereas one can agree with E.D. Hirsch (1987) that we need to be literate in our shared cultural heritage, we also need to become culturally literate in hitherto invisible cultures, as Anthony Appiah, Henry Louis Gates and their colleagues have been arguing in their proposals for multicultural education (1998).

Social literacy should also be taught throughout the educational systems, ranging from a focus on how to relate and get along with a variety of individuals, negotiate differences, resolve conflicts, and communicate and socially interact in a diversity of situations. Social literacy involves ethical training in values and norms, delineating proper and improper individual and social values (which may differ in various regions and countries). It also requires knowledge of contemporary societies and thus overlaps with social and natural science training. In fact, in light of the significant role of science and technology in the contemporary world, threats to the environment, and the need to preserve and enhance the natural as well as social and cultural worlds, it is scandalous how illiterate some overdeveloped societies, like the US, are concerning science, nature, and even peoples' bodies. An *ecoliteracy* should thus appropriately teach competency in interpreting and interacting with our natural environment, ranging from our bodies to natural habitats like forests, oceans, lakes, and deserts.

The challenge for education today is thus to develop multiple critical literacies to empower students and citizens to use emergent technologies to enhance their lives and to create a better culture and society based on respect for multicultural differences and aiming at fuller democratic participation of individuals and groups primarily excluded from wealth and power in the previous modern society. A positive postmodernity would thus involve the creation of a more egalitarian and democratic society in which more individuals and groups were empowered to participate. A great danger facing us is that globalization and emergent technologies will increase the current inequalities based on class, gender, and racial divisions.

Privileged groups have had more direct and immediate access to emergent technologies and literacy training in many locales. It is, therefore, a challenge of education today to provide access to multiple technologies and to the literacies needed for competence to excluded or oppressed individuals and groups to overcome some of the divisions and inequalities that have plagued contemporary societies during the entire modern age.

Radical educators must attempt to connect the phenomenon of evolving technologies and the technological revolution and the multicultural explosion and drama of conflicting ethnicities, classes, genders, religions, and so on, so that differences can create diversity, tolerance, and an enhanced and strengthened democracy and society and not increasing conflict, intolerance, division, and violence. It is not just a question of talking about media literacy, computer literacy, or other multiple literacies from a technological viewpoint, but thinking together emergent technologies and multiculturalism, with technological and social transformation.

Thus, a challenge for critical educators is to discover how multiple technologies and critical literacies can serve the interests of multiculturalism, making teachers, students, and citizens aware of how the proliferating technologies are transforming everything from education to work to war, the challenges involved, the multiple critical literacies needed, and the opportunities for educational reform and social reconstruction.

To be sure, legitimate concerns have been raised regarding the possibilities that emergent technologies will increase the regnant inequalities in relation to privileged class, gender, and racial groupings. As is well known, the original computer culture was largely a white, male middle to upper class "geek," or "nerd," culture that tended to exclude women, people of color, and members of classes without access to computer technologies. As multiple technologies become a more central aspect of schooling, work, and everyday life, however, more and more women and members of groups previously excluded from computer culture are now becoming participants as they gain access to computers, multimedia technologies, digital devices, and social media in schools, in the workplace, and at home. Of course, the question of access to multiple technologies becomes increasingly important as work, education, and every other aspect of social life is undergoing transformation, making multiple critical literacies essential to work, cultural, educational, and political exigencies of the future. If the previously disadvantaged and marginalized groups will not gain access to the emerging technologies, class, gender, race, and other divisions will exponentially grow, creating ever more virulent divisions and the prospects of social upheaval and turbulence.

Yet there are aspects of the forms of literacy being spawned by information technologies and multimedia culture that are potentially democratizing and empowering for individuals and groups previously on the bottom end of prevailing configurations of class, gender, and racial power. The increased informality, closeness to speech patterns, and spontaneity of e-mail composition and participation in chat rooms and computer-mediated communications and forums provide access to individuals and groups whose literacies and modes of writing were deemed inferior or deficient from more standard classical print-media perspectives. Indeed, the openness of many forums of computer-mediated communication, the possibility of ever more individuals able to produce their own websites and social media, and to gain access to volumes of information previously limited to those who had access to elite libraries potentially democratize education, cultural production, and participation in cultural and political dialogue and movements.

Thus, issues of access and exclusion about multiple technologies and critical literacies are crucial to realizing the promises of democracy. Yet, there are potential threats in the mushrooming of seductive information, communication, and entertainment technologies. The danger is that youth will become immersed in an alluring world of hi-tech experience and lose their social connectedness and ability to communicate and relate concretely to other people interpersonally. Informal modes of computer communication can create private languages and subcultures, and disadvantage participants in broader cultural communication and participation.

Statistics suggest that more and more youth sectors can access cyberspace and that college students with Internet accounts are spending as much as four hours a day in the novel realm of technological experience.[2] Increasingly, the media have been generating a moral panic concerning allegedly growing dangers in cyberspace with lurid stories of young boys and girls lured into dangerous sex or running away from home, endless accounts of how pornography on the Internet is proliferating, and the publicizing of calls for increasing control, censorship, and surveillance of communication – usually by politicians or others who are computer illiterate. The solution, however, is not to ban access to those technologies, but to teach students and citizens how to use them so that they can be employed for productive and creative, rather than problematical, ends.

To be sure, there are dangers in cyberspace as well as elsewhere, but the threats to adolescents are significantly higher through the danger of family violence and abuse than seduction by strangers on the Internet. And while there is a flourishing trade in pornography on the Internet, this material has become increasingly available in a variety of venues from the local video shop to the newspaper stand. So, it seems unfair to demonize the Internet. Attempts at

Internet censorship are part of the attack on youth, which would circumscribe their rights to obtain entertainment and information, and create their own subcultures.[3] Consequently, devices like the V-chip that would exclude sex and violence on television, or block computer access to objectionable material, is more an expression of adult hysteria and moral panic than genuine dangers to youth which certainly exist, but much more strikingly in the real world than in the sphere of hyperreality.

Throughout this century, there has been a demonization of new media and forms of media culture, ranging from comic books to film to popular music to television and now to the Internet. As Jenkins argues (1997), this demonization is supported by an assumption of the innocence of childhood, that children are merely passive receptacles, easily seduced by cultural images, and in need of protection from nefarious and harmful cultural content. But as he also contends (1997: 30f), the myth of "childhood innocence" strips children of active agency, of being capable of any thoughts of their own, and of having the ability to decode and process media materials themselves. Of course, children need media education. They need to be involved in an active learning process concerning their culture. But censorship and vilification of media does not help young people become active critics, and participants in their culture.

Accordingly, Jon Katz (1996) has argued for children's "cyber-rights," asserting that our youth's access to Internet cyberculture and media culture in general is necessary for their participation in the larger culture and their own education and development. Mastery of the culture can be the difference between economic success and hardship, between social connectedness or isolation. The Internet allows participation in many dimensions of social and cultural life and the cultivation of those technical skills that can help children in later life.

Therefore, it is necessary to divest ourselves of myths of childhood innocence and the passivity of children's media consumption, positing instead the possibility of active and creative use of media material in which media education is seen as part of youth's self-development and constitution. Accordingly, Henry Jenkins proposes "a new kind of radical media education based on the assumption that children are active participants within popular culture rather than passive victims. We must help our children become more critically reflective about the media they use and the popular culture they embrace. Yet, we can only achieve this by recognizing and respecting their existing investments, skills, and knowledge as media users. Ultimately, our goals must be not to protect our children but to empower them" (Jenkins 1997: 31).

Rather than demonizing and rejecting out of hand all new technologies, we should criticize their misuse and see how they can be used constructively and positively. In studying the kaleidoscopic array of discourses that characterize the evolving technologies, I am somewhat bemused by the extent to whether they expose either a technophilic theory that presents new technologies as salvation that will solve crucial contemporary problems or they embody a technophobic discourse that sees technology as damnation, demonizing it as the significant source of present-day issues. Similar one-sided and contrasting theories greeted the introduction of other new technologies this century, often hysterically. It is indeed curious that a polarized response emerges whenever an innovative technology is introduced about its novelty and differences from previous technologies. New technologies attract both advocates and champions and critics and detractors. This was historically the case with mass media and now computers.

Film, for instance, was celebrated by early theorists as providing a marvelous documentary depiction of reality. Siegfried Kraucauer published a book on film the "Redemption of reality," and it was described early on as an innovative art form, as well as providing novel modes of mass education and entertainment. Likewise, it was soon demonized for promoting sexual promiscuity, juvenile delinquency and crime, violence, and other forms of immorality and evil. Its demonization led in the United States to a Production Code that rigorously regulated the content of Hollywood films from 1934 until the 1950s and 1960s – no open-mouthed kissing was permitted, crime could not pay, drug use or attacks on religion could not be portrayed, and a censorship office rigorously surveyed all films to make sure that no subversive or illicit content emerged.

Similar extreme hopes and fears were projected onto radio, television, and now computers. It appears whenever there are new technologies, people project all sorts of fantasies, fears, hopes, and dreams onto them. This is now happening with computers and multimedia technologies. It is indeed striking that the literature on computer and information technologies is either highly celebratory and technophilic, or sharply derogatory and technophobic. A critical theory of technology, however, and critical pedagogy, should avoid either demonizing or deifying emergent technologies and should instead develop pedagogies that will help teachers, students, and citizens use technology to enhance education and life, and to criticize the limitations and false promises made on behalf of ever proliferating technologies.

Certainly there is no doubt that the cyberspace of computer worlds contains as much banality and stupidity as real life. One can waste much time in useless activity. Yet compared to the bleak and violent urban worlds portrayed in rap music and youth films like *American Me* (1992), *Menace II Society* (1993), *Kids* (1995), *Elephant* (2003), or *Brick* (2006), the technological worlds are havens of information, entertainment, interaction, and connection where youth can gain valuable skills, knowledge, and power necessary to survive the postmodern adventure. Youth can create alternative, more multiple and flexible selves in cyberspace as well as their own subcultures and communities. Indeed, it is exciting to cruise the Internet and to discover how many interesting Websites that young people and others have established, often containing valuable educational and political material. There is, of course, the danger that corporate and commercial interests will come to colonize the Internet, but it is likely that there will continue to be spaces where individuals can empower themselves and create their own communities and identities. A main challenge for youth (and others) is to learn to use the Internet for positive cultural and political projects, rather than just entertainment and passive consumption (see Best and Kellner 2001 and Kahn and Kellner 2003).

Reflecting on the growing social significance of digital technologies and devices makes it clear that it is of essential importance for youth today to gain various kinds of literacy to empower themselves for the emerging cybersociety (this is true of teachers and adults as well). To survive in a postmodern world, individuals of all ages need to gain skills of critical media and computer literacy to enable ourselves to negotiate the overload of media images and spectacles. We all need to learn technological skills to use media and computer technologies to interact and succeed in the hi-tech economy and to form our own cultures and communities. Youth, especially, need street smarts and survival skills to cope with the drugs, violence, and uncertainty in today's predatory culture (McLaren, 1995), as well as new forms of multiple literacy to navigate the digital worlds safely and productively.

It is, therefore, extremely important for the future of democracy to make sure that youth of all classes, races, genders, and regions gain access to information and multimedia technology. This requires training in media and computer literacy skills to provide the opportunities to enter the hi-tech job market and fully participate in the future society, to prevent an exacerbation of class, gender, and race inequalities. And while multiple forms of new literacies will be necessary, traditional print literacy skills are even more important in a cyber-age of word-processing, information gathering, and Internet communication. Moreover, critical multiple literacies involve training in philosophy, social theory, ethics, value thinking, and the humanities which is necessary today more than ever. In fact, *how* the Internet and emergent technologies will be used depends on the overall education of youth and the skills and interests they bring to the technologies, which can be used to access educational and valuable cultural and political material or pornography and the banal wares of cyber shopping malls.

Thus, the concept of multiple critical literacies and the postmodern pedagogy that I envisage maintains that it is not a question of either/or, e.g., either print literacy or multimedia literacy, either the classical curriculum or a new hi-tech curriculum, but it is instead a question of both/and that preserves the best from classical education, that enhances the emphasis on print literacy, but that also develops critical multiple literacies to engage the emergent technologies. Cyberlife is just one dimension of experience, and one still needs to learn to interact in the "real world" of school, jobs, relationships, politics, and community. Youth – indeed, all of us! – need to negotiate many dimensions of social reality and to gain a diversity of forms of literacy and skills that will enable individuals to create identities, relationships, and communities that will nurture and develop the full spectrum of their potentialities and satisfy a wide array of needs. Contemporary lives are more multidimensional than ever, so part of the postmodern adventure is learning to live in a variety of social spaces and to adapt to intense change and transformation (Best & Kellner, 2001). Education, too, must meet these challenges and both utilize new technologies to improve teaching and to devise pedagogical strategies in which technologies can be deployed to create a more democratic and egalitarian multicultural society.

In the light of the neo-liberal projects to dismantle the Welfare State, colonize the public sphere, and control globalization, it is up to citizens, activists, and educators to create alternative public spheres, politics, and pedagogies. In these spaces, that could include progressive classrooms, students and citizens could learn to use information and multimedia technologies to discuss what kinds of society people today want, and to oppose the society against which people resist and struggle. This involves, minimally, demands for more education, health care, welfare, and benefits from the state, and to struggle to create a more democratic and egalitarian society. Yet one cannot expect that generous corporations and a beneficent state are going to make available to citizens the bounties and benefits of the globalized information economy. Rather, it is up to individuals and groups to promote democratization and progressive social change.

Thus, in opposition to the globalization of corporate and state capitalism, I would advocate an oppositional democratic, pedagogical, and cosmopolitan globalization, which supports individuals and groups using information and multimedia technologies to create a more multicultural, egalitarian, democratic, and ecological globalization. Of course, the emergent technologies might exacerbate existing inequalities in the current class, gender, race, and regional configurations of power and give dominant corporate forces powerful tools to advance their interests. In this situation, it is up to people of good will to devise strategies to use technologies to promote democratization and social justice. For as the proliferating technologies become ever more central to everyday life, developing an oppositional technopolitics in alternative public spheres and pedagogical sites will become increasingly important. Changes in the economy, politics, and social life demand a constant rethinking of education and transformative praxis in the light of globalization and the technological revolution, requiring critical and oppositional thinking as a response to ever-changing historical conditions.

Notes

1 · The "digital divide" has emerged as the buzzword for perceived divisions between information technology have and have-nots in the current economy and society. A U.S. Department of Commerce report released in July 1999 claimed that the digital divide in relation to race is dramatically escalating and the Clinton administration and media picked up on this theme (See the report National Telecommunications & Information Administration "Americans in the information age falling through the net,", U.S. Dept of Commerce: Washington, DC, 1999 at <https://otan.us/Resources/Home/OtanLibraryDetails/608> (accessed June 20, 2024)). In any case, it is clear that there is a gaping division between information technology haves and have nots, that this is a major challenge to developing an egalitarian and democratic society, and that something needs to be done about the problem. My contribution involves the argument that empowering the have nots requires the dissemination of new literacies and thus empowering groups and individuals previously excluded from economic opportunities and socio-political participation; see Kellner 2002.

2 · *Wired* magazine is a good source for statistics and data concerning growing computer and Internet use among all sectors of youth and documents the vicissitudes of cyberculture. Studies of Internet addiction, however, raise concerns about negative implications of excessive usage. The *Chronicle of Higher Education* has reported that "Students are unusually vulnerable to Internet addiction according to a new quarterly journal called *Cyberpsychology and Behavior*" (Feb. 6. 1998: A25). The study indicated that students from 18 to 22 are especially at risk and point to a correlation between high Internet use and a dropout rate that more than doubled among heavy users. Accordingly, the University of Washington has limited the amount of Internet time available to students to cut down on overuse and

several other colleges have set up support groups for Internet addiction. But such studies do not record the benefits of heavy Internet use or indicate potentially higher productive uses than, say, watching television, drinking, or engaging in traditional forms of collegiate socializing. For a recent take on Internet addiction, see Elizabeth Hartney, BSc., MSc., MA, PhD, "How to Know if you have an Internet Addiction and What to Do About It," *verywell mind*, Updated on September 17, 2020 at <https://www.verywellmind.com/internet-addiction-4157289> (accessed July 5. 2021).Top of Form Bottom of Form.

3 On the attack on youth in contemporary society and culture, see Giroux 1996, 2002, 2003a, 2003b; Males 1996; and Best and Kellner 2003.

References

Appiah, A. A. and Gates, H. L. (1999). *Africana: The Encyclopedia of the African and African American Experience*. New York: BasicCivitas.

Aronowitz, S. and Giroux, H. (1993). *Education Still Under Siege*. Westport, Conn.: Bergin & Garvey.

Barber, Benjamin (1996). *Jihad vs. McWorld*. New York: Ballantine Books.

Barber, Benjamin (2003). *Fear's Empire. War, Terrorism, and Democracy*. New York: Norton.

Best, S. and Kellner, D. (1991). *Postmodern Theory: Critical Interrogations*. London and New York: MacMillan and Guilford.

Best, S. and Kellner, D. (1997). *The Postmodern Turn*. London and New York: Routledge and Guilford Press.

Best, S. and Kellner, D. (2001). *The Postmodern Adventure*. London and New York: Routledge and Guilford Press.

Best, S. and Kellner, D. (2003). "Contemporary Youth and the Postmodern Adventure." *The Review of Education/Pedagogy/Cultural Studies*, 25(2) (April–June 2003): 75–93.

Boggs, C. (2000). *The End of Politics*. New York: Guilford Press.

Bowles, S. and Gintis, H. (1986). *On Democracy*. New York: Basic Books.

Burbach, R. (2001). *Globalization and Postmodern Politics. From Zapatistas to Hi-tech Robber Barons*. London: Pluto Press.

Castells, M. (1996). *The Rise of the Network Society*. Oxford: Blackwell.

Cohen, J. and Rogers, J. (1983). *On Democracy*. New York: Penguin.

Cvetkovich, A. and Kellner, D. (1997). *Articulating the Global and the Local. Globalization and Cultural Studies*. Boulder, Col.: Westview.

Dewey, John (1997 [1916]). *Democracy and Education*. New York: Free Press.

Dyer-Witheford, N. (1999). *Cyber-Marx. Cycles and Circuits of Struggle in Hi-technology Capitalism*. Urbana and Chicago: University of Illinois Press.

Foran, J. (ed.). (2003). *The Future of Revolutions. Rethinking Radical Change in the Age of Globalization*. London: Zed Books.

Friedman, T. (1999). *The Lexus and the Olive Tree*. New York: Farrar Straus Giroux.

Fukuyama, F. (1992). *The End of History and the Last Man*. New York: The Free Press.

Giroux, H. (1996). *Fugitive Cultures: Race, Violence, and Youth*. New York: Routledge.

Giroux, H. (2000). *Stealing Innocence. Youth, Corporate Power, and the Politics of Culture.* New York: Saint Martin's.
Giroux, H. (2003b). *The Abandoned Generation. Democracy Beyond the Culture of Fear.* New York: Palgrave Macmillan.
Hardt, M. and Negri, A. (2000). *Empire.* Cambridge, Mass.: Harvard University Press.
Harvey, D. (1989). *The Condition of Postmodernity.* Cambridge: Blackwell.
Hirsch, E. D. (1988). *Cultural Literacy: What Every American Needs to Know.* New York: Vintage.
Jenkins, H. (1997). "Empowering Children in the Digital Age: Towards a Radical Media Pedagogy." *Radical Teacher,* 50, (Spring): 30–36.
Kahn, R. and Kellner, D. (2003). "Internet Subcultures and Oppositional Politics", in D. Muggleton (ed.), *The Post-subcultures Reader.* London: Berg.
Kellner, D. (1995a). *Media Culture.* London and New York: Routledge.
Kellner, D. (1995b). "Intellectuals and New Technologies". *Media, Culture, and Society,* 17: 201–217.
Kellner, D. (1997). "Intellectuals, the New Public Spheres, and Technopolitics". *Science New Political,* 41–42 (Fall): 169–188.
Kellner, D. (1998). "Multiple Literacies and Critical Pedagogy in a Multicultural Society". *Educational Theory,* 48(1): 103–122.
Kellner, D. (1999a). "Theorizing McDonaldization: A Multiperspectivist Approach", in: *Resisting McDonaldization,* edited by B. Smart. London: Sage Publications, pp. 186–206.
Kellner, D. (1999b). "Globalization From Below? Toward a Radical Democratic Technopolitics". *Angelaki,* 4(2): 101–113.
Kellner, D. (2000). "New Technologies/New Literacies: Reconstructing Education for the New Millennium". *Teaching Education,* 11(3): 245–265.
Kellner, D. (2002). "Technological Revolution, Multiple Literacies, and the Restructuring of Education," in Ilana Snyder (ed.), *Silicon Literacies.* London and New York: Routledge, pp. 154–169.
Kellner, D. (2003a). *Media Spectacle.* London and New York: Routledge.
Kellner, D. (2003b). *From September 11 to Terror War: The Dangers of the Bush Legacy.* Lanham, MD: Rowman and Littlefield.
Kellner, D. (2003c). "Postmodern Military and Permanent War," in *Masters of War. Militarism and Blowback in the Era of the American Empire,* edited by Carl Boggs. New York and London: Routledge, 2003, pp. 229–244.
Kahn, R. and Kellner, D. (2003). "Internet Subcultures and Oppositional Politics," in D. Muggleton (ed.), *The Post-subcultures Reader.* London: Berg.
Lash, S. (1990). *The Sociology of Postmodernism.* New York and London: Routledge.
Luke, A. and Luke, C. (2000). "A Situated Perspective on Cultural Globalization", in: *Globalization and Education,* edited by N. Burbules and C. Torres. London and New York: Routledge, pp. 275–298.
Males, Mike (1996). *The Scapegoat Generation.* Boston: Common Courage Press.
Mander, J. and Goldsmith, E. (1996). *The Case Against the Global Economy.* San Francisco: Sierra Club Books.

Marx, K. and Engels, F. (1978). *The Marx-Engels Reader*, second edition, R. Tucker, ed. New York: Norton.
McChesney, Robert (1997). *Corporate Media and the Threat to Democracy*. New York: Seven Stories Press.
McChesney, Robert (2000). *Rich Media, Poor Democracy*. New York: The New Press.
McLaren, Peter (1995). *Critical Pedagogy and Predatory Culture*. New York: Routledge.
Moody, K. (1988). *An Injury to One*. London: Verso.
Moody, K. (1997). "Towards an International Social-Movement Unionism". *New Left Review*, 225: 52–72.
Peters, M. (forthcoming). "War as Globalization: The 'Education' of the Iraqi People". *Education in the Age of Terrorism*.
Ritzer, G. (1993 revised edition 1996). *The McDonaldization of Society*. Thousand Oaks, CA: Pine Forge Press.
Stiglitz, J. (2002). *Globalization and Its Discontents*. New York: Norton.
Waterman, P. (1992). "International Labour Communication by Computer: The Fifth International?", *Working Paper Series* 129 (The Hague: Institute of Social Studies).
Watson, J. (ed.). (1998). *Golden Arches East: McDonald's in East Asia*. Palo Alto, California: Stanford Univ. Press.

· 7 ·

CRITICAL REFLECTIONS ON MARCUSE, FREIRE, AND RADICAL PEDAGOGY

In this penultimate chapter of my two-volume collection of essays on radical pedagogy and the critical theory of education, I want to engage the work of two thinkers who have had a decisive influence on my theory and practice of education and are of utmost importance for succeeding and future generations. Both Paulo Freire and Herbert Marcuse see education in the context of social life in specific socio-historical locations and periods, and both develop philosophies of education that promote radical critique of the existing education system and propose radical alternatives. In the following study, I will begin by indicating how Marcuse and Freire share fundamental elements of their critical theories of education and transformative practices while engaging their different origins and, in some cases, their differing emphases and positions.

In essays throughout this volume, I have addressed the education wars of the contemporary era and provided critiques of the right-wing assault on education while providing progressive defenses of education and its importance for democracy a la Dewey. I have been providing models of a radical and transformative pedagogy to reconstruct education to meet the challenges of a multicultural and global society and to provide models of education, promoting democracy, social justice, peace, and the construction of a good society and life worthy of a human being.

Combining the theoretical, political, and personal, I will also discuss the profound influence Marcuse and Freire had on me and others who came of age in their university studies and moved toward radical theory and politics in the 1960s and 1970s and how their works have influenced succeeding generations through the present and into the foreseeable future. In other terms, I will discuss how Marcuse and Freire have become classical thinkers in the philosophy of education and promoters of a radical pedagogy who present starting points for critical theory and democratic politics and pedagogy today. Furthermore, as part of the education wars I have been describing in this book, there are rightwing attacks on Marcuse and Freire, and have been for decades, as well as defenses of their work which has grown to the extent that we can observe Freire Wars and Marcuse wars as subsections of the Education wars. I will address these battles and their relevance for transformative education and radical democracy. Finally, I will emphasize that becoming either a Marcusean or a Freirean is unnecessary. Both can be combined to develop a radical pedagogy, critical theory of society, and transformative praxis in the interests of democracy, social justice, and peace in the contemporary moment—in conjunction with feminist theory, critical race theory, and other progressive theories, as I have been arguing throughout this book. Both Freire and Marcuse presented education as a key development of active and engaged humans to participate in democratic and transformative practice to confront and struggle with present challenges in the highly contested and volatile contemporary era.[1]

First, Marcuse and Freire are macro theorists who base their analysis on a critical theory of society as a whole and envisage systematic social critique and transformation. They are both BIG THINKERS whose radical pedagogies and visions of educational and social transformation imagine and project radical and global transformative change of pedagogy, the individual, and society. Both are socialist humanists who ground their pedagogies in a critical theory of capitalism and a global theory of imperialism and see forces of resistance, liberation, and revolution globally. Both thus operate in their theories, pedagogies, and practices with a dialectic of domination and liberation that criticizes how current educational systems under capitalism promote the reproduction of existing systems of oppression. Both envisage education as a liberation and transformative practice that creates new social relations and society, starting with relations between teachers and students.

Marcuse and Freire value the individual and posit dialectics between the individual subject and the world, and they both strive and sketch out models of individual liberation and a liberated subject becoming fully human and not merely an object of domination and oppression. Further, both Marcuse and Freire develop theories of revolution and socialism and see radical pedagogy as playing a key role in the process of revolutionary social transformation. Both therefore are valuable for the current war against education by the right and the war for progressive democratic transformation for those interested in social justice and a democratic society.

Radical pedagogy today needs to develop the theoretical and practical bases for countering the rightwing war against education and for supporting a progressive education for democracy and social justice, and I argue that Marcuse and Freire are allies of education for democracy and social justice who provide valuable resources for the past and future.

Herbert Marcuse, 1968, and Dramas of the New Left

Marcuse's social theory and radical pedagogy are grounded in Frankfurt School studies of advanced capitalist societies and their Critical Theory of Society (see Kellner 1989). Frankfurt School critical theory operates on a level of global generalization that encompassed both advanced capitalist society and Soviet Marxism and its block of communist countries in its post-war World War II and was during the war grounded in a theory and critique of fascism, with Marcuse and other members of the Frankfurt School working with the U.S. Operations of Secret Services (OSS) in the fight against fascism (Kellner 1988).

In the post-World War II period, Marcuse became a critic of imperialism and advocate of third world revolution, while becoming renowned as a theorist of the New Left and then of global revolution in the 1960s and 1970s until his death in 1979. While both Marcuse and Freire had a profound impact on me, I encountered Marcuse's work first, reading his *Reason and Revolution* (1940) in Graduate School at Columbia University in New York, and thought the text was the best introduction to Hegel, Marx, and social theory, thus encouraging my research in these areas. I found Marcuse's next book, *Eros and* Civilization (1955) to be what I took as the best introduction to Freud and his critique of Western Civilization. I found *One-Dimensional Man* (1964) to be the best critique of US society and advanced capitalism I had encountered when it was published in 1964.

Marcuse's work is grounded in a dialectic of domination and liberation, and in his key works critiques the forces of domination and articulates perspectives on human liberation and visions of an emancipated society. He sees education as a transformative process for emancipated human beings and, like Dewey and Freire, as essential in creating a free and democratic society. In the 1960s, he emerged as a major figure in creating a New Left, which I became associated with as a graduate student at Columbia University.[2]

In 1968, the year before I met Marcuse, there was a student uprising at Columbia that began with the occupation of the President's office, marking what, in retrospect, was the mushrooming of radical student rebellion, anticipating the Occupy Movement of 2011 and the pro-Palestinian movements of 2024 which also involved occupation and encampment to protest war and demand that Universities be responsive to student needs and interests. The Columbia occupation of 1968 was also replicated worldwide, as Herbert Marcuse quickly became world renown as the Father of the New Left and proponent of revolution, traveling all over delivering critiques of capitalism and imperialism while advocating socialism and revolution.

My philosophical allegiances at the time were primarily to Phenomenology and Existentialism, and while I was unprepared for the explosiveness and impact of the student rebellion, I became active in New Left politics, participating in major anti-war and other demonstrations of the epoch. Indeed, students all over the United States, Europe, and all around the world were demonstrating against the Vietnam War, taking over University buildings and even campuses, and in Paris in May '68, it appeared that a new French revolution was in the making.

At that time in 1968, I was studying for my philosophy comprehensive exams at Columbia and teaching my first course, when the student uprising erupted, with SDS radicals occupying the President's Office, while black radicals occupied another campus building. During the protests and student occupations of key buildings at Columbia, an activist with the Students for a Democratic Society, Bob Feldman, discovered documents indicating Columbia's institutional affiliation with the Institute for Defense Analyses (IDA), and it was also discovered that Columbia University professors were doing research for the CIA and aiding in the Vietnam war effort.

There were on-going protests as well concerning Columbia's plan to take city park land bordering on Harlem and turning it into a gymnasium, in which the bottom half would be open to Harlem residents while the top half was reserved for students and members of Columbia. On April 23, 1968, students attempted to enter the main administration building, Low Memorial Library, were rebuffed, marched to the Harlem gym site, where they clashed with police, and then returned to the Columbia campus to occupy Hamilton Hall, which had both classrooms and the offices of the Columbia College Administration.

In the protests and occupation of Hamilton Hall, the SDS students were joined by members of the Student Afro Society (SAS) group. To the surprise of SDS and white students, the African American students in Hamilton told the white students to occupy another building since their agendas were different. After both groups deliberated, the SDS group and other white students decided to take over Low Library, which housed the President's office. Since the occupation closely followed the assassination of Martin Luther King, which resulted in riots throughout the country, including New York, the administration was reluctant at first to use force to evict the students and a dramatic standoff and media circus followed.

Other student groups took over other campus buildings at Columbia in one of the first and most dramatic student insurrections of the era. The Grateful Dead came on campus to give us a free concert, and one day Stokley Carmichael, R. Rap Brown, Eldridge Cleaver, and other black radical leaders came on to campus us to tell us we needed to get serious and join with blacks to carry out a real revolution, and not just a campus shutdown.

In retrospect, the Columbia occupation of the President's office and other campus buildings anticipated the Occupy movement of 2011 and pro-Patestinian movements of 2024 and helped generate a wave of campus occupations in the decades to come, continuing into the present. As I was beginning teaching in Columbia College, I joined a group of professors, some from the Great Books program in which I was teaching, as well as some of my professors from the Philosophy Department, who began meeting and immediately decided to surround in solidarity the occupied buildings in order to protect the student occupiers from getting beat up by conservative groups of mostly jocks and frat guys who were themselves converging on the occupied building threatening to physically remove the students within.

At first, my faculty group confrontation with the right-wing students, who adopted the name "Majority Coalition," was tense, with the short-haired conservative students declaiming that they wanted to "kill the long-haired pukes" who had taken over the campus. However, the faculty and progressive graduate students who joined our ranks quickly convinced them that the radical students had the right to protest policies with which they disagreed, and perhaps the respect that conservative students had for faculty and authority led them to step down in their threats, resulting in a stand-off.

After a few days of drama and accelerating media attention, in the early morning hours of April 30, 1968, the New York Police Department (NYDP) violently crushed the demonstrations, using tear gas and then attacking both the demonstrators in Hamilton Hall and the Low Library, as police did again at Columbia, UCLA, and other universities in 2024. Ironically, Hamilton Hall was cleared peacefully as the African-American students had assembled lawyers and media observers, and a largely African American group of police officers peacefully led the African American students out of Hamilton Hall. The buildings occupied by white students, however, were cleared violently as hordes of police wielding clubs and threatening demonstrators with guns, beat up scores of students and some faculty members who tried to stop the police assault with approximately 132 students treated for injuries while over 700 protesters were arrested.

The night of the raid, I was at home sleeping, as the faculty/graduate student group that I was participating in was organized in 12 hour shifts to protect the students. As I approached the campus early dawn, I noticed commotion and the roar of voices, hurried to the campus, and encountered my Philosophy professor Sidney Morgenbesser, a fellow member of the faculty who were protecting the students who occupied Columbia, with a bloodied head, holding white bandages to stop the blood flow. Sidney described how the police had stormed Low Library occupied by the SDS students, and how he and other professors surrounding the building to try to protect the students, attempted to stop the police. Sidney described how the police proceeded to beat up and arrest students and faculty alike and I convinced Sidney to find a doctor to take care of his head injuries (he survived and continued to be a solid supporter of the Left).

Classes were suspended for the spring semester at Columbia in 1968, and we were happy to receive A's in all our seminars, even though we didn't have to write final papers; many of our professors had joined many of us in the demonstrations, so a closeness between students and professors, rare in U.S. academia at the time, emerged. Yet, one of my Professors, Paul Oskar Kristeller, said he was worried about the student demonstrations because he had seen Nazi student demonstrations previewing the rise of fascism in Germany in the 1930s, but I assured him that the Columbia students were neither fascists nor communists. Kristeller also told me that his Professor at Freiburg University in German, Martin Heidegger, had gotten him a scholarship to study Renaissance philosophy in Italy during the Nazi period, which saved Kristeller's life because he was Jewish.

In the euphoria of the accelerating protests of 1968, we had the feeling that we were at the heart of revolutionary upheavals in the U.S. and globally when a representative from France came and told us of the French student and worker uprising that was shutting down the whole of Paris and briefly was erupting throughout France in May 1968. The gym in Morningside Park which offended the Harlem residents and black radicals was never built, Columbia severed its relations with the IDA, and many of us experienced the euphoria of radical upheaval and were radicalized by the experience.

During this time, the Vietnam War was raging and many of my generation were being sent over as cannon fodder for a cause that we did not understand or support. One day around 1968 I went over to Barnard College and heard a packed lecture by Noam Chomsky. Chomsky, at the time a Professor of Philosophy at MIT, was known to philosophy students for his controversial philosophy of mind and linguistic theory. Chomsky proved himself a brilliant public lecturer, providing an entire history of post-World War II Vietnam, the National Liberation Movement that drove out the French, the raging Civil War in the country, and how the US intervened against the Communist North in support of a corrupt South Vietnamese government, providing a sharp critique of U.S. interventionism and imperialism. I walked away with a much deeper understanding of the dynamics of Vietnam and with great respect for Noam Chomsky who I would later meet and whose writings had an impact on my view of media and politics. Moreover, Chomsky and Marcuse were ideals for me of a Public Intellectual, using their academic knowledge and skills to address issues of public importance, and I have aspired to this ideal my whole career.

Again in 1969 at Columbia, there was an attempt at a replay of the 1968 demonstrations which quickly dissipated and some of the disillusioned SDS members formed the Weather underground which became notorious after some bombings in which their leaders literally went underground. At this time of turmoil in the University, students organized reading groups where some professors, graduate students like me, and others proposed courses organized around topics or books, and I organized a reading group focusing on *One-Dimensional Man*. I remember sitting outdoors on the lawn at Columbia with a small group of students, including Nancy and Steve Fraser (Nancy became famous later as a leading Feminist-Marxist philosopher and a close comrade of mine, and her then husband Steve became a successful editor for a big publishing house). Anyway, the close reading and passionate discussion of the text *One-Dimensional Man* sealed the deal convincing me that Marcuse had the most radical and pertinent critique of contemporary US culture and society of the era that best captured its dynamics. Hence, to help understand the momentous political upheavals of the epoch, I carefully studied the works of Herbert Marcuse, and by the time of the publication of *An Essay on Liberation* (1969), I both better understood Marcuse's writings and the philosophical underpinnings of the student movement to which I was increasingly attracted and involved.

At Columbia in May 1969, I heard Herbert Marcuse lecture one evening and talked with him for the first time the next day during a reception in the Philosophy Department. We asked Marcuse about Heidegger, his study with him, and what he thought of Heidegger today. Marcuse joked that he heard Heidegger was chiseling his philosophy in stone in Germany, highlighting what he took as the reactionary and archaic nature of Heidegger's thought which he expounded upon as a whole. We then asked him about Adorno, and he replied, "Theodore W. Adorno is one of the most important thinkers of our time," and expounded upon some of Adorno's ideas. None of the philosophy professors showed up, and at one point, Marcuse asked other graduate students and me to escort him to the West End Bar where earlier Alan Ginsberg and the Beat poets hung out and where at the time, my fellow graduate students also, ate, drank, and discussed philosophy, politics, and other issues of the day.

As we crossed the campus in front of the Philosophy Department, some major militants in the Weather Underground approached me and said, "We want to rap with Marcuse." I asked Herbert, and he agreed, and we all sat down on the grass. One of the Weather Underground dudes explained that they planned to burn down the office of a Columbia Professor doing research for the US government that facilitated certain heinous practices in the Vietnam war. Almost immediately, Herbert said that he thought this was not a good idea, that it would probably backfire and bring on major repression, and argued that the University should be used as a site to recruit and train revolutionaries, going on to say that the University was a relative utopia in U.S. society where one could read and study, develop critiques of US capitalism and imperialism, could organize radical groups, and prepare for the revolution. He was passionate and convincing on this point, and after a brief discussion, the Weather Dudes got up, thanked Marcuse for his advice, and got up to leave. As they were parting, Marcuse joked, "Now if you were planning to burn down a bank, I might not be so negative" – and shortly thereafter, the Bank of America in Santa Barbara was burned down, the subject of a Newsreel documentary, and the Weather Underground took credit.

At the West End bar where we went for a beer, I was won over by Marcuse's humor, humanity, and the power of his ideas. We discussed philosophy but also Jack Kerouac, Allen Ginsberg, and other noteworthy of the Beatnik movement. Shortly thereafter, in reading Kerouac's autobiographical novel as a Columbia student, *Vanity of Duluoz* (1968), I was fascinated to note that Jack Duluoz, the main character of the novel and a stand-in for Kerouac, lived in a fifth-story walk-up apartment on the corner of 105th Street and West End Avenue and every Saturday morning heard the gongs of a Buddhist temple summoning worshipers, and I realized: "Hot Damn! I've living in the same pad as F – ing Jack Kerouac!" Those were the good old days!

The year before, I lived on 108th off Amsterdam and later learned that this was the same block on which Barack Obama first lived when he was a student at Columbia in the 1980s. I immediately read Obama's two books on his life and political views when he announced his surprising presidential run in 2008. I remember vividly asking myself, "Who the F is this guy!" and quickly turning to read his books to find out (Obama 2004; 2007). Obama claims he left his apartment on 108th Street because of poor heating, and I remember being awakened with loud heat pipes giving off steam, so I know what he was talking about. Barack, however, lived on the bourgie side of Amsterdam Avenue, while I lived on the ghetto side, merging into Spanish Harlem. After my apartment was robbed, I had to leave this pad, typewriter, and favorite Norwegian sweater from my Junior Year abroad in Scandinavia. My Puerto Rican neighbors explained how junkies would break into houses through fire escape windows. After the second robbery in which my door was broken down, I gave up and luckily found the groovy pad described in above on 105th Street. However, once I witnessed a shooting out the window and walked over a bloodstain on the sidewalk for some weeks thereafter, knowing that while living in a utopian dream world, I was also living in an urban war zone.

Marcuse continued to strongly shape my thoughts and actions as a New Left student activist and then radical teacher when I got my first tenure track job at the University of Texas-Austin in 1973. Curiously, but I suppose not accidentally, I was hired to teach Marxism at UT, and I always included a Marcuse text in the course, and used as primary text *The Marx-Engels Reader* (Tucker, ed. 1978), a course which I will discuss below after first engaging my initial confrontation with the writings of Paulo Freire and my emergence as a radical pedagogue.

Teaching Freire and Radical Pedagogy

While teaching at Austin, I first encountered the work of Paulo Freire, which deeply influenced me and made me a lifelong advocate of radical pedagogy. Freire was born in 1921 in a poor region of Northern Brazil and experienced poverty as a youth. Growing up in the 1930s global Depression, Freire experienced hunger and vowed to fight poverty and side with the poor, a vow Freire faithfully kept. Later, he went to university in his hometown of Recife and ultimately became a professor of education at the University. Freire was teaching adult literacy programs to peasants in Brazil when the military junta came into power in 1964, and he was imprisoned, released, and "invited" to leave the country. He then taught in Chile, the US, and Europe before returning to Brazil in the early 1980s when there was a liberalization process.

Freire's global reputation as a critical pedagogue was established when he published his first book, *Education as the Practice of Freedom,* in 1967, followed in 1968 by *Pedagogy of the Oppressed,* published in English in 1970 and translated into many languages. It achieved a global reception, establishing Freire as the father of critical pedagogy. In his Preface to *Pedagogy of the Oppressed,* Freire discusses the origin and genesis of the book and defends the project of promoting **critical consciousness** (*conscientizacao* or conscientization) through participatory adult education and answer criticisms that such a pedagogy is negative and merely destructive. To answer such criticism, he sketches out its role in human liberation and the struggle for social justice. Freire claims that grasping and overcoming contradictions between oppressor and oppressed enables individuals to become a subject, participate in their own self-development and social transformation, and thus realize their full humanity. Education for Freire is the path to self-development and becoming a subject, who can determine one's own life not and is not simply an object of domination and control, as were the oppressed under colonial rule, or as an object of authoritarian education.

For Freire, our ontological vocation is to become a subject, be free and develop ourselves and become fully human. This critical and dialectical Humanism was influenced by Hegel, Marx, Fanon, Che, Fromm, and Marcuse, among others, and exhibits a Marxian concern with class, oppression, and revolution. Freire's texts also have affinities with the Christian Left, the theology of liberation, and existentialism, all of which emphasize personal liberation and freedom. Becoming a subject for Freire involves overcoming what Erich Fromm calls "fear of freedom" and choosing a biophilic over a necrophiliac orientation, i.e., choosing love of life and nurturing of life over hatred of life and its destruction.

Freire defends himself against charges of idealism, claiming that promoting love, humanity, justice, and other moral values encourages the realization of one's basic humanity and social being, establishing the foundation of a community (1970, p. 21). Freire attacks the sectarianism of the left and the right, insisting that the pedagogy of the oppressed is a task for radicals that sectarians cannot carry out, as it is anti-dogmatic and anti-sectarian, guided by philosophical perspectives on liberation and humanization, and the dialectic of domination and liberation, aiming at freedom and self-determination.

In Chapter 2 of the *Pedagogy of the Oppressed*, Freire develops his pedagogy of liberation, educational practice, and teaching as a process of liberation. His pedagogy is based on a distinction between the banking conception of education and a dialogical concept that sees education as taking place in conversations between teachers and students. Thus, while the banking concept involves the professor lecturing to students who passively receive the information, Freire sees education as a dialogue rooted in concrete historical conditions of oppression, struggle, and the possibilities of liberation. He claims that the oppressed's great humanistic and historical task is to liberate themselves and their oppressors, while the teacher is to side with the oppressed in their/our struggle for liberation. For Freire, the liberation of the oppressed can only be the work of the oppressed themselves (a paraphrase of Marx that the liberation of the working class must become the task of the working class itself). Hence, the teacher who wants to help the oppressed must help them/us to liberate (i.e., educate) themselves/ourselves and join in the social process of liberation and self-development.

Hence, the pedagogy of the oppressed must be forged with and not for the oppressed in a dialogue, communication, and co-participation process that is dialogical and democratic and not top-down and authoritarian. Freire insists that the pedagogy of the oppressed must avoid objectivism (determinism) and subjectivism (voluntarism). By contrast, the critical pedagogue must see reality as a dialectical synthesis of the subjective and the objective, the constraining and limiting contrasted to the enabling and possible, and search with the students for ways to overcome oppression and seek liberation and self-realization.

Finally, Freirean pedagogy is motivated by generative themes, defined as the key themes of the epoch that emerge in dialogue between students, teachers and community members and inspire education and pedagogical praxis toward liberation. For Freire, revolution was *the* generative theme of the 1960s and 1970s, especially for the developing countries, but throughout the world, including the US. Thus, the concluding chapter of Freire's *Pedagogy* is geared toward revolutionary practice, putting Freire's thought in the same radical matrix as Marcuse.[3]

As noted, Freire became world-renowned in the 1970s with his *Pedagogy of the Oppressed* publication, which appeared in Brazil in the late 1960s and was translated and published in English in 1970. Like Marcuse, Freire was a global revolutionary thinker during this period, traveling the world with his critical pedagogy, which he continued developing and promoting until he died in 1997.

Before my avid reading of Freire on critical teaching, the prospect of a more participatory and active educational process already appealed to me. It afforded a helpful pedagogical practice as I approached the first class I ever taught (in the Freshman Great Books Humanities Program at Columbia) while still a graduate student. Every year, a couple of philosophy grad students got positions while still students teaching courses in the Great Books or Western Civilization programs to Columbia undergraduates (who at the time were all male, while Barnard College across the street taught young women, a segregation of the sexes that was finally broken at Columbia after I left).[4]

To say that I was overwhelmed by good fortune was an understatement, and I adopted what I would later identify as a Freirean pedagogy in my course. I knew the students had probably gone to elite prep schools and read some of the Great Books I was to teach, maybe even in Latin or Greek, so they conceivably knew the texts better than I did. Hence, I wisely vowed to learn with and from the students.

I walked into the classroom, sat on the desk, with long hair and blue jeans, looking kind of 1960's radical, and told the students I'd been honored as a Grad Student to teach this course, but I had never taught before at all and confessed that they might know more about the books we were going to read than I do. So, I told them that we should discuss the texts and learn from each other, making it clear that I was counting on their help and that we would read, learn, and discuss these books together. Now, I would bet that the students had never heard this sort of introduction before, so I hoped that it would create the beginning of possible bonding and that we would work together to learn the texts that we would engage.

Next, I told the students that I had never studied Homer (we began the course with Homer's *Iliad* and *Odyssey*) but was looking forward to it; that I had read our following text, The *Book of Job* in the Old Testament in Vacation Bible School, so I was fine with teaching this. I informed the students that I was especially psyched to teach Plato and Aristotle, who I had studied in my philosophy seminars at Columbia – although, I then confessed that I hadn't read much of the Greek playwrights or any of the Latin texts like Vergil's *Aeneid*. I assured them, however, that I looked forward to rapping with them about the books and hoped that we all could read and discuss the books and have a good experience (I should note here that in the '60s, "rapping" meant freewheeling talking about things of interest, while it later became a genre of music...).

The students were excellent with this process, so in my first course, I adopted what would soon become known globally as a Freirean pedagogy with dialogue with the students, problem-posing, and generative questions as both teacher and students raised questions about what issues were critical in the class Humanities texts we were reading. Thus, we were learning together in a community of scholars interested in how these classical texts still related to our lives and had important messages for us today. At the same time, we engaged the cultural differences as well in the themes of the Greek, Latin, Medieval, and early modern texts, and how some themes in these writings were specific to their specific lives and times and the society in which they emerged, while other pieces were more universal and relevant to our lives and experiences today. As a final comment on this course, I would argue that it is essential to give students engagement in these classic Humanities texts, as I would also argue that it is of crucial importance to have a grounding in the multicultural texts of our contemporary U.S. society that include some key U.S. texts that deal with race, sexuality, gender, or other controversial topics that the war on education apparatchiks are banning.

Hence, just as it is essential for someone in our Western Civilization to gain knowledge and to engage the Great Books of our tradition, it is crucial to engage contemporary literature and texts on critical issues of our times. Interestingly and revealingly, some of the same cultural warriors attacking "woke education" attacked Humanities courses in both earlier and contemporary education cultural wars, arguing that students should study disciplines geared toward job training and contributing to the economy. By contrast, Marcuse, Freire, Dewey, and classical philosophers of education defended the Humanities and Philosophy as an essential component of education to be a fully rounded human being.[5]

During the same period that Marcuse was emerging as a significant figure in the New Left and as a social critic and philosopher of liberation on a global scale, Paulo Freire published *Pedagogy of the Oppressed*, which was translated all over the world, hitting the US in 1970 which I immediately closely read as a Bible for teaching. In 1973, I received my Philosophy Degree Ph.D. from Columbia and got my first tenure-track job at the University of Texas-Austin. Beginning my 25 years of teaching philosophy at UT-Austin, I strode confidently into class this time, unlike at the first University lecture I had ever taught at Columbia, where I wasn't sure what to do. Now, however, I was a Freirean, a critical pedagogue, and a critical theorist and revolutionist, combining Freire and Marcuse. Fortunately, since my first class at UT taught Marxism, it wasn't hard to attack capitalism and imperialism, advocate revolution and socialism and use texts by Marcuse and Freire to engage these issues.

Regarding Freire, I remarked in note 3 below that liberal Freireans tended to read or promote the early chapters of *Pedagogy of the Oppressed*, while it is in Chapter 4 that he advocates revolution and socialism, which I had read and taught with particular interest. Hence, from this optic, Freire is correctly interpreted as a revolutionary socialist thinker, just like Marcuse.

Towards a Radical Pedagogy and Reconstruction of Education

Hence, I started using Freire and Marcuse in my classes, focusing my writing and scholarship on Marcusean themes and using Marcuse's and Freire's pedagogy in the classroom. In the mid-1990s, however, I received a job offer as a Philosophy of Education chair at the University of California at Los Angeles, UCLA. In my Philosophy of Education seminar at UCLA in the Graduate School of Education and Information Studies, I began with Plato's *Republic*. Still, since UCLA was on a quarter system, it took too much of the limited ten week/ten seminar time, so I restricted myself in following years to teaching Philosophy of Education in the modern era, starting with Rousseau, moving to Mary Wollstonecraft who provided a feminist answer to Rousseau, then moving to John Dewey with his progressivist era *Democracy and Education*, and then, of course, using Paulo Freire's *Pedagogy of the Oppressed*.

I supplemented these readings with Toni Morrison's novel *The Bluest Eye*, a profoundly critical meditation on the life of a young African American girl in the aftermath of the Great Depression. From the beginning of teaching Philosophy of Education at UCLA, I always added a novel to the curriculum. Morrison's brilliant Bildungsroman dramatically demonstrated how we are shaped by our house, family, community, and the mass media, all of which play a role in our education and socialization. Morrison's novel portrayed how a young black girl was traumatized by the media representations of Shirley Temple as the All-American Girl and dreamed of having, like Temple, The Bluest Eye, showing how media shape young girls' view of beauty and self-worth.

The Bluest Eye was so successful with my students that I cut back on early modern Philosophy of Education classics and added Selected Papers of contemporary critical theorists of education, including at various times W.E.B. DuBois, Herbert Marcuse, Gloria Anzahldua, Ivan Illich, Taoism or Asian Philosophies of education. Since UCLA has a lot of Asian students, I would always let one or more introduce Asian philosophies of education in the seminar, which derived from the major religions of the area, like Buddhism or Taoism.

During this time, I was chosen to edit Marcuse's unpublished and/or uncollected texts by Peter Marcuse in the 1990s and subsequently produced six volumes of Marcuse's unpublished or uncollected writings. These texts were published by Routledge from 1998 to 2014 in six volumes, including books on Marcuse's writings on war, technology, and fascism; on society, culture, and politics; on philosophy, Marxism, and utopia; on the New Left; on philosophy and psychoanalysis; on art and aesthetics; and education.

My students and I were among the first to pursue the topic of Herbert Marcuse and education with two co-authored books, one on *Marcuse's Challenge to Education*, co-edited with K. Daniel Cho, Tyson E. Lewis, and Clayton Pierce (2009). This text is the first systematic critical engaging of Marcuse's critique of education and vision of educational alternatives. Emerging from an AERA panel that my students and I organized on Marcuse and education, we first published some articles in a journal, *Policy Futures in Education*, edited by Michael Peters. We were published thereafter in book form, opening with two previously unknown lectures from the Marcuse archive explicitly addressing educational issues.[6]

A closing chapter by Charles Reitz valorized Marcuse on the key role of the humanities and the liberal arts in developing a critical, "second-dimensional" understanding. Reitz also related Marcuse to recent battles in higher education on speech codes and political correctness, defending Marcuse against a right-wing demonization by counterrevolutionary culture warriors like Pat Buchanan and Allan Bloom for supposedly promoting a "closing of the American mind." Marcuse had presented well-established critical perspectives of the sort that the right now derides as "woke" – Marxism and feminism, critical race theory, ecology, gay and lesbian theory, and other critical insights. A long introduction by myself and the other editors situates Marcuse's contributions to education in the context of debates over schooling in the post-World War

II era, and compares his work with John Dewey, Paulo Freire, Ivan Illich, and other critics of education.

Continuing the ground-breaking work on Herbert Marcuse and education, I co-authored with Tyson E. Lewis and Clayton Pierce a short biography of Marcuse, focused on his contributions to education, titled *On Marcuse: Critique, Liberation, and Reschooling in the Radical Pedagogy of Herbert Marcuse* 2009). This text provides a succinct introduction and overview of the key ideas of Marcuse, particularly as they pertain to education, laying out his critique of education in relation to his theory of one-dimensional society and his alternative perspectives on radical pedagogy.

Reschooling in Marcuse is a retort to Ivan Ivan Illich and his notion of deschooling (2000 [1971]). Illich argues that schools are so hopelessly organized that it is better to take students outside of school and provide "tools of conviviality" (Illich 1973) by which groups of students with helpful older mentors could engage with each other in reading and discussing books, surfing the Internet, and discussing particular topics, studying broadcasting and social media, teaching critical literacies and critiquing broadcasting and social media. While these concerns are all important, some communities need a focus on public education, and with Marcuse, I think we need to reschool education, teaching students things that matter. Further, we should provide critical literacy and other skills which, through using the word, we can see, understand, critique, and change the world – to adopt a key Freirean phrase.

In conclusion, I would argue that rather than privileging Marcuse or Freire, we should mediate them and use them both, as well as other valuable radical pedagogues, many of whom I have been discussing in the essays and this book and its predecessor volume on *The Philosophy of Education*. Freire in *Pedagogy of the Oppressed* and later works, and Marcuse's critical theory approach to education have powerful perspectives that can be combined. I might note that Marcuse was the first major Western thinker to advocate feminism, critical race theory, and queer studies, and we should emulate him in this regard. Marcuse also stressed the preservation of nature and the importance of being-in-nature for human life (1955). He was one of the first critical theorists to engage ecology and the environmental movement, a theme and practice he supported until he died in 1979.[7]

Interestingly, some right-wing ideologues continue to condemn Marcuse for introducing into education today these critical theories and oppositional studies,[8] but obviously, it was people from these movements who introduced these important components of a critical theory of education. Marcuse merely anticipated these later movements, although he actively participated in the Civil Rights, Anti-War, feminist, ecological, and other radical movements of the time, advocating a critical theory of society that related theory to revolutionary practice and that fought racism, sexism, homophobia, and other forms of prejudice while advocating revolutionary anti-capitalist and anti-imperialist perspectives.

Freire too was part of the radical movements of the 1960s and 1970s and a fearless fighter against authoritarianism and the fascism emerging in Latin American countries which exiled him at certain junctures of his career. Freire's *Pedagogy of the Oppressed* was criticized at the time for neglecting gender and race, theorizing the oppressed solely as a class category, as well as neglecting ecology, but he later apologizes and integrates these issues and perspectives into his evolving theory.[9]

Moreover, not only did radical pedagogues in the Freirean tradition address ecology as I document in Note 7, but many made the intersectionalities of race, gender, class, and sexuality foundational to their radical social theories and pedagogies, such as bell hooks. In *Teaching to transgress: education as the practice of freedom* (1994), hooks produces a neo-Freirean "engaged pedagogy" adapted to conditions in the U.S. and Western democracies where education faces barriers of institutionalized classism, racism, sexism, homophobia, and other bias which "education as the practice of freedom," as Freire argued, serves to attack all forms of oppression. Throughout the works of her last decades, she targeted White Hetero-Patriarchal Capitalism as a major source of oppression and participated in movements to create a more free, just and equitable society liberated from the oppressions of the past.

In a distinguished career from the 1970s to her death in 2021, hooks also developed an engaged pedagogy linked with radical political practice putting education in the service of the struggles for democratic freedoms and against racism, sexism, classism, and other forms of oppression, while also advocating a philosophy of peace and love in *All About Love: New Visions* (hooks 2000), and several subsequent books on the topic.

Marcuse was one of the first Marxist thinkers of his generation to embrace interconnecting critiques of class, with critique of race and racism, gender and feminism, sexuality, and liberation of all forms, while defending the movements that participated in these struggles. Marcuse's student Angela Davis became famous for, among many other things, interconnecting race, gender, class, and sexuality in a critical theory and revolutionary politics, becoming one of the vanguard thinkers and activists of her generation (see Davis 1974 and 1981, among many of her important books).[10]

Freire and Marcuse both dealt with the key issues of their day and radical pedagogy and critical social theories concerned with the themes of human liberation and democratic social transformation. Moreover, as the discussion above indicates, both left legacies of radical struggle and have inspired future generations, hence both their theories and politics are relevant to the contemporary moment. The fact that the establishment have unleashed such extreme and still proliferating attacks on them testifies to their relevance for critical social theory and radical pedagogy today. Hence, I conclude that Marcuse and Freire are highly compatible, and both give us important components radical theories of contemporary society and radical pedagogy for the present age.

Notes

1 In other chapters in this study, I highlight the importance of John Dewey and other radical pedagogues, but, combining the personal and the political, I am focusing on the powerful influences Marcuse and Freire made on me already during my graduate studies at Columbia and in my initial teaching efforts at Columbia and then the University of Texas-Austin which I sketch out here. Since I studied philosophy at Columbia University during the middle to late 1960s, as I sketch out in this chapter, my fellow students and I systematically studied John Dewey's writings as part of our comprehensive exams, and his benevolent portrait was shining down upon us in our seminar room, as we were engaged in our philosophical studies and adventures. Moreover, one day a perplexed secretary was upset because they were providing new furniture for the *Journal of Philosophy* office of the journal that Dewey founded and were throwing out Dewey's desk! "No way!" I interjected and helpfully said I would occupy the desk myself for my graduate studies to commune with the progressive spirit of Dewey. The benevolent secretary smiled and assented, and soon I and four of my fellow graduate students were hauling Dewey's desk on our shoulders, hiking fifteen blocks down Broadway to the bemused stares of our fellow New Yorkers. Then, we plowed five flights up the stairs of my walk-up apartment on the corner of 105th street and West End Avenue, and thereafter Dewey was a material part of my early grounding in philosophy and radical democratic pedagogy.
2 On Marcuse and the New Left, see Kellner 1988 and *Herbert Marcuse. The New Left and the 1960s.* Volume Three of Six Volumes, *Collected Papers of Herbert Marcuse,* edited with Introduction by Douglas Kellner. London and New York: Routledge, 2004.
3 Liberal Freireans focus on the earlier chapters of *Pedagogy of the Oppressed* and tend to ignore or downplay the importance of Chapter 4 of the text; that illustrates his revolutionary perspectives that I see as a key to his philosophy and a significant point of convergence with Marcuse.

4 For details on my teaching of the Great Books program at Columbia, see the Interview in Chapter 7. In this chapter, I am going into the political context of my Columbia University teaching and then my University of Texas-Austin and UCLA experiences.
5 To engage Marcuse's contributions to the Philosophy of Education and the importance of teaching Philosophy, Humanities, and the classics and contemporary literature by a diverse range of writers, see the works on Marcuse by my former Ph.D. students cited in the Reference List by Kellner, D., Lewis, T. and Pierce, C. (2008) and Kellner, D., Lewis, T. Pierce, C. and Cho, D.K. (eds) (2009). Also, see the ground-breaking work on education by Charles Reitz, *Art, Alienation and the Humanities: A Critical Engagement with Herbert Marcuse* (2000). This study documents how Marcuse's philosophical writing explicitly critiques education. Reitz argued that the general framework of Marcuse's social theory transformed (through dialectical negation, preservation, and elevation) a central assumption of classical European philosophy: higher education can cultivate both the aesthetic sense and the political will to accomplish our humanization. Yet higher education has become predominantly scientific and technical and primarily serves the needs of commerce, industry, and the military. Ed today, even the liberal arts curriculum, reproduces a politics of class, race, and gender through a conservative curriculum. Higher education, reconstructed in Marcuse's view of the emancipatory elements of the Liberal Arts, Humanities, and critically oriented social sciences, can act *against alienation and for the cosmopolitan dehumanization of culture.*
6 Curiously, Herbert Marcuse was earlier blamed in the 1970s for the wave of Marxism in the Universities by rightwing critics. His influence and embrace feminism, Queer theory, and embrace of browns, blacks, and people of color in progressive social movements led to his being attacked as a foundation for Critical Race Theory and other radical theories of gender, sexuality, and multiculturalism in later and more recent critiques of his work; I should state that the wave of often off-the-wall and over-the-top right-wing critiques of Marcuse during the past decades indicates his long-time and continuing importance for critical social theory, radical pedagogy, and revolutionary politics from the 1960s to the present. For rightwing post-1960s critiques of Marcuse blaming him for the extreme left and counterculture in U.S. universities and cultural spaces, see Bloom (1987) and D'Souza (1992).
7 See Marcuse's article "Ecology and the Critique of Modern Society" (1992) and my study "Herbert Marcuse and Radical Ecology," buried in the deep net at <https://pages.gseis.ucla.edu/faculty/kellner/Illumina%20Folder/kell11.htm> (accessed April 1, 2023) and available in print as Kellner 1992.
8 For recent attacks accusing Marcuse of being the source of contemporary Marxism, critical race studies, radical feminism, and other "woke" theories and movements, see pseudoliberal Matt Taibbi, "Marcuse-Anon: Cult of the Pseudo-Intellectual. Reviewing "Repressive Tolerance" and other works by Herbert Marcuse, the quack who became America's most influential thinker," *Substack*, February 16, 2021 at <https://taibbi.substack.com/p/marcuse-anon-cult-of-the-pseudo-intellectual-1d3>(accessed March 31, 2023), and rightwing commentator Liz Wheeler, "Critical race theory is repackaged Marxism," *Newsweek*, June 14, 2021 at <https://www.newsweek.com/critical-race-theory-repackaged-marxism-opinion-1599557>(accessed March 31, 2023). For positive views of Marcuse's effect on recent generations and defense of Marcuse in the Marcuse's Cultural Wars, see Charles

Reitz, "Herbert Marcuse and the New Culture Wars: Campus Codes, Hate Speech, and the Critique of Pure Tolerance" in Kellner, Lewis, Pierce, and Cho (eds) (2009); George Katsiaficas, "Behind Recent Attacks on Herbert Marcuse," International Herbert Marcuse Society (www.MarcuseSociety.org), December 14, 2021; and Višić (2023).

9 Freirean pedagogy is thought especially fruitful as a foundation for ecopedagogy because it honors culturally relevant knowledge of nature and society. See Richard Kahn, *Critical Pedagogy, Ecoliteracy, & Planetary Crisis* (New York: Peter Lang, 2010) and Greg William Misiaszek, *Freire and Environmentalism Ecopedagogy* (London: Bloomsbury Academic, 2023). However, C.A. Bowers and certain co-authors from the Global South on the other hand charge that Freire's work is inadequate for an understanding the cultural roots of the ecology crisis because of Freire's philosophical and political foundations in the Western intellectual tradition. See *Rethinking Freire: Globalization and the Environmental Crisis* edited by C.A. Bowers and Frédérique Apffel-Marglin (Mahwah, NJ: Erlbaum, 2005). In a recent email Greg Misiaszek discussed Freire regretting that he had neglected nature and ecology in *Pedagogy of the Oppressed*, imagined a fifth chapter on these topics in a new edition, and was working on the topic in his last years.

10 On the connection between Davis and Marcuse, see Andrew T. Lamas, "Angela Davis," in *Routledge Handbook of Marxism and Post-Marxism*, ed. Alex Callinicos, Stathis Kouvelakis, and Lucia Pradella (London: Routledge, 2021), 410–418.

References

Bloom, A. (1987). *The Closing of the American Mind*. New York: Simon & Schuster.
Davis, A. (1974). *An Autobiography*. New York: Random House.
Davis, A. (1981). *Women, Race and Class*. New York: Random House.
D'Souza, D. (1992). *Illiberal Education. The Politics of Race and Sex on Campus*. New York: Vintage.
Freire, P. (1970). *Pedagogy of the Oppressed*. New York: Continuum.
Freire, P. (1976 [1967]). *Education as the Practice of Freedom*. London: Writers and Readers Publishing Cooperative.
hooks, b. (1990). *Yearning: Race, Gender, and Cultural Politics*. Boston, Massachusetts: South End Press.
hooks, b. (1994). *Teaching to Transgress: Education as the Practice of Freedom*. New York: Routledge.
hooks, b. (2000). *All About Love: New Visions*. New York: William Morrow.
Illich, I. (2000 [1971]). *Deschooling Society*. Marion Boyars Publishers Ltd; New edition.
Illich, I. (1973). *Tools for Conviviality*. New York: Harper & Row.
Kahn, R. (2010). *Critical Pedagogy, Ecoliteracy, & Planetary Crisis*. New York: Peter Lang.
Kellner, D. (1984). *Herbert Marcuse and the Crisis of Marxism*. Berkeley and London: University of California Press (USA) and Macmillan Press (England).
Kellner, D. (1989). *Critical Theory, Marxism, and Modernity*. Cambridge, UK and Baltimore, MD: Polity Press and John Hopkins University Press.
Kellner, D. (1992). "Herbert Marcuse and Radical Ecology." *Capitalism, Nature, and Socialism*, 3(3) (Sept. 1992): 43–46.

Kellner, D. (ed. 2004). *Herbert Marcuse. The New Left and the 1960s*. Volume Three, *Collected Papers of Herbert Marcuse*, edited with Introduction by Douglas Kellner. London and New York: Routledge.

Kellner, D. (2008). Kellner, D., Lewis, T. and Pierce, C. *On Marcuse: Critique, Liberation, and Reschooling in the Radical Pedagogy of Herbert Marcuse*. Rotterdam, The Netherlands: Brill Publishers.

Kellner, D., Lewis, T. Pierce, C. and Cho, D. K. (eds.). (2009). *Marcuse's Challenge to Education*. Lanham, MD: Rowman & Littlefield.

Marcuse, H. (1940). *Reason and Revolution*. Boston: Beacon Press.

Marcuse, H. (1955). *Eros and Civilization*. Boston: Beacon Press.

Marcuse, H. (1964). *One-Dimensional Man*. Boston: Beacon Press.

Marcuse, H. (1969). *An Essay on Liberation*. Boston: Beacon Press.

Marcuse, H. (1992). "Ecology and the Critique of Modern Society." *Capitalism, Nature, and Socialism*, 3(3) (Sept. 1992): 43–46.

Misiaszek, G. W. (2023). *Freire and Environmentalism Ecopedagogy*. London: Bloomsbury Academic.

Obama, B. (2004). *Dreams from My Father: A Story of Race and Inheritance*. New York: Crown Books.

Obama, B. (2007). *The Audacity of Hope: Thoughts on Reclaiming the American Dream*. New York: Broadway Books.

Reitz, C. (2000). *Art, Alienation and the Humanities: A Critical Engagement with Herbert Marcuse*. Albany, NY: SUNY Press.

Tucker, R. (Tucker, ed. 1978). *The Marx-Engels Reader*. New York: Norton Press.

Višić, M. (2023). "Onwards and Upwards to the Kingdom of Beauty and Love. Herbert Marcuse's Trajectory to Socialism," *Filozofija i društvo* at <https://www.ceeol.com/search/journal-detail?id=93> (accessed April 1, 2023).

· 8 ·

CONCLUDING THOUGHTS ON MULTIPLE CRITICAL LITERACIES AND THE RECONSTRUCTION OF EDUCATION

Many of the studies on critical media and digital literacies that I have presented here so far highlight the ways that the Internet, new digital technologies, and social media are dramatically transforming the circulation of information, images, and various modes of culture, and thus require Reconstruction of Education in the Spirit of John Dewey, Paulo Freire, and Herbert Marcuse. And so in the following sections that are looking toward education in the 21st century, I want to emphasize in conclusion the importance of students learning multiple forms of critical digital literacies that involve both how to use computer culture and digital technologies to do research and gather information, communicate, interact, and present and debate ideas, as well as to perceive the cyberculture of the 21st century as a cultural terrain which contains texts, spectacles, games, social media and new interactive multimedia which requires new modes of critical literacies.

Digital culture today is a discursive and political location in which students, teachers, and citizens can all intervene, engaging in discussion groups and collaborative research projects, creating their web sites and social media, producing new multimedia for cultural dissemination, and engaging in multiple modes of social interaction and learning. Digital culture enables individuals to actively participate in the production of culture, ranging from discussion of public issues to creation of their own cultural forms.

However, to take part in this culture requires not only accelerated forms of traditional modes of print literacy which are often restricted to the growing elite of students who are privileged to attend competent and superior public and private schools, but also demands teaching and learning multiple forms of critical digital literacies as well, thus posing significant challenges to education in the contemporary era.

It is indeed a salient fact of the present age that digital culture is proliferating and so we have to begin teaching critical digital literacies from an early age on. Critical digital literacies, however, need to be theorized and expanded. Often the term "computer literacy" is synonymous with technical ability to use computers, to master existing programs, and maybe engage in some programming and coding oneself. I want, however, to suggest expanding the conception of computer and digital literacies from using computer programs and software to a broader concept of critical media and digital literacies that include gaining skills in the decoding, interpretation and critique of media, proficiencies in the finding, evaluating and storing of information, and developing, in addition, more sophisticated abilities in traditional reading and writing, as well as the capability to critically dissect cultural forms taught as part of critical media literacy and new forms of multiple literacy (see Kellner and Share 2019).

Critical information literacy involves both the accessing and processing of diverse sorts of information proliferating in our infotainment society.[1] It encompasses learning to find sources of information ranging from traditional sites like libraries and print media to new Internet websites and search engines, and, crucially, to discern solid and sourced factual information from disinformation and misinformation that permeates our highly politicized and contested culture and society.

Thus, on this conception, genuine critical computer and information literacies involve not just technical knowledge and skills, but refined reading, writing, research, and communicating ability that involves heightened capacities for critically accessing, analyzing, interpreting, and processing print, image, sound, and multimedia material. Computer literacy involves the ability to discover and access information and intensified abilities to read, to scan texts and computer data bases and websites, and to download or print the information in a form appropriate for further information processing. Utilizing information accessed in an educational context further requires putting it together in meaningful patterns and mosaics, to construct meanings and interpretations, to contextualize and evaluate, and to discuss and articulate one's own views.

Within computer culture, visual literacy takes on increased importance. On the whole, computer screens are more graphic, visual, and interactive than conventional print fields which disconcerted many of us when first confronted with the new environments. Icons, windows, mouses, and the various clicking, linking, and interaction required by computer-mediated hypertext requires new competencies and a dramatic expansion of literacy. Visuality is obviously crucial, requiring one to quickly scan visual fields, perceive and interact with icons and graphics, and use technical devices like a mouse to access the desired material and field. One must also learn navigational skills of how to proceed from one field and screen to another, how to search for information on the Internet and computer data bases, and how to move from one program to another if one operates, as most now do, in a window-based computer environment.

The new multimedia environments require a diversity of multisemiotic and multimodal interaction, involving interfacing with words and print material and often images, graphics, and multiple forms of audio and video material. The New London Group early on produced the concept of "multiliteracy" to describe the types of literacy required to engage new multimedia technology, while Semali and Watts Pailliotet and their collaborators (2019) propose the concept "Intermediality" to call attention the need to generate literacies that allow interaction between various media and new multimedia, and that promote interdisciplinary and interactive education in an attempt to create education that promotes democratic social change. In a similar vein, individuals involved in the University of California at Los Angeles and San Diego with the *la classa magica* project are using new computer and multimedia technology to teach basic reading and writing skills, as well as new computer and multimedia literacy and forms of social cooperation and interaction.[2]

As technological convergence develops apace, one needs to combine the skills of critical media literacy with traditional print literacy and new forms of multiliteracy to access the new multimedia hypertext environments.[3] Literacy in my conception involves socially-constructed forms of communication and representation and the corresponding competencies involved in effectively using them. Thus, reading and interpreting print was the appropriate mode of literacy for books, while critical media literacy requires reading and interpreting discourse, images, spectacle, narratives, and the forms and genres of media culture (Kellner and Share 2019; Kellner 2020). Forms of multimedia communication involve print, speech, visuality, and audio, in a hybrid field which combines these forms, all of which involve skills of interpreting and critique.

Obviously, here the key root is the multiple, the proliferation of media and forms that require a multiplicity of competencies and skills and abilities to navigate and construct a new semiotic terrain – hence the term multiliteracy and the notion of multiple literacies that I develop in the next section. Multiliteracies involve reading across multiple and hybrid semiotic fields and being able to critically and hermeneutically process print, graphics, images, and perhaps moving images and sounds. The term "hybridity" suggests the combination and interaction of diverse media and the need to synthesize the various forms in an active process of the construction of meaning. Reading a music video, for instance, involves processing images, music, spectacle, and sometimes narrative in a multisemiotic process that simultaneously draws on diverse aesthetic forms. Interacting with a website or digital devices involves scanning text, graphics, often moving images, and clicking onto the fields that one seeks to peruse and appropriate. This might involve combining video, audio, print, and graphics in new interactive learning or entertainment environments.

While traditional literacies involve practices in contexts that are governed by rules and conventions, the conventions and rules of multiliteracies are currently evolving so that their pedagogies is a new although quite bustling and competitive field. Multimedia fields are not entirely new, however. Multisemiotic textuality was first evident in newspapers (consider the difference between *The New York Times* and *U.S.A. Today* in terms of image, text, color graphics, design, and content) and is now evident in textbooks that are much more visual, graphic, and multimodal than the previously linear and discursive texts of old. Yet it is multimedia web sites, and new multimedia forms of communication, information and entertainment that are the most distinctively multimodal and multisemiotic forms. These sites are the new frontier of learning and literacy, the great challenge to education in the contemporary era.

As we proceed into the 21st century, we need to theorize the literacies necessary to navigate and interact in these new multimedia environments and to gain the skills that will enable us to learn, work, and create in new cultural spaces and domains. Parenthetically, I might note that we are soon going to have to rethink SATs and standard tests in relation to the new technologies; having the literacy and skills to successfully navigate, communicate, work, and create within computer and multimedia culture is quite different from reading and writing in the mode of print literacy and while this mode of literacy continues to be of utmost importance it is sublated within multiliteracy, so eventually an entirely different sort of test is going to need to be devised to register individuals' multiliteracy competency and to predict success in a new technological and educational environment.[4]

Thus, in my expanded conception, critical digital literacies involve technical abilities concerning developing basic typing skills, mastering computer programs and coding, accessing information, and using computer and digital technologies for a variety of purposes ranging from verbal communication to artistic expression to political debate. There are ever more hybrid implosions between media and computer culture as audio and video material becomes part of the Internet, as multimedia develop, and as novel digital technologies and devices become part and parcel of the home, school, and workplace.

Therefore, the skills of decoding images, sounds, and spectacle learned in critical media literacy training can also be valuable as part of critical digital literacies as well. Furthermore, print literacy takes on increasing importance in computer world as one needs to critically scrutinize and scroll tremendous amounts of information, putting new emphasis on developing reading and writing abilities. In fact, Internet discussion groups, chat rooms, email, and various forums require writing skills in which a new emphasis on the importance of clarity and precision is emerging as communications proliferate. In this context of information saturation, it becomes an ethical imperative not to contribute to cultural and information overload, and to concisely communicate one's thoughts and feelings.

In a certain sense, digital technologies and cyberculture are becoming the technological equivalent of Hegel's Absolute Idea, able to absorb everything into its form and medium. Computers are now not only repositories of text and print-based data, but also contain a wealth of images, multimedia sights and sounds, and interactive environments that, like the media, are themselves a form of education that require a critical pedagogy of electronic, digitized culture and communication. From this conception, critical media and digital literacies constitute something like a Hegelian synthesis of print and visual literacy, technical skills, skills in information-gathering, data processing and communicating, brought together at a new and higher stage. While Neil Postman and others produce a simplistic Manichean dichotomy between print and visual literacy, and between books and media entertainment, we need to learn to think dialectically, to read together text and image, to decipher sight and sound, and to develop forms of computer and multimedia literacy adequate to meet the exigencies of an increasingly high-tech society.

These multiple literacies have been conceptualized as part of a postmodern pedagogy which requires developing critical forms of print, media, computer, and multiliteracy, all of which are of crucial importance in the new techno-culture of the present and fast-approaching future.[5] Whereas modern pedagogy tended to be specialized, fragmented, and differentiated, and was focused on print culture, a postmodern pedagogy involves developing multiple literacies and critically analyzing, dissecting, and engaging a multiplicity of cultural forms, some of which are the products of emergent technologies and social media, requiring developing new critical literacies to engage the evolving cultural forms and media.

In fact, contemporary culture is marked by a proliferation of cultural machines which generate a panoply of diverse aesthetic artifacts within which we wander, trying to make our way through this forest of symbols, spectacles, and semiotic novelties. New critical multimedia literacies require the ability to scan, interact with, traverse, organize, and create innovative multimedia educational environments. Multimedia literacy thus involves not just reading, but interacting: clicking to move from one field to another if one is involved in a hypertext environment such as one finds on web sites or multimedia texts; capturing, saving, downloading, and perhaps printing material relevant to one's own projects; and maybe responding verbally or adding one's own material if it is a site that invites genuinely interactive participation. These reflections require an analysis of postmodern culture and education that has been a highly contested field.

Musings on Postmodern Education and Culture

From the perspective of postmodern theory, modern education is seen as the mass education that began in the 19th century with standardized curriculum, grades, degrees, and public accreditation. It is criticized as homogenizing, normalizing, and imposing the norms, practices, and values of the dominant society on the young. Modern education, from this perspective, corresponds in the field of education to mass production and consumption characterizing modern societies, and an era dominated by corporations, the State, military, and educational institutions marked by bureaucracy, a technical system of instrumentalized rules and regulations, and mass conformity.

Modern education is also connected to an era of print technology and literacy based on reading books. As Marshall McLuhan argued (1964), different societies have various dominant media that provide diverse modes of society, culture, and education. McLuhan distinguishes between premodern oral culture and traditions, modern print culture, and (postmodern) electronic culture. In traditional, premodern societies, education is oral and transmits relatively fixed and changing traditions and a hierarchic, authoritarian social structure.

For McLuhan, the major instrument of modernity was the emergence of print technology that created an entirely new modern culture, and modes of education and subjectivity with print media dominant. Modern culture and education were highly nationalistic, often determined by the state and reproducing and focusing on national cultures. Modern education tended to be secular, following the enlightenment and predicated on a separation of church and state. Modern education was organized on the factory and industrial system with public and private buildings and grounds, and classes organized around time periods.

In McLuhan's view, new electronic technologies create new modes of culture connected to media like radio, film, television, and now computers, social media, and digital technologies that are creating new forms of subjectivity which are more sensory, multimodal, fragmented, and decentered. For McLuhan, there is a misfit between the experiences of students in a rationalized, abstract, book culture environment of schooling, and the more kaleidoscopic and aestheticized media culture in which they are immersed.

Sherry Turkle (1995) describes the emergence of personal computer technologies and the novel forms of interaction, identities, and experiences that they are producing. She interprets the shift from big mainframe computers to personal computers as symptomatic of a postmodern shift to an innovative type of computer technology and novel forms of subjectivity and culture. For Turkle, big IBM mainframe computers are bound up with centralization, massification, hierarchy, big government and corporations, and are thus a figure for modernity itself. Further, modern computers are connected with mechanistic science that is universalist, rationalist (there is one way to do it), and top-down, with a cult of experts and hierarchy; it is also for Turkle rooted in hard masculine science which is logical and abstract.

By contrast, Turkle claims that personal computers are bound up with a postmodern logic and aesthetics. On her account, postmodern computer technologies are "soft" and "feminine" (e.g., more concrete and ductile), subject to tinkering, more graphic and multimedia, and more expressive, merging art and technology. Whereas modern mainframe computers required highly specialized knowledge and were only accessible to a techno-elite, postmodern personal computers are "user-friendly" and lend themselves to experimental activity and promote creative and multifaceted selves. PCs thus nourish a postmodern culture of the iconic surface, for while old modern computers required depth-oriented thinking and in-depth technological know-how to get behind the screen, current computers operate on the surface, requiring only that one point and click to navigate cyberspace.

Furthermore, personal computers, on Turkle's analysis, enable a more decentralized, individualist, and variegated culture which can generate postmodern selves – multiple, fragmented, constructed and provisional, subject to experiment and change. "Windows" for Turkle is the privileged metaphor for postmodern subjectivity – dispersed, decentered, and constructed. Computer software windows open the subject not only to the work-world of texts and word-processing, but also to the emerging realms of simulation, cyberspace, and interactive multimedia culture.

From these postmodern perspectives, education needs to be reconstructed to overcome the divisions between students' everyday life in a media and computer culture, and to generate new literacies that will enable students to interact in the contemporary world. Allan and Carmen Luke argue (2001) that broad-ranging and robust new pedagogies are needed to grasp the changing social and psychological conditions of life in a globalized, high-tech and digitized world. They also argue that dramatic transformations of education are necessary to create subjects and practices appropriate to a new global society, digitized culture, and world of new identities, social relations, and cultural forms.

Indeed, many educators have been arguing for a reconstruction of education based on developing new literacies to engage new technologies variously described as multiliteracies, multiple literacies, or multiple technoliteracies (see Cazden et al. 1996, Kellner 1998, the articles in Snyder 2002; Kellner and Share 2005; 2019; and Kahn and Kellner 2006). Projects for a postmodern reconstruction of education also build on Dewey's pedagogy, and particularly his calls for the democratization of education to produce more robust democratic societies (Kellner 1998; Kellner and Share 2005; 2019).

Ironically, during the opening decade of the third millennium when postmodern critiques of modern education were widely circulated and reconstructive programs were being advanced, the Bush administration in the United States was pushing a program predicated on standardized testing, focusing on print literacy and mathematics, and generally reproducing what critics believed to be problematic aspects of modern education. And as we have seen in early chapters, reactionaries have been attacking education itself, banning books, imposing rightwing ideological curriculum, and needless to add, totally ignoring the technological revolution and its impact on education that serious critical pedagogues are addressing.

However, in an era of continuous technological development and the emergence of evolving technologies, critiques of modern education will persist and new proposals for the postmodern reconstruction of education will continue to circulate. In addition to the linear cognitive skills needed for traditional reading of print material, multimedia literacy thus requires a multisemiotic ability to read hypertexts that are often multidimensional requiring the connecting of images, graphics, texts, and sometimes audio-video material. It also involves new forms of intertextuality and contextualizing multimedia material. Multimedia thus involves making connections between the complex and multilayered cyberworld and its connection with the real world. As Carmen Luke reminds us: "Since all meaning is situated relationally – that is, connected and cross-referenced to other media and genres, and to related meanings in other cultural contexts – a critical literacy relies on broad-based notions of intertextuality" (1997: 10). Intertextuality draws attention to the complex ways that language, image, and types of texts are related to various genres, forms, narratives, and modes of meaning such as visual design.

Thus, on one hand, one must learn to read multimedia forms that are themselves overlapping and interrelated, switching from text to graphics to video to audio, decoding in turn sight, sound, and text. In a global information environment, this also may involve switching from sites from one country to another requiring contextual understanding and literacy that is able to read and interact with people and sites from different cultures. As Carmen Luke puts it: "[N]ew [forms of] virtual communication are emerging, which require an intertextual understanding of how meanings shift across media, genres, and cultural frames of reference. Whether one `visits' the Louvre on-line, joins an international newsgroup of parents of Downs Syndrome children, or visits the site of an agricultural college in Kenya, cross-cultural understanding and `netiquette' is increasingly crucial for participating effectively in global communications" (Luke 1997: 10).

Crucially, multimedia literacy should be contextual, it requires thematizing the background and power relations of cultural forms (i.e., including analysis of the political economy of the media and technology, of how corporate organizations control production and dissemination, and how oppositional and alternative media and uses are possible; see Kellner 2020), as well as the context and power relations of the specific media use in question (i.e., the differences between television watching in the classroom, at home with one's family, with one's friends or alone; or the differences between computer use for research, data organization, email, or playing games, etc.). Multimedia literacy also envisages new modes of collaborative work on research projects or web sites, new forms of student/teacher participation and interaction, and new pedagogical uses for the new technologies which may often appear exotic in the present, but which will become increasingly commonplace in the future and will force a rethinking of education.

Finally, multiliteracy must become critical, and in response to excessive hype concerning new technologies and digital devices, it is necessary to maintain the critical dimension. After an excellent discussion of new modes of literacy and the need to rethink education, Gunther Kress argues that we must move from critique to design, beyond a negative deconstruction to more positive construction (1997). Yet rather than following such modern logic of either/or, we need to pursue the logic of both/and, seeing design and critique, deconstruction and reconstruction, as complementary and supplementary rather than as antithetical choices.

Certainly, we need to design new technologies, pedagogies, and curricula for the future, and should attempt to design new social and pedagogical relations as well, but we need to criticize misuse, inappropriate use, overinflated claims, and exclusions and oppressions involved in the introduction of new technologies into education – resisting at the same time the attacks on education itself from rightwing ideologues. The critical dimension is needed more than ever as we attempt to develop *new* teaching strategies and pedagogy, as we design new technologies and curricula, we must be constantly critical, practicing critique and self-criticism, putting in question our assumptions, discourses, and practices as we experimentally develop new critical literacies and pedagogy.

In such an experimental and evolving educational project, obviously critique is of fundamental importance. From the Deweyean perspective, progressive education involves experiment and the experimental method which involves critique of limitations, failures, and flawed design. In discussing new media and digital technologies and multiliteracies, one also needs to constantly raise the question, whose interests are these new technologies and pedagogies serving, are they serving all social groups and individuals, who is being excluded and why? We also need to raise the question both of the extent to which new technologies and literacies are preparing students and citizens for the present and future and producing conditions for a more vibrant democratic society, or simply reproducing existing inequalities and inequity.

New Life Conditions, Subjectivities and Literacies in Alan and Carmen Lukes' Reconstructive Project

> It is surely not difficult to see that our time is a time of birth and transition to a new period. The spirit has broken with what was hitherto the world of its existence and imagination and is about to submerge all this in the past; it is at work giving itself a new form. To be sure, the spirit is never at rest but always engaged in ever progressing motion... the spirit that educates itself matures slowly and quietly toward the new form, dissolving one particle of the edifice of its previous world after the other,.... This gradual crumbling... is interrupted by the break of day that, like lightning, all at once reveals the edifice of the new world. Hegel, *The Phenomenology of Spirit*, 1807.

I was pleased some years ago to see that in their paper "Adolescence Lost/Childhood Regained: On Early Intervention and the Emergence of the Techno-Subject," Allan and Carmen Luke (2001) deployed a critical poststructuralist Hegelian framework to articulate transformations in the situation of youth and the need to reconstruct education and promote new literacies appropriate to the new material conditions, transformations, and subjectivities emerging in the contemporary era. While some educational applications of poststructuralism, feminism, and postmodern theories reject Hegelian and other modern discourses out of hand as excessively totalizing or reductive, the Lukes' convincingly argue that broad-ranging and robust new theories are needed to grasp the changing social and psychological conditions of life in a globalized, high-tech and digitized world. They also convincingly argue that dramatic transformations of education are necessary to create subjects and practices appropriate to a new global society, digitized culture, and world of new identities, social relations, and cultural forms.

I would agree that something like a quasi-Hegelian and Marxian theory of society and history is necessary to describe and map the new historical stages, developments, and breaks, while certain forms of postmodern theory derived from Lyotard, Baudrillard, and others reject the very theoretical resources needed to analyze the "postmodern condition" that postmodern theorists evoke. For a too radical postmodern theory fetishizes breaks and differences (i.e., Baudrillard) whereas more dialectical theories can present continuities and discontinuities, theorizing ruptures and novel conditions as well as connections with the past.

Of course, some versions of the Hegelian philosophy of history are excessively totalizing, idealist, reductive, teleological and ideological, and the Lukes avoid these pitfalls by mediating Hegelian/modern conceptions with poststructuralist epistemologies and analyses of emergent postmodern conditions that put in question previous pedagogies and educational philosophies. They also suggestively deploy poststructuralist ideas to democratize and reconstruct education, combining modern and postmodern perspectives, theory and practice.

My remarks will address three dimensions of what I take to be the Lukes' contributions in their important 2001 article to philosophy of education today: (1) Articulating the novel life conditions, subjectivities, and identities of youth; (2) cultivating new multiple critical literacies to respond to new technologies and the challenges of globalization; and (3) on the basis of these analyses to propose a radical restructuring and democratization of education.

New Life Conditions, Subjectivities, and Identities

Alan and Carmen Luke (2001) argue that current educational systems, curricula, and pedagogies were designed for the production of a laboring subject who has become an "endangered species" in the current economic, social, and cultural system. Modern education was constructed to develop a compliant work force who would gain skills of print literacy and discipline that would enable them to function in modern corporations and a corporate economy based on rational accounting, commercial organization, and discursive communicative practices, supported by manual labor and service jobs. The life trajectory for a laboring modern subject was assumed to be stable and mappable, progressing through K-12 schooling, to Universities and perhaps onto professional schools or higher degrees, to well-paying jobs that would themselves offer life-time employment, a stable career, and solid identities.

All of this, the Lukes suggest, has changed in a global economy marked by constant restructuring, flux and rapid change, and new material conditions and subjectivities. Students coming into schools have been shaped by years of computer and video games, television, a variety of music technologies and forms, and new spheres of multimedia and interactive cyberculture. Moreover, the steady jobs that were waiting for well-disciplined and performing students of the previous generation are disappearing, while new jobs are appearing in the high-tech sector, itself subject to chaotic booms, busts, and restructuring. And as the September 11 terrorist attacks on the U.S. and their chaotic aftermath have demonstrated, life in a high-tech and global society is much more complicated, fragile, and subject to dramatic disruptions and transformations than was previously perceived.

There is thus a fundamental misfit between youth life-experience and schooling, the expectations of an older generation concerning labor and new work conditions, and the previous print-based and organizational economy and culture in contrast to the new digital and multimedia based culture and hybridized global economy. Postmodern theorists have amassed cultural capital theorizing such breaks and ruptures, but have had few positive recommendations on how to restructure institutions like schooling (although there are stacks of books, generally of little worth, on how to succeed in the new economy). The Lukes' analysis is distinguished by an attempt to draw the consequences for restructuring education and democratizing society from reflection on new life conditions, experiences, and subjectivities in the light of the connection between the re-formation of labor and new social constructions of subjectivity.

New Technologies/New Critical Literacies

Schooling in the modern era has been largely organized around the transmission of print literacies and segregated academic knowledges based on a modern division of disciplines into such things as social science, literature, or physical education. Schooling authorities have been in a moral panic, the Lukes suggest, by declining literacy test scores and have recommended correctives such as early intervention to help produce stronger print literacy skills at younger ages. The Lukes argue (2001), however, that such projects are misguided because they fail to take account of the new technologies, subjectivities, and demands for the new economy and culture that requires multiple literacies, more flexible subjects, and new skills. The solution, they suggest, is to cultivate in the sphere of education new literacies that will respond to new technologies and cultural conditions and empower students to participate in the new high-tech culture and economy.

In this context, the Lukes argue that early print literacy intervention strategies fail to adequately prepare students with the literacies they need to navigate and negotiate the new economy and culture, and may perpetuate obsolete forms of schooling and culture. I would add here that the increasing emphasis on testing and quantitative scoring that is the basis of the Bush administration and conservative educational philosophy in the U.S. is also woefully flawed and already obsolete as it is rolled out, as are the SAT and most tests that measure student capabilities. These tests are educational technologies with genealogies in an earlier era marked by different social and economic imperatives, cognitive skills necessary for the economy and culture, and different subjectivities. The tests are thus now seriously outdated and in need of change to respond to the challenge of new technologies and a new era of globalization.

However, the new technologies and new literacies require a careful rethinking of education and literacy in response to its new challenges that will involve an era of Deweyan experimental education, trial and error, and research and discovery. In many parts of the world, there are the equivalent of early intervention print projects in the realm of computers, in which computers are put in children's hands at an ever earlier age in the hopes of developing multiple computer literacies. There is a raging debate, however, concerning the proper age to expose children to computers and cultivate computer literacy, just as there have been and still are debates over the proper time to begin cultivating print literacy in children.

In the Hegelian concept of *Geist*, the subject develops through mediations of culture and society in specific historical ways, but encounters contradictions and blockages which are overcome by sublation or *Aufhebung*, i.e., overcoming obsolete or oppressive conditions that are transcended. In the Lukes' version of the Hegelian dialectic, the new technologies and conditions of postmodern life are producing new experiences and subjectivities that come into conflict with schooling, itself based on earlier historical subjectivities and congealed institutions, discourses, and practices, modeled on the industrial factory system (i.e., time-parceled segments, staying immobile at a specific site to perform labor, submitting to the discipline of bosses). The optimistic Hegelian scenario is that this conflict can be overcome through an *Aufhebung* that sublates (i.e., negates, preserves, takes to higher stage) the positivities in the conflict and negates the obsolete aspects. Put more concretely: when there are contradictions between, say, a print-based curriculum and new subjectivities mediated by multimedia, then resolving the contradiction requires going to a higher level; e.g., restructuring schooling to preserve, for instance, the importance of print-based culture and literacy, but also bringing in new literacies and pedagogies to respond to, mediate, and develop in pedagogically progressive ways new technologies that make possible new forms of education and culture.

An Hegelian critique would thus perceive some forms of life, such as schooling, as obsolete, as too-print based in the conception of literacy, and as exhibiting moral panic in the face of new literacies and experiences. In Hegelian terms, schooling is seen as out of phase with the most advanced aspects of the culture and society, and must be transformed to harmonize with the new economy, technology and culture.

As noted, in the 1960s, Marshall McLuhan made the argument that there was a misfit between education and children's subjectivities largely because of TV and pop culture-based experience of kids' perceptions and subjectivities in terms of mosaics, patterns, oral culture, and images. In Hegelian (world-historical) terms, however, I don't think you could justify a restructuring of education on the basis of children's immersion in television and media culture. McLuhan's critique overburdens the allegedly transformative effects of television and popular culture on '60s youth. Moreover, the McLuhan vision arguably exaggerates the role of oral and tribal culture in the construction of new subjectivities, in addition to deploying problematic distinctions between hot and cool media and making a host of hyperbolic claims.

However, I do believe that by substituting computers and new multimedia technology for television and the media of McLuhan's day, one can argue that there are now significant transformations of the economy and culture that lend more credence to sweeping McLuhanesque proclamations concerning the obsolescence of modern education institutions. For one thing, the economic and cultural global restructuring going on in the world today is done on the basis of the most advanced sector of the new economy and culture (i.e., information and multimedia technology) penetrating ever more realms of life from entertainment to labor to schooling. Thus, the reconstruction of education on the grounds that socio-economic, cultural, and the material conditions of everyday life and labor are changing is a reasonable response to the great transformations now underway.

Thus, following the calls of some neo-McLuhanites and the digerati, we need to transform education to bring us it in line with new technologies, the global economy and culture, and the new multimedia cyberculture, in order to meet the demands of new digitally-mediated economy, polity, and culture, and to make education relevant to the contemporary world. There are, however, several caveats necessary in pursuing this argument. First, one needs to take seriously the Hegelian notion of *Aufhebung*, or sublation, in relation to print literacy since the ability to read and write linguistic texts and communication is arguably more important than ever in the new multimedia environment which is still significantly text-based (i.e., e-mail, chat rooms, list-serves, even much of the world wide web consists of text-based archives).

To be sure, new multimedia and computer literacies are necessary but they need to be articulated with print literacy, in which multiple literacies enable students and citizens to negotiate word, image, graphics, video, and multimedia digitized culture. Moreover, one needs to reconstruct education not to fulfill the agenda of capital and the high-tech industries, but to radically democratize education in order to advance Deweyan, Frierean, and Marcusean conceptions of the development of individuality and multidimensional selves, the promotion of citizenship and community, and the strengthening of democractic participation in all modes of life. Thus, one needs to accompany demands for multiple critical literacies and a restructuring of education with a program of the democratization of education, as I suggest in my concluding remarks.

Toward a Radical Reconstruction and Democratization of Education

In calling for the reconstruction of education to promote critical media and digital literacies as a response to the continuing development of digital technologies, social media, and globalization, one encounters the problem of the "digital divide." It has been well-documented that some communities, or individuals in privileged groups, are exposed to more advanced technologies and given access to more high-tech skills and cultural capital than those in less privileged communities. One way to overcome the divide, and thus a whole new set of inequalities that mirror or supplement modern divides of class, gender, race, and education, is to restructure education so that all students have access to new technologies and new literacies, so that education is democratized, and the very learning process and relation between student and teacher is rethought.

The Lukes suggestively note (2001) that the Hegelian Master/Slave dialectic characterizes relations between students and teachers today in which teachers force their curricula and agendas onto students in a situation in which there may be a mismatch between generational cultural and social experiences and even subjectivities. Educators, students, and citizens must recognize this generational divide and work to overcome conflicts and make differences more productive. That is, many students may be more technologically skilled than teachers and can themselves be important pedagogical resources. I know that much of what I've learned about how to use computers I've learned from students, and continue to draw upon them both in and out of class to help me navigate the new high-tech culture and to devise productive pedagogies and practices for the contemporary era.

In general, democratizing education can be enhanced by more interactive and participatory forms of education such as list-serves, class blogs and discussion sessions, archived Zoom sessions, the collective building of websites, online discussion, and collaborative computer-based research projects. Yet the restructuring of education also requires cultivating critical information literacies concerning limitations of Internet-based knowledge and the need for library inquiry and accessing books as important pedagogical resources, as well as the skills of differentiating reliable information and research sources on the internet from misinformation and unreliable sources. For learning and teaching, books and print-based materials and multimedia web-based materials should be seen as supplementary and not as oppositional, in which one is uncritically favored over the other, as some traditionalists privilege print literacy and book culture, while some of our contemporaries excessively celebrate the Internet, cyberculture, and web resources.

In addition, a Hegelian-Deweyan-Frierean philosophy of education would envisage merging classroom-based Socratic discussion with computer research and online projects that would combine oral, written, and multimedia cultural forms in the process of education without privileging one or the other. Some educators still insist that face-to-face dialogue in the classroom is the alpha and omega of good education and while there are times that classroom dialogue is extremely productive, it is a mistake, I believe, to fetishize face-to-face conversation, books and print media, or new multimedia or online teaching sites such as Zoom. Rather the challenge is to draw upon in an experimental and supplemental way all of these dimensions of the educational process to restructure and democratize education.

Finally, I would suggest that since concrete reconstructions of education will take place in specific local and national contexts, the mix between classroom pedagogy, books and reading print-material, and multimedia and Internet-based education will vary according to locale, age, and the needs and interests of students and teachers. The idea behind critical multiliteracies is that diverse and multimodal forms of culture blend in lived experience to form new subjectivities. The problem with educational institutions is that they become fixed in monomodal instruction with homogenized lesson plans, curricula, and pedagogy.

New digital media and technologies enable teachers and students to break with these models and to engage in Deweyan experimental education. New critical pedagogies could help create subjects better able to negotiate the complexities of emergent forms of everyday life, labor, and culture, as we evolve in the new millennium. Whereas modern mass education tended to see life in a linear fashion based on print models and developed pedagogies which broke experience into discrete moments and behavioral bits, new pedagogies could produce skills that enable individuals to better navigate the multiple realms and challenges of contemporary life. Deweyan education focused on problem-solving, goal-seeking projects, and the courage to be experimental, and it is this sort of education and spirit that will help produce new pedagogies for a new millennium. It is the virtue of the work of critical pedagogues and theorists to raise these issues and I look forward to future discussion and developments in the philosophy of education in response to ever-changing cultural, social, political, and technological developments.

Notes

1 In 1991, the Association of Supervision and Curriculum Development (ASCD) concluded: "Information literacy equips individuals to take advantage of the opportunities inherent in the global information society. Information literacy should be a part of every student's educational experience. ASCD urges schools, colleges, and universities to integrate information literacy programs into learning programs for all students" (AASL 1996). The project has been taken up by the national Forum on Information Literacy (NFIL). Building on these projects, it is thus important to see that computer literacy involves developing a wide range of information literacies, and that the latter also involve develop multiliteracies that access and interpret images, media spectacles, narratives, and new cultural sites in an expanded concept of information that resists its reduction to print paradigms alone.
2 For other conceptions of multimedia literacy, see the discussions of literacies needed for reading hypertext in Burbules and Callister 1996; the concept of multiliteracy in the New London Group 1996 and Luke 1997; the concept of hyperreading in Burbules, 1997, and the papers in Snyder 1997 and Semali and Watts Pailliotet, 2019.
3 There are two major modes and concepts of hypertext, one that is primarily literary, that involves new literary/writing strategies and practices and one that is more multimedia, multisemiotic, and multimodal. Hypertext was initially seen as an innovative and exciting new mode of communication that increased potentials for writers to explore new modes of textuality and expression and to expand the field of writing. As multimedia hypertext developed, it was soon theorized as a multisemiotic and multimodal form of communication. Yet some early advocates of hypertext attacked the emergence of the World Wide Web as a debased medium which brought back into play the field of earlier media, like television, forcing the word to renegotiate its power with the image and spectacles of sight and sound, once again decentering the written word (see, for instance, Joyce 1997; on hypertext, see Landow 1992 and 1997; Snyder 1996 and the articles in Snyder 1997).

4   While I have not myself researched the policy literature on this issue, in the many discussions of SAT tests and their biases which I have read, I have not encountered critiques that indicate the obsolescence of many standardized tests in a new technological environment and the need to come up with new testing procedures based on the new cultural and social fields that we are increasingly immersed in. Yet proposals for devising new standardized tests are emerging and this issue will be hotly debated and contested in the future. Indeed, there are signs that the SAT exams are now being questioned and phased out in some areas; the University of California, for instance, abandoned the SAT and ACT exams in 2020 as a freshman admission requirement and decided to develop its own substitute standardized test by 2025. See Larry Gordon, "In historic action, UC moves to drop SAT/ACT and develop a replacement exam for admissions. UC's move is expected to have influence nationally. Supporters expect it will result in more ethnic and income diversity on campuses." *EdSource*, May 17, 2020 at <https://edsource.org/2020/in-historic-action-uc-moves-to-drop-sat-act-and-develop-a-replacement-exam-for-admissions/632174> (accessed March 14, 2021).
5   For my take on postmodern theory, see Kellner 1989b and 1989c; Best and Kellner 1991, 1997, and 2001For an earlier sketch of postmodern pedagogy, see Kellner 1989c.

References

Best, Steven and Douglas Kellner (1991). *Postmodern Theory: Critical Interrogations*, Co-authored with. London and New York: Macmillan and Guilford Press.
Best, Steven and Douglas Kellner (1997). *The Postmodern Turn*. New York and London: Guilford Press and Routledge.
Best, Steven and Douglas Kellner (2001). *The Postmodern Adventure. Science, Technology, and Cultural Studies at the Third Millennium*. New York and London: Guilford and Routledge.
Cazden, Courtney, Cope, Bill, Fairclough, Norman, Gee, James, Kalantzis, Mary, Kress, Gunter, Luke, Allan, Luke, Carmen, Michaels, Sarah and Nakata, Martin (1996). "A Pedagogy of Multiliteracies: Designing Social Futures." *Harvard Educational Review* 66: 60–92.
Kahn, Richard and Douglas Kellner (2006). "Reconstructing Technoliteracy: A Multiple Literacies Approach," in *Defining Technological Literacy*, edited by John R. Dakers. New York and England: Palgrave Macmillan: 253–274.
Kellner, Douglas (1998). "Multiple Literacies and Critical Pedagogy in a Multicultural Society." *Educational Theory*, 48(1): 103–122.
Kellner, Douglas (1995; 2020). *Media Culture*. Second Edition (completely revised). New York and London: Routledge.
Kellner, Douglas and Jeff Share (2005). "Toward Critical Media Literacy: Core Concepts, Debates, Organization, and Policy." *Discourse: Studies in the Cultural Politics of Education*, 26(3) (September): 369–386.
Kellner, Douglas and Jeff Share (2019). *The Critical Media Literacy Guide: Engaging Media and Transforming Education*. Rotterdam, The Netherlands: Brill-Sense Publishers, 2019.
Luke, Allan and Carmen (2001). "Adolescence Lost/Childhood Regained: On Early Intervention and the Emergence of the Techno-Subject." *Journal of Early Childhood Literacy*, 1(1): 91–120.

McLuhan, Marshall (1964). *Understanding Media: The Extensions of Man*. New York: Signet Books.
Semali, Ladislaus and Ann Watts Pailliotet (2019). *Intermediality: Teachers' Handbook of Critical Media Literacy*. New York and London: Routledge.
Snyder, Ilana (2002) (ed.). *Silicon Literacies*. London and New York: Routledge.
Turkle, Sherry (1995). *Life on Screen. Identity in the Age of the Internet*. New York: Simon and Schuster.

AFTERWORD

Crises of the University and Student Movements

For me, the current wave of student protests on US university campuses over Israel's war on Gaza remind me of the horrendous U.S. war on Vietnam in the 1960s and the 1970s and the protest movement rolling from one campus to another. This wave of unprecedented student protests helped to form a New Left, an ever stronger Civil Rights movements, a new wave of feminism, and many other progressive movement ranging from ecology to peace and disarmament.[1]

One hopes that the current wave of protests against Israel's war on the Palestinians with U.S. military support will be equally productive and have inaugurated a new generation into protest movements and progressive political commitment among the current generation. The protesting students, on this analysis, are on the right side of history, as I wish to argue in an Afterword that addresses crises of the University with attacks on education, student protestors, and University governance from the Right and the Left.

By coincidence, I was a graduate student in Philosophy at Columbia University in 1968 when the protests against the Vietnam war were taking place and Columbia University was occupied by students. At the time, I was a third year graduate student and was awarded a class to teach the first year Great Books course to in-coming Columbia freshmen—my first teaching experience.

When the 1968 Occupation happened at Columbia, I joined a Faculty group that ringed the buildings which students had occupied to protect them against right-wing students and outsiders who wanted to invade the occupied camps and beat up and pull out the students. When this group (parallel to the recent May 2024 UCLA counter-protestors who I describe below) saw the Faculty protecting the Columbia students, they did not invade the building, but formed a ring around the Faculty group, leading to cooling off of tensions.

This peaceful situation was disrupted, however, when the University called in the NYPD who beat up Professors and students alike, as they arrested students who had occupied the Columbia buildings. I was not at the protest site when the police arrived as our faculty group had 12 hour shifts and I was just returning to campus for my shift when the police arrived. As I entered the 113th street Columbia entrance, I saw one of my Philosophy Professors, Sidney Morgenbesser, who had been part of the barricade of Faculty protecting the students, coming out, his head profusely bleeding, holding a white scarf to his head to stem the blood. I took Sidney for medical treatment and he told me how the police had brutally attacked the Columbia encampments and how the Faculty standing around the occupied buildings were the first to be attacked by the brutal police (and Sidney walking out to try to reason with the police was one of the first to be brutally beaten).

There was a strike for the rest of the year at Columbia and the students in the Graduate School of Philosophy at Columbia all got straight A's for our courses, as many of our Professors supported the student protest groups and some constituted the Progressive Faculty Group that defended the students. After the police raid, I and fellow graduate students created study groups on campus that were as valuable as classes. Moreover, I was able to forge close relations with other Professors during the Occupation who had supported the student as the Faculty group I joined had numerous meetings of how to resolve the crisis and support the students that led a large number of us to form the supposedly protective barrier around the Columbia occupation.

We did keep the counter-protestors from attacking the occupying and protesting students safe from student attack and thus prevented the horrible student violence that the world watched the on May 1-2, 2024 at UCLA,[2] but we could not protect the students from the police and my message from all of this is: ADMINISTRATORS: DO NOT CALL IN THE POLICE! NEGOTIATE!

AFTERWORD

DIALOGUE! REMEMBER AND ENGAGE Paulo Freire who in his classic *The Pedagogy of the Oppressed* urged dialogue, mutual understanding and consensus as a way of engaging difficult problem.

The failure of dialogue and peace negotiations resulted in the Vietnam war ending in a fiasco for the United States as the US pulled out of Vietnam in 1975, the Communist troops from the North took over and over 50,000 US lives and over a million of Vietnamese lives were lost. Vietnam Vets returned to the U.S. traumatized from the war experience and many have never recovered. The opponents of the war and anti-war movement that I was part of were certainly historically correct that the war against Vietnam was a bad war that was not in US interests, and so the anti-war demonstrators were on the right side of history, part of the Arc of Progress that Dr. Martin Luther King extolled.

I went from Columbia to the University of Texas at Austin after receiving my Ph.D. in 1973 and taught philosophy there until the mid-1990s when I came to UCLA. During my Texas years, an anti-Apartheid movement emerged against the racial discrimination and oppression in South Africa and UT-Austin had a student group that called for the University to divest all investments in South Africa and I spoke at anti-Apartheid rallies supporting the divestment movement. As I remember, there were few, if any, that supported South Africa and its Apartheid State, and the University of Texas soon divested.

Hence, I conclude from this episode, the anti-Apartheid students were on the right side of history and the many Universities that supported the anti-Apartheid movements were likewise part of a movement that created a global movement against South African Apartheid that led to the end of the Apartheid regime and a democratic South Africa state that was universally supported.

As the anti-Vietnam war movement and the anti-Apartheid movement were on the right side of history, so too is the pro-Palestine student movement calling for an end to the war against Palestine and University divestments from Israel. Already some Universities have negotiated divestment from Israel through dialogues with student, faculty, and administration reaching consensus that divestment from Israel is morally justified, strengthening these Universities and putting them on the right side of the Arc of History.

This was not the case with UCLA, where I have taught for the past twenty-five years after leaving the University of Texas at Austin. For weeks, UCLA students established a pro-Palestine encampment in the UCLA quad between Royce Hall and Powell Library. While the encampment students were peaceful, groups of pro-Israel students were organizing and harassing them and on Tuesday April 30th a group of pro-Israeli counter-demonstrators attacked the encampment around 11:00 pm at night, wielding batons, tear-gas, fire-crackers and other weapons. They assaulted the encampment, trying to tear away barriers and physically confronting the students. In the words of UCLA Professor David N. Myers, who witnessed the attack, wrote:

> UCLA, the top-rated public university in the United States, experienced one of the darkest nights in its 105-year history on Tuesday, May 1. Over the course of my 33-year career at UCLA, I have never seen anything so terrifying take place.
> Around 11 p.m., a group of masked counter-demonstrators made their way to the Royce Quad in the heart of campus and began to attack the encampment set up last week by demonstrators opposing the war in Gaza. They threw a firecracker into the encampment, tore down its outer walls, threw heavy objects at demonstrators and instigated direct physical confrontations. Those in the encampment were left to fend for themselves against a violent band of thugs intent on inflicting damage.
> The incident marked a total systems failure by the university, the city of Los Angeles, and the state of California.[3]

I myself watched this event with horror live on cable TV as the invading thugs tried to wreck the peaceful protest camp, brutally hitting the protestors with clubs, attempting to destroy the camp, throwing firecrackers into their midst, spraying tear-gas on the student protestors, and otherwise terrorizing the protestors. This spectacle of horror was broadcast for hours on live TV, showing a mob of rampaging counter-protestors with no police in sight for hours.

In the newspaper and TV accounts of the attack on the protest camp the next day, evidently there were UCLA police sent to protect students, but like the cowardly Texas police at Uvalde, Texas tasked to protect students against a rampaging school shooter, who walked around for hours doing nothing to intervene as ordered, the UCLA police also failed to intervene and protect students from the mob. Later, when interviewed, the UCLA police said that they were ordered by the University to protect property and not to confront the students, so it appears this was an administrative failure.

The next day watching cable TV coverage of the UCLA counter-protestors attack on the peaceful encampment, I saw an interview with UCLA Professor David Meyer who had written of his experience watching the counter-protester attacks the camp which he published in *The Forward* that I cited above. He noted, as he did in the article, that he heard some of the counter-protesters speaking Hebrew, which makes me think that some of the thugs were IDF-trained and applying their tactics as if the people in the peace encampment were enemies of the state to be destroyed (the speculation is not far fetched as every young Israeli male and female undergoes a year or more of compulsive military training — although there are exemptions for some religious groups and others).

There is, in fact, currently hot debate in Israel for the religious exemptions as it is seen as grossly unfair, as young Israeli men and women have been brutalized by the war against Palestine since October 7, which has produced not only over 40,000 Palestinian deaths, the destruction of most of Gaza, and the alienation of Israel from almost every country in the region and most of the world, but has produced the traumatization and death of many Israeli soldiers, as well as its citizens and many supporters of Israel abroad who oppose the brutal war against Palestine.

All of my Israeli friends and my Jewish colleagues in the UCLA community passionately oppose Netanyahu's war and support the Palestinians and the global call by the UN and every Humanitarian group for the end of the war and release of all hostages, so the generation long task of rebuilding Gaza and bringing Israel back into the world of peace and humanity can begin.

The protesting UCLA students, on this analysis, are on the right side of history, as were the students protesting the Vietnam war and the apartheid in South Africa where students successfully protested the regime and gotten many Universities and corporations to divest from South Africa, which contributed to the Apartheid regime in South Africa. So, once again, it is likely that the students protesting against Israel's horrific war on Gaza will be vindicated by being on the side of justice in the Arc of History.

It is all the more horrific, that after suffering brutality and trauma at the hands of violent counter-protestors—-while UCLA police stood by and witnessed the assault without doing anything and the LAPD did not arrive to quell the counter-protester attack for hours--the next day as the student protestors were trying to get over the trauma of the assault of their camp and the brutality they'd experienced, the UCLA Administration called in the police to tear down the camp that same night leading into May 1. While the LAPD failed for hours to arrive to protect the protestors in the encampment, this time it was the LAPD that were the assault force, tearing down the camp and arresting over 200 students. Jem Bartholomew reports:

> Hundreds of law enforcement officers breached a Gaza solidarity encampment at the University of California, Los Angeles campus on Thursday morning, removing barricades and threatening students with arrest.

> LAPD officers in tactical gear filed on to the UCLA campus around sunset on Wednesday and began to force their way into the encampment at about 3.1am PDT. They were met with about 300 to 500 protesters in the encampment – and another 2,00 people gathered outside the barricades in support – who shouted "shame on you". It is the latest crackdown on pro-Palestinian protesters demanding universities divest from companies linked to Israel's war effort in Gaza, and comes amid ongoing fallout from events on Tuesday, when counter-demonstrators attacked the UCLA encampment.[4]

This was especially horrendous since the UCLA protesters had been terrorized by the pro-Israeli group just hours before, subjecting them to more extreme trauma as they were arrested, watched their encampment torn down, and were hauled away to the Los Angeles police station to be booked. Yet some news footage the next day showed a UCLA support group meeting the arrested protesters at the police station with cheers and offers to take them home, provide counseling, and solidarity, demonstrating the goodness of the pro-Palestine encampment compared to the thug counter-protesters who had just assaulted them hours before and the UCLA Administration who ordered their camp torn down and hundreds arrested.

It's never too late to change directions and I hope that the UCLA community, including students, faculty, and administrators, will help the UCLA administration recognize its grave mistake in bringing in the police and enabling mob attack groups to besmirch the reputation of UCLA globally. This issue will not soon disappear and it is of grave importance that every student, faculty member, and administrator engage themselves in the issues and debates raised by the pro-Palestinian students and that UCLA can become part of the solution rather than part of the problem, as we used to say in the 1960s, a bon mot still relevant today.

Notes

1 Edward Helmore, "Echoes of Vietnam era as pro-Palestinian student protests roil US campuses. Calls for divestment continue despite hundreds of arrests, with more demonstrations planned for Democratic national convention, *The Guardian*, April 28, 2024 at https://www.theguardian.com/world/2024/apr/28/us-student-protests-gaza-israel (accessed April 28, 2024).

2 Interestingly, Faculty Groups at Columbia, UCLA, and other campuses also joined students to attempt to provide protection from assault. See Anemona Hartocollis, "Taking Cues From Students, U.C.L.A. Faculty Members Join the Protests Taking Cues From Students, U.C.L.A. Faculty Members Join the Protests. At U.C.L.A., a few professors helped negotiate

with the university. At Columbia, they guarded the encampment. But not all faculty members are on board. *The New York Times*, May 3, 2024 at https://www.nytimes.com/2024/05/02/us/columbia-protests-professors-support.html (accessed May 2, 2024).

3 David N. Myers, "I'm a UCLA professor. Why didn't the administration stop last night's egregious violence? The university should have anticipated Tuesday night's chaos — but security personnel were nowhere to be found," *The Forward*, May 1, 2024 at https://forward.com/opinion/608479/ucla-violence-campus-protests/(accessed May 3, 2024).

4 Jem Bartholomew, "Police move in on pro-Palestinian encampment at UCLA. LAPD action at University of California, Los Angeles marks latest flashpoint in mounting tensions on US college campuses." *The Guardian*, May 3, 2024 at https://www.theguardian.com/us-news/article/2024/may/02/first-thing-police-move-in-on-pro-palestinian-encampment-at-ucla (accessed on May 3, 2024).

Studies in Criticality

Series Editor
Shirley R. Steinberg

Counterpoints publishes the most compelling and imaginative books being written in Education and Cultural Studies today. Grounded on the theoretical advances in critical theory, feminism, and postcolonialism in the last two decades of the twentieth century, Counterpoints engages the meaning of these innovations in various forms of educational expression. Committed to the proposition that theoretical literature should be accessible to a variety of audiences, the series insists that its authors avoid esoteric and jargonistic languages that transform educational scholarship into an elite discourse for the initiated. Scholarly work matters only to the degree it affects consciousness and practice at multiple sites. The editorial policy of *Counterpoints* is based on these principles and the ability of scholars to break new ground, to open new conversations, to go where educators have never gone before.

For additional information about this series or for the submission of manuscripts, please contact:

> Shirley R. Steinberg, Series Editor
> msgramsci@gmail.com

To order other books in this series, please contact our Customer Service Department:

> peterlang@presswarehouse.com (within the U.S.)
> orders@peterlang.com (outside the U.S.)

Or browse online by series:

> www.peterlang.com

Milton Keynes UK
Ingram Content Group UK Ltd.
UKHW021527021224
3319UKWH00043B/1318